Rethinking Theories of Governance

RETHINKING POLITICAL SCIENCE AND INTERNATIONAL STUDIES

This series is a forum for innovative scholarly writing from across all substantive fields of political science and international studies. The series aims to enrich the study of these fields by promoting a cutting-edge approach to thought and analysis. Academic scrutiny and challenge is an essential component in the development of political science and international studies as fields of study, and the act of re-thinking and re-examining principles and precepts that may have been long-held is imperative.

Rethinking Political Science and International Studies showcases authored books that address the field from a new angle, expose the weaknesses of existing concepts and arguments, or 're-frame' the topic in some way. This might be through the introduction of radical ideas, through the integration of perspectives from other fields or even disciplines, through challenging existing paradigms, or simply through a level of analysis that elevates or sharpens our understanding of a subject.

For a full list of Edward Elgar published titles, including the titles in this series, visit our website at www.e-elgar.com

Rethinking Theories of Governance

Christopher Ansell

Professor of Political Science, University of California, Berkeley, USA

RETHINKING POLITICAL SCIENCE AND INTERNATIONAL STUDIES

Cheltenham, UK • Northampton, MA, USA

© Christopher Ansell 2023

All rights reserved. No part of this publication may be reproduced, stored in a retrieval system or transmitted in any form or by any means, electronic, mechanical or photocopying, recording, or otherwise without the prior permission of the publisher.

Published by
Edward Elgar Publishing Limited
The Lypiatts
15 Lansdown Road
Cheltenham
Glos GL50 2JA
UK

Edward Elgar Publishing, Inc.
William Pratt House
9 Dewey Court
Northampton
Massachusetts 01060
USA

A catalogue record for this book
is available from the British Library

Library of Congress Control Number: 2023943182

This book is available electronically in the **Elgar**online
Political Science and Public Policy subject collection
http://dx.doi.org/10.4337/9781789909197

Printed on elemental chlorine free (ECF)
recycled paper containing 30% Post-Consumer Waste

ISBN 978 1 78990 918 0 (cased)
ISBN 978 1 78990 919 7 (eBook)

Printed and bound in the USA

For my brilliant sister, Julie Jeannine Ansell

Contents

Preface		viii
1	Do governance theories rise to the challenge?	1
2	Addressing challenging public problems	12
3	Effective and accountable agencies: political conditions	30
4	Effective and accountable agencies: administrative conditions	47
5	Building effective and accountable governance	63
6	Enhancing democratic legitimacy and managing political conflict	86
7	Improving global cooperation and coordination	106
8	Reducing poverty and inequality	126
9	Managing the commons and transitioning to sustainability	153
10	Rethinking theories of governance	174
References		192
Index		238

Preface

More than once, and perhaps every day during the researching and writing of this book, I found myself thinking that I had bitten off more than I could chew. At the beginning of nearly every section I felt like opening with the phrase "This is a vast subject...." In contrast to Caesar's *Veni, Vidi, Vici* (I came, I saw, I conquered), my motto should be *Veni, Vidi, Vidi, Vidi...* etc.

Still, the synthesizing mission of the book is a good one. As my friend and colleague Todd LaPorte is fond of reminding us, "we know more and more about less and less." While we are all most comfortable in our own highly specialized bailiwicks, any real appreciation of governance theories requires that we go beyond them.

A note of thanks goes to Harry Fabian, the Commissioning Editor at Edward Elgar, who suggested this book project to me and was generous in his patience. I also have several friends and colleagues who have been very important in shaping the ideas that go into this book, though none merit blame for the result. Our Women's Faculty Club lunch group—Louise Comfort, Ann Keller, Todd LaPorte, and Paul Schulman—has been a special source of inspiration over many years. Thanks also to Martin Bartenberger, Patrick Baur, Mark Bevir, Arjen Boin, Mathilde Bourrier, Margaretha Breese, Sevie Chatzopoulou, Tom Christensen, Ruth Collier, Scott Douglas, Alison Gash, Ruth Langridge, Satoshi Miura, Paul 't Hart, Philipp Trein, Jarle Trondal, and Thenia Vagionaki. My Saturday zoom call with Joe Babarsky, Jeff Brown, Bob Feath, Tom Fitch, Dave Rivard, Jim Rogers, Jim Rowe, and Mike Vitez helped deliver me through COVID-19 with all but my ego intact. I owe a special debt of gratitude to Kevin O'Brien, Eva Sørensen, and Jacob Torfing for their friendship and intellectual camaraderie, and to my wife, Suzanne Ryan, for simply putting up with me.

1. Do governance theories rise to the challenge?

We live in challenging times. Do governance theories help us meet those challenges? Are they a useful resource? The social psychologist Kurt Lewin famously observed that "there is nothing as practical as a good theory" (Lewin, 1943, 118). But it is not always evident that theory is practical or necessarily clear what makes a good theory. Some might say that the purpose of theory is understanding, not practical action. Others might point out that our collective dilemmas have more to do with deep-rooted political constraints than with the sufficiency or insufficiency of our theories of governance. Although such claims and caveats have merit, this book takes on the somewhat quixotic task of rethinking our theories from the perspective of whether they are useful.

The task is quixotic because judging the usefulness of a theory—not to mention theories—is a problem without a "stopping rule." Whether a theory is useful is, at least in part, in the eyes of the beholders—that is, those potentially interested in using it. These beholders are diverse and have different skills, needs, interests and agendas, so judging "usefulness" as if theory had a universal utility is certainly problematic. The book also goes broad rather than deep in order to learn what we can from juxtaposing many different theoretical perspectives. Governance theories cover an enormous number of topics ranging from water governance at the scale of a watershed to the efforts to reduce poverty on a global scale.

The book adopts two strategies to bound the task. First, it does not judge how useful governance theories have proven to be. Doing so would require an analysis of how they have been used and whether their use has been successful. More modestly, the book reflects on *how* theories become useful, arguing that they become useful when they are warranted, diagnostic and dialogical. It then evaluates various theories of governance according to how well they meet these criteria. Second, the book cannot evaluate all governance theories, even according to this more modest standard. There are simply too many that merit recognition to credibly tackle them all. To focus the analysis, each chapter is organized around a practical challenge. Chapter 1, for example, asks whether and how theories of governance help us understand and tackle difficult public problems. Chapter 10 asks if governance theories help us manage the commons and the transition to a more sustainable world. This strategy focuses

1

the analysis but also certainly leaves out some important theoretical work on governance.

To understand what counts as a governance theory, we must first have a sense of what the term "governance" means. The difficulty of writing a book about governance theories is that the term is either so broad that it becomes a catchall for everything related to politics, policy and administration, or very specific, referring to a distinct set of debates about governing that have appeared over the last several decades. Very broadly, the term "governance" refers to the process of governing, which is the exercise of authority, rules, coercion, deliberation, persuasion, or other political or institutional measures, to achieve collective ends. However, the term began to be used in the 1990s across a range of disciplines, where it assumed a variety of specific and sometimes conflicting meanings (Rhodes, 1996; Pierre, 2000; Chhotray and Stoker, 2009; Ansell and Torfing, 2016; Torfing, 2023). Before delving into the issue of what makes a theory useful, it is important to first consider what "governance" means, at least for the purposes of this book.

WHAT IS GOVERNANCE?

The challenge of navigating between a broad and specific view of governance is exacerbated by the fact that different disciplines and discussions have developed quite different, and sometimes opposing, conceptions of governance. For example, one very important strand of the governance literature developed by the World Bank and the development community was related to concerns about government corruption and accountability (Rose-Ackerman, 2017). This led to the concept of "good governance," which stressed the importance of developing effective state institutions. This approach to governance is focused on the quality of government, as suggested by Fukuyama's (2013, 350) definition of governance as "government's ability to make and enforce rules, and to deliver services, regardless of whether that government is democratic or not."

In other fields, very different conceptions of governance grew up. For instance, in the field of public administration, Rhodes (1996) championed the definition of governance as "self-organizing networks." A key implication of this perspective, he argued, was that governance was a broader term than government and stressed the interdependence between organizations and their interaction and negotiation. Other fields—like global governance or environmental governance—stressed the collective action dilemmas at the heart of governance, as reflected in Oran Young's (2021, 36) definition: "Governance is a social function centered on steering societies away from collectively undesirable outcomes and toward collectively good ones."

There has been quite a bit of push-back against the elastic and even faddish nature of the concept of governance. Pollitt and Hupe (2011, 653), for example, describe "governance" as a "magic concept" and write that:

> Magic concepts have advantages and limitations. They can perform the functions of advertising, focusing and legitimizing certain ways of looking at the world and in recruiting support for certain broad lines of action. However, they should not be mistaken for clear-cut scientific, technical or operational terms. To struggle to standardize their usage is to invite frustration.

Speaking to the public administration field, Frederickson (2005) argued that governance had become too expansive a concept, swallowing up our traditional approach to public administration. Building on the analogy of regime theory in international relations, he proposed that governance should focus on interjurisdictional, third-party and public non-governmental dimensions of governing.

These conceptual shoals are navigated in this book by calling attention to three broad meanings that distinguish governance:

1. First, the term governance is often used when we are talking about how specific issues are managed—fisheries governance, water governance, etc. People often find the vocabulary of governance useful when they are focused on the management of specific societal problems and when they are talking about governing in the trenches.

2. Second, the term governance is typically used when we are talking about the structure and process of interaction among many different groups and organizations engaged in governing. Thus, governance is often discussed in terms of the coordination of collective action, which some governance theorists describe as steering—a systems concept that comes from the German concept of *Steuerung* and arises from discussions of how government can direct, coordinate and control relatively autonomous societal subsystems (Mayntz, 1993). Peters and Pierre (2020), for instance, define governance as steering the economy and society toward collective goals.

3. Third, and perhaps most importantly, governance often implies widening the lens beyond "government" to include interaction between public and private actors or between the state and civil society (Kooiman, 1993). However, although the concept can accommodate interest in purely private governance, this does not imply that government has been replaced by self-organizing private actors.

While the term is not—and cannot be—crisp, it is used in this book to refer to the collective interaction of government and non-government actors engaged in the governing of specific public problems. While the overall focus is on this interaction, in most cases "government" remains the primary authorizer, organizer and sponsor of this interaction.

A key question emerging out of this discussion is whether we are talking about a theory or theories of governance. Pierre and Peters (2020) ask whether it is possible to have a unified theory of governance and they build on their earlier work (Peters and Pierre, 2016) to suggest that decision-making is a common theoretical denominator. All accounts of governance assume the central importance of decision-making, though who makes decisions varies significantly on a spectrum that runs from states making governing decisions unilaterally to non-state actors making governing decisions without the involvement of states.

Bevir (2013) offers a theory of governance that builds on an interpretive postfoundational philosophy. It rejects modernist and neoliberal accounts of governance as reifying governing institutions and instead calls for seeing governance as "something akin to a political contest based on competing and contingent narratives" (2013, 26–27). From Bevir's perspective, Peters and Pierre are "modernists" who strive for formal and ahistorical generalizations based on an account that starts with institutions, structures and mechanisms— typically forgetting individual agency in the process (Bevir and Krupicka, 2011).

Although these ideas about a unified governance theory are worthy of consideration, the purpose of this book is not to grasp, evaluate or debate *the* theory of governance. The focus on usefulness enjoins us to consider the many different theoretical ideas that have grown up under the umbrella of the concept of governance. This strategy creates a major difficulty of its own: what to exclude? For practical, division-of-labor reasons, the book leaves aside many potentially relevant discussions. For instance, it does not address policy process theories or the enormous body of research on corporate governance. Ultimately, the reader will have to judge whether the book has found the sweet spot in terms of the governance theories it reviews.

A final caveat that readers should appreciate at the outset is that theories are rarely tidy statements. They develop out of sustained discussions among scholarly and practitioner communities, accumulating ideas and evidence over time. They are rarely rationalized with a tidy bow and what counts as a theory can be hard to pinpoint. Most theories have an open-ended quality, with a mix of empirical evidence (pro and con) and there is rarely a comprehensive statement or test of theory across a wide range of circumstances. In addition, different theories often grow up to describe similar issues from different perspectives, and they often talk past one another. None of this is meant as a criticism of theory. For better or worse, this is just the way that theory develops in the social sciences—and probably elsewhere as well.

WHAT IS THEORY AND WHAT DOES IT DO?

To consider how a theory can be useful, we must first ask: what is theory and what does it do? Is joe-blow pundit on the nightly news expressing a theory? In colloquial terms, the answer is often "yes" if the pundit is making a claim or an interpretation to be evaluated by subsequent events. In this book, however, the focus is on the practice of systematically elaborating explicit claims and interpretations for the purpose of evaluating them. Theory is the "work that researchers do in pursuit of making *informed* knowledge claims" (Cornelissen et al., 2021, 3). This is typically a scholarly activity, though practitioners sometimes engage in explicit theory-building.

There are many possible meanings of "theory." Abend (2008, 182) distinguishes no less than seven in sociology and argues that the semantic problem of the concept of theory "stem[s] from the erroneous belief that there is something—indeed, one thing—out there for the word 'theory' to really correspond to." An enviably succinct claim is that theory logically explicates concepts and makes causal arguments that answer the query "why?" (Sutton and Staw, 1995). This perspective is valuable but too narrow. Conceptualization is certainly fundamental to all theorizing, but theories do not necessarily need to make causal claims. Theory may be descriptive or designed to orient us to a particular phenomenon. While theory is also certainly informed, it is often as much about speculation as it is about fact. Thus, as a first cut, theory is *a body of interrelated concepts and propositions that purports to describe, interpret, explain, evaluate or critique a particular phenomenon*.

What makes a theory useful, or as Lindblom and Cohen (1979) reframe the question, what makes knowledge usable? A fundamental challenge is that theory is an abstraction or generalization. Yet the usefulness of theory generally refers to its practical application to a specific case or context. By their very nature, theories are general rather than concrete and they do not—cannot—provide a complete representation of the contexts in which they might apply. However, useful theories can describe key scope conditions under which they apply and give potential users of the theory a sense of how they might analyze a concrete situation.

Scholars uphold different perspectives on what makes a theory useful. As editor of *Public Administration Review*, James Perry (2012, 479) called for authors to submit more "usable knowledge," by which he meant knowledge that:

> meets users' priorities and needs and is research of high scientific quality. It is scholarship that consciously attends to managing the trade-offs between the ability to make causal statements and generalize those statements to other settings (i.e.,

internal and external validity) and the ability of a broader audience to accept and apply them.

In the field of social psychology, "[a] practical theory is one that suggests actionable steps toward solving a problem that currently exists in a particular context in the real world" (Berkman and Wilson, 2021, 864). It is also testable, coherent, parsimonious, generalizable and explains known findings (Higgins, 2004). The philosopher Karl Popper (1963) argued that good theory is falsifiable and hence, "the more a theory forbids, the better it is." But organization theorists have described the value of theory as "enlightenment" or "disciplined imagination" (Weick, 1989; DiMaggio, 1995) and a survey of sociological theory finds that "[t]he difference between one theory and another is in comparative candlepower" (Martindale, 2013, vii).

We see here tensions between the practical relevance, scientific validity, and enlightenment value of theories, and these tensions run through the field of governance. Recalling Herbert Simon's (1946) famous criticisms of the "proverbs" of public administration, for example, the "good governance" agenda has been described as "a set of well-meaning but problematic proverbs" (Andrews, 2008, 379) and the "policy network" literature has been criticized for being primarily metaphoric (Dowding, 1995). Others, however, see these governance "heuristics" as effective analytical devices because they "can grapple with the detail and the unique characteristics of particular public policy decision-making cases" (Toke, 2010, 778) and they find "folk theories" of global governance useful for helping international organizations grapple with diversity and accountability challenges (Halliday, 2018).

How does theory make a difference that might be called useful? One potential answer is that theory—or at least, empirically validated theory—should tell us what to do to achieve some desired outcome. While this view is alluring, it is also limited in a number of ways. Most scholars see the value of developing a strong knowledge base for policymaking, but there has been significant critique of the idea of "evidence-based policymaking" and its goals of providing prescriptive knowledge (Greenhalgh and Russell, 2009; Head, 2016; Ansell and Geyer, 2017; Cairney, 2018). Cairney (2022) describes evidence-based policymaking as a "myth" designed to project control and rationality. It embodies a kind of engineering or technocratic view of governance that ignores its political dimensions (Chhotray and Stoker, 2009). Most importantly, from the perspective of this book, overestimating the applicability of generalized theoretical claims leads to the problems that confront "blueprint" or "best practice" strategies—that is, ignoring the context in which they apply (Ostrom, 2007; Andrews et al., 2013). Yet if the usefulness of theories does not lie in their ability to tell us what to do, how should we think about their usefulness?

THEORY AS WARRANTED ASSERTIBILITY, DIALOGUE AND DIAGNOSIS

The philosopher John Dewey (1941) argued that too often our understanding of knowledge disconnects it from inquiry and subordinates inquiry to the production of knowledge. Dewey stresses the fallibility of knowledge, which is by nature selective, conditional and sensitive to shifting perspectives and changing interpretations of problems. Moreover, it depends on continually evaluating it in practice and finding out whether it holds under the conditions evaluated. His stress on the fallibility of knowledge, his emphasis on inquiry, his critique of the notion of objective truth and his emphasis on experience all lead him to stress that "warranted assertibility"—mouthful that it is—is a better way to think about knowledge. Knowledge claims are warranted when they arise out of inquiry, practice and empirical evaluation, but warranted is not the same thing as infallible or true.

The evidence-based and warranted assertibility views converge in valuing empirical assessment of theoretical claims, and other things being equal, they share the view that a knowledge claim is more warranted when the quality of evidence for a claim is high, as judged by prevailing scientific standards. However, there remains a difference in emphasis. A warranted assertibility perspective is concerned about how warranted a theory is for a specific user occupying a specific situation and having a specific purpose and is less inclined to accept the universalistic nature of knowledge claims. Theoretical knowledge is more warranted when it is derived from situations that are similar or analogous to the situation or experience in which it might be used. As a result, case study evidence may have more warranted assertibility than experimental results in some circumstances. Theory is also more warranted when it has been demonstrated to robustly hold across a wide range of circumstances.

While these differences are a matter of emphasis, a second aspect of the warranted assertibility perspective is more fundamental for thinking about theoretical usefulness. For Dewey, knowledge is not only the end point of inquiry, but also its starting point. An application of warranted knowledge about governance still requires further inquiry into the circumstances in which it is applied. From this perspective, theoretical knowledge is not a prescription of what to do, but rather a framework for guiding and assisting inquiry. This point reflects the larger epistemological tradition that Dewey advances: knowledge is not an independent truth, but a tool for structuring and solving problems. As Alexander George (1994, 162) writes in an essay on bridging the gap between theory and policymaking, "[t]heory and generic knowledge are best conceived as aids to policy analysis and to the judgement of the policy-maker."

There are at least two closely related ways to think about how theories can usefully guide inquiry. Very simply, theories can help us to *diagnose* a situation and *dialogue* with it. A diagnostic theory helps us understand the context or situation in which theoretical knowledge is to be applied. Rather than telling us to do *x*, it helps us understand what we need to know in order to evaluate whether to do *x*, *y* or *z* (George, 1994; Ostrom, 2011). For example, a theory might help us to identify the factors likely to be drivers or barriers in the way of addressing a particular challenge. A dialogical view helps us to engage with a context or situation in a dynamic way, aiding us to refine and adapt our queries and strategies as the context or situation itself changes. The dialogue is between the theory and the situation, as well as between the different features of the situation as they interact (Rule and John, 2015).

One way to think about the usefulness of a theory that follows from this diagnostic and dialogical perspective is that they help us by "organizing perspective." Stoker (1998, 26) has argued that governance theory is really an "organizing perspective," that "makes its theoretical contribution at a general level in providing a set of assumptions and research questions." To do this, the theory provides something like an "ontology" of a given context. It suggests who the important actors are likely to be and how they can be expected to behave. An organizing perspective can help us to see where or how we might intervene and to anticipate issues that might arise if we do intervene. For example, the theory of street-level bureaucracy focuses our attention on the critical role of public employees in interpreting and giving meaning to public policy. This organizing perspective identifies a phenomenon of importance and then identifies the factors that affect the role of these employees in policy implementation (e.g., time and resource constraints) and the types of effects these factors might produce (e.g., rationing of social services; stereotyping etc.).

Diagnostic and dialogical theory does not simply articulate solutions to problems. Instead, a critical aspect of this perspective is that theories can help structure problems so that they can be better addressed (Hoppe, 2018). However, many theories set out abstract categories and do not really encourage deeper inquiry or investigation. Diagnostic and dialogical theory stimulate reflection, help us to imagine alternatives and anticipate problems, and above all to ask questions. Useful theories facilitate the collection of critical empirical information that may lead to theory elaboration, revision or rejection.

Another element of this perspective might be called "discernment." A useful theory help users discern critical aspects of a situation that might have important consequences or implications for action or understanding. For example, building on conceptual distinctions developed in the multi-level governance literature, Maggetti and Trein (2019, 358) argue that the implications of multi-level governance for problem-solving capacity and for problem genera-

Do governance theories rise to the challenge? 9

tion depend on whether the "denationalization" process led to an unbundling of authority "upwards, downwards or sideways." This theoretical argument is intended to help users of the theory discern different situations that produce different consequences, with implications for problem-solving or problem generation.

Environmental governance scholar Oran Young (2002) has advocated a diagnostic approach to governance that navigates a course between "universal" design principles and the contrary claim that every context is completely unique. Young (2019, 2) proposes the concept of a diagnostic tree, which moves from general considerations about a situation and then branches down to more specific concerns. A diagnostic tree formulates a set of focused queries that can be addressed in a stepwise fashion, such that the answer to each query might lead you down a different branch in the tree where you will meet new queries.

Most generally, a diagnostic and dialogical approach to theory shifts attention from "what to do" to "what to ask." Theories should invite further inquiry and support a "questioning" perspective that prompts us to ask fruitful questions that might assist design or action (Turnbull, 2013). Dunn (1997, 278) described "erotetic rationality" as a form of "questioning and answering" that requires probing the context of any policy problem. Building on Aristotle, Isaacs (2001) argues that dialogical inquiry requires challenging the tacit assumptions that generate our experience.

Useful theories also self-problematize. That is, they alert us to the conditions under which they are likely to go astray or where it is not clear they are applicable. To some degree, this is about posing the scope conditions for the argument. But it is also about calling attention to points of uncertainty or ambiguity. Theory is also enriched if it generates a community of scholars who build on and around it, revising and adapting it as it is applied or evaluated.

Finally, a theory is generally more useful when it opens up the proverbial black box. Doing so generally requires specifying causal mechanisms and their potential linkages and describing the dynamics of the system. However, a useful theory does not have to be causal, but may instead give you the descriptive richness that allows you to perceive how a system works and suggests how to investigate it in order to understand it more deeply (Weick, 2007). Table 1.1 summarizes the key points of an approach to theoretical usefulness that emphasizes the value of diagnosis and dialogue.

WHAT'S COMING?

The next eight chapters investigate the usefulness of governance theories from the perspective of whether they are warranted, diagnostic and dialogical. Chapter 2 sets the tone by examining whether governance theories help us

Table 1.1   Theory as dialogue and diagnosis

- Shifts attention from what to do to what to ask
- Helps to structure a problem and understand what we need to know in order to act
- Helps us to discern and probe important structures, dynamics and causal mechanisms
- Identifies possible strategies or capacities needed to address an issue and aids inquiry into their relative efficacy under different circumstances
- Helps us to ask questions that critically anticipate the negative consequences of our actions
- Helps to stimulate our imagination and encourages further inquiry
- Theory self-problematizes by suggesting its scope conditions and by discussing where it can go wrong or mislead
- Opens up the black box of phenomena and invites closer inspection

understand and address why public problems are so nettlesome. The focus here is not on the analysis of specific problems like homelessness or biodiversity loss. Rather, the focus is on more generic theories of public problems, such as the wicked problem framework. The first part of this chapter explores whether and how general theories of public problems help us to analyze or diagnose them. The second part analyzes what these perspectives can tell us about managing or solving these difficult problems.

Chapters 3–5 explore twin concerns that run through much of the governance literature: the question of what makes governance effective and accountable. Chapter 3 investigates the political conditions that governance theories identify as supporting or detracting from the effectiveness and accountability of public organizations, with the first part of this chapter considering the broad issue of how politics and administration interact and the second half zeroing in on issues related to accountability. Chapter 4 then examines the administrative and managerial aspects of the effectiveness and accountability of public agencies, broadly contrasting a New Public Management and an institutionalist perspective. Chapter 5 extends the analysis of effectiveness and accountability to the state's role in governance and then evaluates two topics that lie at the core of many governance theories: network and collaborative governance.

Chapter 6 shifts the focus from effectiveness and accountability to the question of what governance theories contribute to our understanding of democratic legitimacy and the management of societal conflict. After reflecting on some broad theoretical discussions of democracy and legitimacy, the analysis examines what governance theories can tell us about the various governance mechanisms that shape the relationship between the democratic state and civil society. This chapter then concludes with a consideration of what governance theories contribute to the management of societal conflict.

Chapter 7 asks what theories of global governance tell us about how to address the challenge of global cooperation and coordination. The chapter first considers the "global governance gap" and examines some of the basic institutional features of global governance. The chapter then investigates what governance theories tell us about how governance networks operate on a global scale and explores some specific strategies for increasing global cooperation and coordination.

Chapter 8 asks what governance theories contribute to addressing a public problem of global concern—poverty and inequality. The first part of this chapter focuses primarily on the issue of poverty reduction and examines what both state-centric and society-centric perspectives contribute to understanding and addressing this topic. The second part of the chapter focuses on the theme of inequality and considers several ways that governance theories contribute to our understanding of equity, inclusion and justice.

Chapter 9 takes up another central global concern: how can we manage the environmental commons and how can we make the difficult transition to sustainability? The first part of the chapter focuses on what governance theories tell us about successfully governing the commons, while the second part of the chapter investigates governance theories that help us understand transitions to sustainability.

Finally, Chapter 10 summarizes the findings from Chapters 2–9 and then considers some of the cross-cutting themes that might help us to "rethink governance." The central message is that rather than envisioning governance as a move away from government, we should place more priority on examining how governance structures and processes encourage a "state–society synergy." Although some governance research already points in this direction, framing a governance research agenda in this way can help us to focus governance theories in constructive ways and can encourage a new line of inquiry into the structures and processes of governance. This chapter concludes with a general discussion of how we theorize and suggests that a better integration of instrumental, critical and explanatory aspects of governance theories might serve us well.

2. Addressing challenging public problems

It is a common perception that public problems are accumulating faster than we can solve them. Yet whether the world has more or more serious problems in 2023 than in 1823 or 1923 is difficult if not impossible to say. Poverty, child labor, and domestic violence were probably worse in the Dickensian London of Oliver Twist than in contemporary London, but these issues have quite a different meaning and more urgency for Londoners today. The London of the 1820s suffered from cholera and smoke pollution; the London of today must deal with pandemics and climate change. Judging whether our problems are worse or more numerous than our predecessor's problems is a tricky business.

A better way to think about public problems is that our expectations about whether they can be solved have changed and the political dynamics of thinking about public problems have been dramatically transformed. After two centuries of economic growth, the development of modern marvels of engineering, technology and science, and the consolidation of stable and peaceful democratic rule in much of the world, it feels like we should be able to solve problems of homelessness, drug addiction, climate change, income inequality, and loss of biodiversity. Alas, it often feels that we cannot, or least in any definitive sense.

This chapter focuses on theories of governance that tell us something about how we can address challenging public problems. It does not try to evaluate theories targeted toward addressing specific problems like homelessness or climate change. Such problems invariably have extensive literatures discussing their specific challenges, which are beyond the scope of this book. Instead, this chapter will focus on theories of governance that provide relatively generic accounts of how to understand challenging public problems and how to develop solutions to those problems.

DIAGNOSING PROBLEMS

Wicked Problems

The most famous theoretical framework for understanding the challenge of public problems is the concept of "wicked problems," which was formulated

Addressing challenging public problems

by two scholars of urban planning—Horst Rittel and Melvin Webber—in the early 1970s. The duo posed the provocative question, "why are planning problems not like engineering problems?" (For valuable genealogies of the wicked problem concept, see Gruendel (2022) and Crowley and Head (2017)). In response, Rittel and Webber (1973) set out a ten-point framework of what made planning problems "wicked," in the sense of being difficult to manage and solve. Table 2.1 lists the ten major points in their framework.

Table 2.1   The wicked problems framework

1. There is no definitive formulation of a wicked problem

2. Wicked problems have no stopping rule

3. Solutions to wicked problems are not true-or-false, but good-or-bad

4. There is no immediate and no ultimate test of a solution to a wicked problem

5. Every solution to a wicked problem is a "one-shot operation"; because there is no opportunity to learn by trial-and-error and every attempt counts significantly

6. Wicked problems do not have an enumerable (or an exhaustively describable) set of potential solutions, nor is there a well-described set of permissible operations that may be incorporated into the plan

7. Every wicked problem is essentially unique

8. Every wicked problem can be considered to be a symptom of another problem

9. The existence of a discrepancy representing a wicked problem can be explained in numerous ways. The choice of explanation determines the nature of the problem's resolution

10. The planner has no right to be wrong

Source: Rittel and Webber (1973).

These ten characteristics of wicked problems describe why planning problems are difficult to manage and solve. A key to appreciating both the power and the limits of this framework is that it emphasizes *why* wicked problems are not engineering problems and hence cannot be solved through rational, comprehensive, technocratic planning (the limits to which had already been persuasively argued by Charles Lindblom (1959)).

These characteristics are not set out as falsifiable causal hypotheses. Rather, the wicked problems framework is an interpretive theory that is intended to orient planners toward the nature of social problems, helping them interpret why planning problems are so difficult. Although the original framework did not tell us what to do to address wicked problems, it suggested some important implications. One of the most important is that if the planner approaches a "wicked problem" as if it is a "tame problem" and tries to solve it using rational planning procedures, the planner is likely to fail or be disappointed.

Another valuable aspect of this interpretive framework is that it enhances the planners' understanding of planning problems. To some degree, the ten points are framed as "paradoxes," telling us the ways wicked problems behave in a fashion that feels both definitive (note the declarative form of each statement) and untenable. As a framework of understanding, this paradoxical style has its limits. It does not really encourage fine-grained analysis, though the shock of the statements does disabuse planners that they can go about planning in the logical, rational fashion of engineers. A multitude of case studies have used and applied the wicked problems framework to difficult problems. In this sense, there is a kind of prima facie case that the framework is warranted. But it is also appropriate to point out that the claims of the wicked problem framework are themselves rarely evaluated empirically.

To some extent, the wicked problem is both dialogical and diagnostic, in the sense that it invites planners to reflect on the distinctive nature of public problems and to reflect critically on their basic orientation to public problems and their style of intervening. As Brian Head observes, "The attraction of the 'wicked problem' concept is that it seems to provide additional insights concerning why many policies and programs generate controversy, fail to achieve their stated goals, cause unforeseen effects, or are impossibly difficult to coordinate and monitor" (2008, 103). Its strength and limitation is that it essentially frames each point as "not X," where X represents the assumptions of a rational, technocratic model.

Moreover, the ten points insist that planning problems are "Y not X," where Y is the paradoxical opposite of X. This contrast limits the diagnostic value of the framework in practice and provides an awkward perspective from which to analyze actual problems. Take, for instance, the claim "The planner has no right to be wrong." This point is typically taken to mean that the planner cannot experiment with solutions because every experiment has subsequent implications. While we can appreciate this point in an abstract way, it is less useful in practice and probably detracts from the idea that solutions to very challenging problems must in some sense adopt an experimental stance.

There is debate in the scholarly literature about whether the concept of wicked problems is useful because "it can be used to highlight limitations of reductionistic approaches for addressing complex societal and environmental problems" versus whether it is "ambiguous and often used rhetorically rather than analytically" (Lönngren and Van Poeck, 2021, 481). In a review of the framework, Lönngren and Van Poeck find that scholarship on wicked problems performs two key rhetorical functions: it challenges existing approaches to problem-solving and it proposes alternative strategies for approaching problems. Although they find that the descriptive/analytical use of the concept is limited by the conceptual pluralism of scholarship, they argue that it is a useful "sensitizing" or "critical" concept. Based on a survey of policy experts, Peters and Tarpey (2019) found that respondents rarely utilize all of Rittel and

Addressing challenging public problems

Webber's ten points and conclude that the wicked problem framework has probably been overused.

While some scholars have sought to condense or refine the original wicked problem criteria (e.g., Duckett et al., 2016), others have expanded them. Levin et al. (2012), for example, describe a class of "super wicked" problems that add four additional characteristics to the wicked problem framework: (1) time is running out; (2) those seeking to end the problem are also causing it; (3) no central authority exists for addressing the problem; and (4) policies discount the future irrationally. Levin et al. establish a "diagnostic framework" that encourages policymakers to probe the conditions that make it difficult to gain traction on super-wicked problems.

Turnbull and Hoppe (2019) argue for replacing the categorical logic of the wicked problems framework with a more "relational" approach based on how different policy actors "question" a problem and whether they pose answers that close down (repress) or open up (express) possibilities for further questioning. Similarly, Alford and Head (2017) reject the "totalizing" character of the original wicked problems framework and instead propose a framework that analyzes problem gradients along two dimensions: complexity and the difficulty of stakeholder relations. As problems become more complex and have more challenging stakeholder relations, they become more wicked. They suggest that this revised framework is more useful for analyzing a problem and developing problem-solving strategies.

Ill-structured, Intractable and Messy Problems

An alternative to the "wicked problems" framework examines whether problems are more or less "structured" (Simon, 1973). Structured problems can be addressed by technical and standardized solutions because there is a significant degree of certainty about the knowledge necessary to solve the problem and agreement about the norms and values underpinning the problem and its solution (Hisschemöller and Hoppe, 1995). By contrast, unstructured problems do not have pre-formed solutions, their knowledge base is uncertain and the norms and values that underpin them are disputed or at least not agreed upon. They are "far from certainty" and "far from agreement" (Hoppe, 2011, 16). The main solution to an "unstructured" problem is to structure it, a process that Hoppe (2011) describes as requiring "puzzling" (analysis), "powering" (exerting pressure and influence) and "participation" (deciding who gets to puzzle and power). Poor problem structuring can lead to what Mitroff and Featheringham (1974) call "solving the wrong problem" or an error of the "third type" (a reference to type 1 and type 2 errors in statistical reasoning).

Wildavsky (1979) argued that policy was as much an art of creating problems as it was of solving them, by which he meant identifying them in ways that could be solved (essentially, problem structuring). Dunn (1997) argues that where problems are ill-structured, problem structuring is more fundamental than problem-solving. The challenge, however, is that we tend to approach ill-structured problems with the same methods that we approach more structured problems (e.g., cost–benefit analysis). Doing so leads us to deny our ignorance and puts us at risk of trying to solve the wrong problem. To gain traction in this situation, he argues, we need to distinguish between the second-order "problem of problems" (the unstructured nature of the problem) before we can address the first-order problem of solving a specific problem. Dunn (1988) identifies several methods of addressing problem structuring, with the overall proviso that these methods must be appropriate to the unstructured nature of the problem.

Another perspective on public problems refers to "intractable problems," a perspective Shön and Rein (1994) use to describe policy controversies that cannot be resolved by appeal to facts because the parties to the dispute either do not accept the same facts or interpret them differently. They suggest that such controversies can be addressed through what they call "frame reflection," a process of experimenting with alternative framings of controversial issues. Hisschemöller and Hoppe (1995) argue that intractable controversies arise when policymakers persist in trying to solve the wrong problem, which occurs when the perspectives or interests of different groups are not considered in the problem structuring process. They describe what might more recently be called a "social learning" or "policy learning" strategy for preventing or resolving intractable problems, with learning helping to align various interests and perspectives with problem structuring. Dunlop and Radaelli (2018) argue that where the tractability of problems is low and the group of actors who should be "at the table" is not well defined, a form of "reflexive learning" is necessary, which essentially requires a deliberative mode of inquiry that allows diverse perspectives to interact.

Policy scholars have also described what they call a "policy mess," which is a "public issue so uncertain, complex, interrupted and disputed that it can't be avoided" (Roe, 2013, 3). Emery Roe argues that policy messes can be managed, but not "cleaned up." He argues that "[t]oo many people insist that the way to clear up policy messes is by reducing uncertainty, simplifying complexity, resolving conflict and completing unfinished business—in short, getting rid of turbulence" (Roe, 2016, 353). Instead, he suggests that we learn about how to effectively manage messes from a group he calls "reliability professionals," who are in the business of managing messes on a regular basis.

Studying the professions who manage the electricity infrastructure, Roe identifies several traits or conditions that allow these managers to reliably manage messes. The first is the overall system design, which sets the basic macro-parameters in which reliability professionals work. Designs that

Addressing challenging public problems 17

provide room for a range of continencies are likely to make the job of mess management more tractable. This latitude allows for "scenario formulation" and for "local contingency scenarios." Mess management is also facilitated when these professionals can bridge and translate between pattern recognition and anticipation at the micro level and contingency scenarios at the meso level.

Like the wicked problems framework, the ill-structured, intractable and policy mess perspectives help to discern the features of problems that make them difficult to "solve." The problem structuring approach advocated by Dunn and Hoppe and the intractable problems approach advanced by Shön and Rein fit particularly well with the diagnosis and dialogue perspective introduced in Chapter 1 of this book. Arguably, these approaches take us deeper inside the process of handling challenging problems than does the wicked problem framework.

Social and Other Traps

Another way that scholars have analyzed social problems is using the metaphor of a "trap." Platt (1973) first introduced the Skinnerian concept of a "social trap," which occurs when a behavior that is undesirable from a collective or long-term point of view is reinforced, and hence repeated. The result is that suboptimal short-term behaviors are "locked-in." The key to getting out of a social trap is to enhance the relative value of the more optimal behaviors by adding incentives, punishments or authority that counter suboptimal behaviors. Platt noted that traps are often "nested," meaning that several interlocking traps reinforce one another. More recently, Young (2021, 103) has argued that incremental strategies are unlikely to break out of social traps, because they typically require a "regime shift."

Platt was building on Garrett Hardin's conception of the tragedy of the commons, which will be discussed more in Chapter 9. However, this "collective action" notion of social traps has also been elaborated by Rothstein (2005) who has analyzed social traps as a cultural or collective phenomenon. Rothstein argues that getting out of a social trap requires collective cooperation, and collective cooperation depends, in turn, upon trust. Both social and institutional trust are important for explaining willingness to support the costly policy efforts required to break out of social traps.

Development economics has used the concept of a "poverty trap" to explain persistent poverty and to explore policy implications. Like the concept of "traps" in general, the concept of "poverty trap" emphasizes self-reinforcing dynamics that lock people and countries into suboptimal equilibria. A range of different self-reinforcing mechanisms, operating at different levels of analysis (individual, household, firm, local, regional or nation, etc.) have been posited, including poor access to credit, corruption, low saving rates, poor nutrition, lack of access to technology, social exclusion, or environmental degradation. Barrett and Swallow (2006) introduced the concept of "fractal poverty traps" to describe how poverty traps are often "multi-level" phenomena and scholars have also increasingly pointed to the multi-dimensional nature of poverty traps (Radosavljevic et al., 2021). Unfortunately, it is difficult to empirically demonstrate the existence of a poverty trap (Barrett and Carter, 2013) and some research finds limited evidence of poverty traps (Kraay and McKenzie, 2014).

Repenning and Sterman (2002) introduced the concept of a "capability trap," arguing that they occur when the energy, time and resources invested in keeping production going at a certain rate prevents energy, time and resources from being expended on efforts to improve production, thus trapping the organization at a certain level of capability. A capability trap is like a social trap in that it is often produced when people or institutions value short-term benefits over long-term consequences. But Repenning and Sterman also discuss how "blame dynamics" can reinforce capability traps by accentuating the wrong response—for example, blaming employees for low production rather than focusing on long-term improvements.

While Repenning and Sterman focus on a capability trap at a single firm, other scholars have brought attention to how they might work at a governance level. A study of the U.S. Highway System, for example, shows how under-funding has led to deferred maintenance, producing a situation that speeds up highway deterioration (Guevara et al., 2017). Another study investigates how a weak evidence base discourages the development of a longer-term strategic response to homelessness and suggests that a community dynamics model can be used to diagnose and address capability traps (Fowler et al., 2019, 349).

The concept of a capability trap has also been used in international development, where they can occur at the individual, organizational, and organizational ecosystem levels and where behaviors at each level can produce suboptimal outcomes. These behaviors can constrain innovation and disincentivize performance and, like nested social traps, produce mutually reinforcing but suboptimal outcomes. Andrews et al. (2013, 2017) argue that "blueprint" or "best practice" strategies of international development tend, despite good intentions, to accentuate these suboptimal behaviors. In a series of African case studies, Mdee and Harrison (2019) have shown how application of best practices in water governance have tended to reinforce capability traps.

A theoretical advantage of the "trap" concept is that it calls our attention to the mechanisms that underpin difficult-to-solve problems. The concept also prompts inquiry into the nature of traps and points to the value of systems dynamics models for diagnosing the interdependent and reinforcing nature of a trap. We have several case-specific illustrations of traps of various sorts, but still limited empirical evaluation of their existence.

Complexity and Problem-Solving

Complexity is a common factor underlying many discussions of difficult-to-solve problems (Peters, 2005; LaPorte, 2015). Like the wicked problems framework, a complexity approach to public problems seeks to avoid more "reductionist" approaches to governing (Colander and Kupers, 2014; Cairney and Geyer, 2017). Complexity cannot easily be reduced or eliminated, so it must be managed or adapted to, or as Wagenaar (2007) suggests, "harnessed." A key point that follows from this perspective is that those who live inside the complexity—even if they are not "experts"—will have knowledge of the complexity that those outside the complexity—even if they are "experts"—may not appreciate. Wagenaar (2007) argues that harnessing complexity means engaging those with inside knowledge and experience, and this, in turn, means engaging with citizens through participatory and deliberative governance.

The idea that governance complexity is negatively related to policy implementation is an old one in the governance literature (Pressman and Wildavsky, 1984), but continues to inspire empirical research. Kirschke and Newig (2017) argue that governance complexity varies along five dimensions: (1) goal conflicts exist; (2) many variables influence goal attainment; (3) these variables are dynamic over time; (4) goals and variables are highly interconnected; and (5) evaluating problem-solving is highly uncertain. They note that all these strategies call for information-gathering, but each dimension also has some specific needs: conflicting goals requires conflict-solving strategies, while many variables requires goal prioritization and dynamic variables, interconnectedness and uncertainty call for modeling, decision support and adaptive decision-making. Kirschke et al. (2017a, 2017b) operationalize this framework and apply it to German water projects.

In addition to discerning different types and dimensions of complexity, scholars have introduced diagnostic perspectives that allow for the assessment of complexity and its implications. Geyer and Rihani (2012), for example, propose the "Stacey Diagram" as a valuable diagnostic tool for evaluating complexity and its implications for public policy. The Stacey Diagram has two axes. One axis refers to certainty and it ranges from "close to certainty" to "far from certainty." The other axis refers to agreement and ranges from "close to agreement" to "far from agreement." The diagram then relates these dimensions to different strategies for dealing with public policy issues. Where the situation is close to certainty and close to agreement, we are in a stable situation where we can be comfortable with rational-technical decision-making. Where the situation is far from uncertainty and far from agreement, we are in an unstable world subject to the potential for disorder and disintegration that can only be addressed by "muddling through." In between, we are in a situation where innovation and improvization become critical strategies for dealing with complexity.

On a critical note, Triantafillou (2020) argues that complexity is the idea that underpins much of the New Public Governance literature and it has become "trapped" by it. He argues that this literature has become so absorbed by dealing with complexity that it overlooks more straightforward strategies of problem-solving.

PROBLEM-SOLVING STRATEGIES

Remedying Wicked Problems

The founders of wicked problems theory, Horst Rittel and Melvin Webber, were pessimistic that wicked problems could be solved and this may have slowed down academic attention to how to tackle such challenges (Crowley and Head, 2017). Peters (2005) has argued that policy problems are more or less "solvable," which is a reference to whether there is a definitive, one-shot solution that can be identified or whether the solution is unclear and unlikely to be resolved once and for all. Interpreting "wickedness" as a function of complexity, uncertainty, and value divergence, Head (2008) points out that since there is no single root cause of these dimensions, there is no one single approach to addressing wicked problems.

In his most recent statement on wicked problems, Head (2022) has identified seven generic strategies for dealing with wicked problems. First, the problem can simply be denied or ignored, which often reflects political incentives to avoid blame. Second, political leaders can more directly tackle wicked problems through executive action or command-and-control regulation. Third, wicked problems can be broken up into smaller and more tractable problems, though this strategy tends to ignore their systemic or interdependent nature. Fourth, a technocratic approach can be applied to wicked problems, which tends to rely on an evidence-based approach to problem-solving. Fifth, wicked problems can be addressed through an incremental and pragmatic problem-solving strategy, often in a fashion that adapts and improves strategy through learning and feedback. Sixth, stakeholder collaboration can help address wicked problems by ensuring cooperation and coordination between parties with different interests and perspectives. Finally, wicked problems may be addressed through developing preventive strategies that attack problems before they manifest themselves.

A simple diagnostic model for deciding on a general strategy for dealing with wicked problems is proposed by Roberts (2000). The first question policymakers should ask themselves is about the type of problem they face. Simple problems exhibit low levels of conflict, while complex problems face conflict

Addressing challenging public problems 21

over solutions, and wicked problems face conflict over both problem definitions and solutions. If policymakers deem problems wicked, then they should proceed to ask a question about whether power over problems and solutions is dispersed or not. If not, then wicked problems can be approached using authoritative coping strategies. If power is dispersed, policymakers should then ask whether power over problems and solutions is contested or not. If it is not contested, then collaborative coping strategies are a good approach. However, if power is contested, then competition is the default coping strategy—those who amass the greatest support and resources get to set the problem-solving strategy.

One strategy for addressing wicked problems is to deepen knowledge about the problem. Head (2008) argues that the most common prescriptions for addressing wicked problems include "better knowledge, better consultation and better use of third-party partners" (2008, 114). Evidence-based policy approaches, however, are particularly tricky and frustrating as public problems become more "wicked" and "intractable" (Parkhurst, 2016; Ansell and Geyer, 2017; Newman and Head, 2017). Therefore, various approaches to knowledge generation have been proposed. Head and Xiang (2016) argue for an "adaptive, participatory and transdisciplinary" approach, while Conklin (2005) has developed a "dialogue mapping" methodology that helps to facilitate collaboration, organize collective knowledge, and analyze the wicked problem itself. Bianchi et al. (2017) have shown how "dynamic performance management" modeling—a type of qualitative dynamic systems modeling—can be useful for addressing wicked problems.

Constructively addressing challenging problems calls not only for reflection on the character of the problem and collection of knowledge about it, but also the ability to update this analysis through time. Hoppe (2018) has proposed a series of heuristics to help policymakers move from ill-structured to structured problems, arguing that they must first reflect on the character of the problem and decompose it into workable chunks, and then work to structure it around approximate and feasible solutions to the right problem. But the analysis does not stop there because policymakers must remain attentive to negative feedback and continue to experiment with alternative approaches. Scholars have also suggested that effectively coping with wicked problems means approaching them with a variety of incremental strategies (Daviter, 2017).

Termeer et al. (2015) argue that four governance capabilities are needed for addressing wicked problems—reflexivity, resilience, responsiveness, and revitalization. Governance actors must have the capacity to reflect on the problem itself (reflexivity), to be resilient in the face of surprises and emerging challenges (resilience), to act responsively to changing demands (responsiveness), and to unblock unproductive situations (revitalization). Using examples from

European agricultural reform, they show how these capabilities are necessary for achieving policy breakthroughs.

In their analysis of "super wicked" problems, Levin et al. (2012) ask policymakers to "reason forward" to consider how they can unleash "progressive incremental" change—that is, to consider how policy choices made in the present create the conditions for subsequent policy changes that extend and deepen the original direction of change. Like the original wicked problems framework, the super wicked problems framework is primarily useful for helping those who will take action to think about how they orient themselves toward problem-solving agendas.

Small Wins

One promising strategy for dealing with difficult-to-solve public problems is the idea of "small wins." Karl Weick (1984) first called attention to "small wins" as a strategy of problem-solving. His basic idea was that scaling down problem-solving strategies such that they produce more immediate positive feedback can enhance both the manageability and the motivational basis of effective problem solving. These small wins can then accumulate to produce more transformative change.

Defining small wins as positive concrete outcomes that produce in-depth change of moderate importance, Termeer and Dewulf (2019) identify six mechanisms that can propel small wins forward to produce more transformative change: *energizing* refers to the positive psychological feedbacks that result from concrete achievements; *learning-by-doing* refers to the way individuals and groups can learn from small achievements how to refine, redirect, or expand their efforts; a *logic of attraction* refers to the way that success can produce a positive flow of resources for subsequent efforts; *bandwagon effects* refer to the way that small wins encourage imitation, which can lead to efforts of greater scale; *coupling* refers to linkages that can develop between small wins operating in different places or on different scales; and *robustness* refers to the ability of smaller efforts to survive scaling-up (Termeer and Dewulf, 2019, 305–307).

Termeer and Metze (2019) demonstrate the usefulness of this framework for understanding "circular economy" initiatives. However, in a study of 17 regional efforts to reduce plastic pollution in the Netherlands, Bours et al. (2021) find that bottom-up small wins efforts are promising, but they also encounter challenging institutional barriers and can fail to scale up or become institutionalized.

Similar in spirit to the small wins approach, Wildavsky (1979, 63) called attention to "The Law of Large Solutions in Public Policy," pointing out that the key to addressing social problems was to keep them small because the solutions to large problems created problems of their own. Building on a perspective on cultural differences outlined by Douglas and Wildavsky (1983), Verweij et al. (2006) argue that complex problems require "clumsy solutions" that combine and bridge different cultural norms rather than trying to optimize around a single cultural system.

Networks and Collaboration

Collaborative or networked governance is commonly seen as necessary for responding to wicked problems because these strategies enable stakeholders to cooperate at the "system" level (Roberts, 2000; Van Bueren et al., 2003; Koppenjan and Klijn, 2004; Weber and Khademian, 2008; Ferlie et al., 2011; Kapucu, 2014; Head and Alford, 2015; Daviter, 2017). A study of chronic homelessness, for example, argues that "collaborative governance can best meet its goals at solving wicked problems like chronic homelessness when it is truly collaborative" (Mosley and Park, 2022, 148). However, Noordegraaf et al. (2019) criticize the wicked problem framework's "romanticized notion" of collaboration, trust and learning as a strategy for dealing with such problems.

A basic insight of this research is that complex problems implicate multiple institutions and stakeholders and hence require some mode of multi-party coordination and cooperation. Although hierarchy could also achieve such coordination, the challenge is that a common hierarchy rarely encompasses or applies to all the relevant parties, which often include multiple "sovereign" public jurisdictions as well as private stakeholders. Thus, "network governance" or "network management" is a kind of de facto best strategy for responding to complexity. Whether or not networks are up to the task of managing complex governance challenges remains an open question (Koppenjan and Koliba, 2013). Networks add their own complexity to problem-solving, because they typically require complex negotiations between multiple parties (Huxham and Vangen, 2000; Kapucu, 2014).

Klijn and Koppenjan (2014) distinguish three types of complexity associated with network governance. *Substantive complexity* is related to the limits on knowledge, which produces multiple and often conflicting perspectives and interpretations. Addressing the challenge of substantive complexity requires a joint framing (or reframing) of relevant knowledge so that stakeholders are operating from the same perspective. *Strategic complexity* arises due to the interaction of different interdependent strategies, which are typically uncoordinated. Addressing this type of complexity requires stakeholders to develop some baseline rules that can coordinate action among their different agendas, a process often facilitated by intermediaries or brokers. *Institutional complexity* occurs when different rules, often governing different domains, interact and clash. This type of complexity can be addressed by making rules more flexible or by removing rules that block progress. Klijn and Koppenjan argue that "network management" is the process of managing these different dimensions of complexity.

"Boundary-spanning leadership" has also been proposed as a critical strategy for achieving more integrated problem-solving. Edelenbos and van Meerkerk (2015, 27) report on survey research on complex water projects that supports the claim that "boundary spanning activities positively affect the throughput legitimacy of governance networks." A similar claim is that "bridging organizations" are critical mechanisms for achieving integration (Berdej and Armitage, 2016).

Adaptive Governance

"Adaptive governance" has also been proposed as a strategy for grappling with complex governance issues, particularly for environmental governance. Chapter 9 takes up the topic of adaptive governance in more detail, but Duit and Galaz (2008), among others, have argued that the concept of "complex adaptive systems" (CAS), as derived from complexity theory, offers a good framework for thinking about how governance can tackle complex and challenging problems. CAS's assume that agents follow different behavioral schemata and that they "self-organize" due to the lack of central direction. The "coevolution" of these agents can lead to unstable and unpredictable system dynamics that produce surprising "threshold" or "cascade" effects.

To respond constructively to such system dynamics, Duit and Galaz argue that it is necessary to have "adaptive capacity," which they interpret in terms of the ability of organizations to engage in both "exploration" (flexibility and experimentation) and "exploitation" (efficient production). A high capacity for both exploitation and exploration will produce "robust" governance, while weak exploitation and exploration capacities will produce "fragile" governance. A high capacity for exploitation but a weak capacity for exploration will tend to produce "rigid" governance, while strong exploration capacity and weak exploitation capacity will tend to produce "flexible" governance. As this typology suggests, a combination of exploration and exploitation capacity produces the best odds for addressing complex problems.

Andrews et al. (2013) also stress the value of adaptation for breaking out of capability traps. Their "problem-driven iterative adaptation" (PDIA) approach emphasizes the importance of customizing problem-solving to the local context, creating a supportive environment for experimentation, adopting the lessons from these experiments and incorporating them into revised strategies, and building broad-based political support for these efforts. Implementation capacity is particularly important for successful PDIA.

Policy Problems and Policy Design

One important argument in the public policy literature is that we can improve our ability to address problems through better policy design (Linder and Peters, 1984; Peters, 2005; Hoornbeek and Peters, 2017). In sketching an early analytical framework for policy design, Linder and Peters (1984) suggested that policy design should be seen as a form of operational problem-solving and that effective policy design must triangulate between an understanding of the characteristics of problems, goals, and policy instruments. Bali et al. (2019) argue that anticipating effective policy designs requires ascertaining the root cause of problems and then selecting policy instruments that address these causes and that are operationally feasible and politically acceptable.

Recent policy design research emphasizes the importance of "policy mixes," the bundles of policy instruments that are deployed in a particular policy area (Howlett et al., 2015). This approach to policy design also widens out the perspective on who is responsible for policy design, acknowledging that design is shaped by diffuse networks of policy advisors. It also widens the analysis of policy instruments beyond technical considerations to consider the source of policy ideas and the fate of policy instruments in different contexts. Moreover, instead of focusing on how one policy design substitutes for another, the new design literature has been sensitized by historical institutionalism to focus on how policies evolve through the layering of new upon existing policies.

Factors affecting the process of policy instrument choice are thus an important consideration for understanding how policies address problems. Complex "policy assemblages" may emerge in a non-designed, evolutionary fashion to address complex problems and may in fact be too messy to be interpreted as designed (Howlett et al., 2015; Hartley and Howlett, 2021). "Non-design" or "muddling through" occurs where governments do not have the intention to design but do have the wherewithal to effect policy design, whereas the inverse situation—where policies have the intention but not the capacity to design—tends to lead to "design by patching" (i.e., tinkering and marginally changing existing design by layering on new policy elements). Policymakers often face incentives to under- or over-react to policy problems, producing "disproportionate" policy designs (Maor, 2017).

Policy design researchers have also begun to think about policy design in terms of its robustness, which refers to whether a policy is able to carry out its functions despite the shocks, setbacks and challenges it encounters (Capano and Woo, 2017, 2018). A robust policy design, for example, might include ensuring that the policy has the capacity to collect information about implementation or about success and failure. It might also include the ability to revise the policy over time, which places a premium on incorporating flexibility into the policy design. Capano and Woo (2018) argue that diversity, redundancy and modularity are key features of robust policy designs, and, taken together, indicate the need for "polycentric decisional structures" (a plurality of semi-independent decision units operating as a system; see Chapter 9 for discussion of the concept of polycentricity). When combined with adequate political and technical capacity, they expect such a structure to contribute to robust policy design.

Public Innovation

Increasing the rate of public innovation is another strategy for dealing with challenging public problems (Torfing, 2016; Crosby et al., 2017). In a systematic review of the literature on public sector innovation, De Vries et al. (2016) identify some key drivers of innovation. Frequently noted external drivers of innovations include the role of media and external networking, while important organizational drivers include the availability of slack resources, the existence of supportive leaders, and the degree to which an organization is risk-averse. With respect to characteristics of innovations, ease-of-use is conducive to successful innovation. Research also points to the importance of creative employees empowered to innovate. Of these different types of innovation drivers, the review finds that organizational drivers are particularly critical.

Torfing (2019) contrasts hierarchical, competitive and collaborative forms of public innovation and outlines the argument in favor of collaboration. The strength of collaboration, he writes, is that it can include a diversity of stakeholders who can bring relevant knowledge, skills, perspectives and support to the innovation process. However, harnessing this diversity can itself be challenging and depends on the motivation of the participants, effective institutional design and integrative leadership. Collaborative innovation is a distinctive process of policymaking that works through reframing existing problems and issues, producing new ideas about how to address problems, learning what works through various forms of experimentation, and engaging in an iterative process of design, assessment and diffusion (Crosby et al., 2017).

Sørensen (2017) argues that it is not sufficient to treat public innovation as an administrative process; we must also acknowledge that it entails *political* innovation. She defines political innovation as constituting "new perceptions of what counts as public value and new ways of transforming these perceptions into authoritative goals, principles and rules for public governance" (2017, 6). Political innovation deserves more attention in public innovation research because it tends to create the context in which policy innovation can materialize.

In a study of public innovation in three major European cities—Barcelona, Copenhagen and Rotterdam—Lewis et al. (2018) develop a conceptual model linking innovation drivers (supportive conditions for innovation), leadership and networking (communicating and working with various groups) to public innovation. Operationalizing these variables with survey questions and measuring innovation as a self-reported capacity for innovation, they find that leadership is the most important variable, with innovation drivers and networking playing a smaller but still significant role. They find that "network governance" leadership was the most important style of leadership in Barcelona and Copenhagen, while an entrepreneurial style of leadership was more important in Rotterdam.

CONCLUSION

How useful are these different theoretical perspectives for helping us address the challenging problems that we face in the twenty-first century? The first part of this chapter begins by considering how governance theories diagnose why social, political and policy problems are so hard to solve. Governance theories characterize these difficult-to-solve problems as wicked, ill-structured, intractable, messy, and complex. These different interpretations all point to reasons why some public problems are difficult to manage and solve, particularly through a linear and rational process.

While the wicked problems framework has been the most prominent and popular of these interpretive theories, governance theorists still struggle with the critical attributes it identifies as important. There have been various efforts to revise, refine or condense these attributes. These efforts raise a challenge that confronts all descriptive theories—how to validate their alternative descriptions of the world. Governance scholars have also suggested alternatives to the wicked problem framework that highlight the ill-structured, intractable or messy nature of problems or their character as traps. Each of these approaches brings something to the table. The ill-structured problems framework points to the importance of decomposing problems and structuring them so they can be solved; the intractable problems framework calls attention to the value of frame reflection; the messy problems framework identifies the important role of reliability professionals; and the concept of traps calls our attention to reinforcing dynamics that prevent movement away from suboptimal situations.

A common feature of many of these discussions is that they call attention to the complex nature of problems, and, indeed, claims that public problems are complex are ubiquitous in the governance literature. One general claim that arises from these discussions is that complex problems cannot be resolved through "reductionist" methods, since complex problems are analogous to "whack the mole" games where problems solved in one form reappear elsewhere in a different form. Only a more systems-oriented approach to problems can begin to grasp their interconnected nature.

28   *Rethinking theories of governance*

While the wicked problems framework is skeptical about the possibility of solving wicked problems, what can we learn from these problem characterizations about how to approach problems constructively? Research suggests that reflection on the characteristics and conditions of a problem and the collection of knowledge about it represent one critical step in addressing challenging problems. Incremental but cumulative strategies with constant updating and collaborative knowledge collection and sharing are generally called for in this literature. A logic of "small wins" is seen as appropriate for grappling with the complexities of challenging public problems.

While incremental strategies seem to be called for, it is also important to appreciate that analyses of complex problems point to the importance of systemic problem-solving that integrates different people, resources, knowledge and agendas. As a result, a common claim of the governance literature is that complex problems are better solved by networks and by collaboration than by hierarchies. Complex and challenging problems are characterized by interdependence that makes it imperative to organize across boundaries. Moreover, these characteristics create a dynamism and interactivity that is sometimes referred to as "non-linear," and that leads to a stress on the adaptive nature of problem-solving. The cross-cutting, flexible and adaptive nature of networks is thus seen as a valuable asset for addressing challenging problems. One way to put this is that a governance strategy must be able to coevolve with the dynamics of the problem.

Policy design research suggests that we can improve our collective ability to successfully address public problems by attending to how we design policy instruments. The recent policy design literature, however, has shifted attention from the selection or design of single policy instruments toward a focus on "policy mixes" and has broadened the perspective on how designs develop. Public policy scholars have also begun to consider how politics can intervene to shape policy designs and how they can be designed in ways that increase their robustness. While early policy design ideas often had a rationalist bias that was somewhat at odds with many of the ideas presented in this chapter, more recent approaches have generally moved in the direction of seeing policy design in collaborative and evolutionary terms.

One final strategy that has gained prominence in recent years is the idea of public innovation. Indeed, the view is that challenging public problems cannot be addressed without increasing the rate of public innovation. This research has investigated the drivers and barriers of public innovation and found that networking, leadership, experimentation and learning are key factors in successful innovation.

The theories reviewed in this chapter are generally interpretive in nature, in the sense that they are designed to help us interpret why some problems are so difficult to solve. While relatively weak on systematic evidence—and hence, warranted assertibility—they are stronger in their diagnostic and dialogic character. They do help us to ask questions about the nature of public problems and to imagine, in a very broad sense, the strategies and capacities for responding constructively.

3. Effective and accountable agencies: political conditions

A central challenge for contemporary governance is how to build effective and accountable public institutions. Indeed, this challenge has been the central concern of the "good governance" movement, which sees effective and accountable institutions as the cornerstone of economic development, citizen well-being, and stable democracy. This concern is also a defining feature of the entire field of public administration. Although the governance literature expands our focus beyond government to the analysis of a wider range of legal and social institutions, these public institutions often remain at the heart of governance processes.

This chapter focuses on one breed of public institution—the administrative agency. While legislative and judicial institutions deserve their own attention, administrative agencies often play a key role in linking the state to governance processes that extend beyond the state. Their role in these processes can be either positive or negative. On the one hand, they deliver welfare benefits and public goods and regulate the economy and society, providing the necessary conditions for public prosperity. On the other hand, public agencies also wield considerable discretionary power and control significant resources, facing many temptations to use this power and these resources in self-serving ways. Thus, we care about both their effectiveness and their accountability.

While administrative agencies are both powerful and central to governance, they certainly do not exist in a vacuum. They typically receive their authorization, legitimacy and funding from external sources and they operate in political, and often highly politicized, environments. How they interact with this political environment is essential for understanding their effectiveness and accountability. In some cases, the political environment will support their effectiveness and enhance their accountability. In other cases, public agencies become pawns in larger political games or they become treasure chests for political clientelism and corruption. This chapter focuses on some of the theoretical perspectives that scholars have advanced about the general political conditions that shape effectiveness and accountability. Clearly, the relationship between public agencies and their political environments is not an easy one and the "modern" discussions on this topic reach back to the end of the nineteenth century.

POLITICS AND ADMINISTRATION

Perhaps the most basic and longstanding idea about how to enhance the effectiveness and accountability of public organizations is to separate politics from administration. This idea is by no means merely "theoretical" and is foundational for civil service reform movements in many parts of the world. Theoretically, however, the concept of a separation between politics and administration is usually attributed to Woodrow Wilson (1887) and Max Weber (1978), who were keen late nineteenth- and early twentieth-century observers of the expanding administrative state. Put very simply, their idea was that politicians should engage in politics, while administrators should execute policy without regard to partisan politics, exercising "neutral competence." While expressing different levels of enthusiasm, both Wilson and Weber envisioned "a formalized, professionalized, hierarchically organized, and meritocratic public administration" (Sager and Rosser, 2009, 1138).

Woodrow Wilson is famous in the public administration literature for his advocacy of a separation of politics and administration, which has led to over a century of research and debate (a debate still not put to rest!). McCandless and Guy (2013, 370) argue that Wilson was not arguing for a strict dichotomy of politics and administration but was attempting to carve out public administration as a distinct field of inquiry. Politicians and administrators are of course interdependent, but effective administration depends on administrators having a degree of discretion that protects them from partisan politics. Wilson stressed that administrative action was strongly rooted in public law and he advocated for a professional civil service (Sager and Rosser, 2009).

Max Weber is famous for his emphasis on bureaucracy as an expression of modern rationality and he stressed the way that this rationality distinguished modern bureaucracy from "patrimonial" forms of administration (Fukuyama, 2013). While Weber saw bureaucracy as an efficient form of state organization, he also feared that this rationality would displace the more value-driven action of democratic politics. As a result, according to Sager and Rosser (2009), he emphasized a stricter separation between politics and administration than did Wilson, stressing the importance of the political neutrality of civil servants.

In many countries, public sector employment is used as a form of political patronage, which reduces the professionalism and effectiveness of the public sector (Grindle and Hilderbrand, 1995). Recent research in the Wilsonian/ Weberian tradition emphasizes the importance of separating the careers of politicians and administrators. In practice, this means that politicians and administrators need to have different paths of recruitment and promotion and Dahlström and Lapuente (2017) stress that this separation must work both ways: bureaucracies cannot be controlled by employees who receive their jobs through party patronage, and by the same token, politics cannot become dominated by high-level civil servants. They argue that such a separation is crucial for effective government because it prevents corruption and creates a system of checks and balances between bureaucrats and politicians. Critically, the careers of civil servants cannot be dependent on the goodwill and support of politicians.

An important implication of Dahlström and Lapuente's argument is that bureaucrats and politicians are held accountable to different norms, standards and actors. Although this argument is close in spirit to a Weberian perspective, they distinguish their argument from what they call the "closed Weberian bureaucracy" model. In the closed model, law is stressed over management and they emphasize that this closed legalistic approach can erode the separation between bureaucracy and politicians—in particular, by making administration a career path to politics. Using a Quality of Government expert survey for 100 countries (from three surveys between 2008 and 2011), their analysis finds that the separation of bureaucratic and political careers will produce less corruption, more government effectiveness, and more successful reform efforts.

An idea closely related to the separation of politics and administration is the argument that the quality of government depends on the impartiality of governing institutions (Rothstein and Teorell, 2008). This concern for impartiality goes beyond the stamping out of corruption and clientelism, as nicely summarized by Holmberg et al. (2009, 141):

> In our view, although a high degree of corruption is clearly an antithesis to high quality governance, the latter encompasses more than merely the absence of corruption. Our definition of good governance would also include the absence of other practices that may or may not be related to corruption, such as clientelism, nepotism, cronyism, patronage, discrimination, and the "capture" of administrative agencies by the interest groups that they are meant to regulate.

From this perspective, impartiality is a key normative principle of good governance, a procedural norm that does not specify the content of government policies (Rothstein and Teorell, 2008). However, Rotberg (2014, 512) advances the following critique of impartiality as the central criteria of good governance: "...impartiality might or might not carry with it the ability to 'deliver,' that is, to 'perform.'"

The separation between politics and administration does not necessarily mean that civil servants will serve as loyal and impartial servants of politicians. Gailmard and Patty (2007) argue that meritocratic civil service systems (inadvertently) create incentives for bureaucrats to invest in the development of expertise, which leads in turn to bureaucracies having policy preferences that often diverge from the preferences of their principals. Moreover, the rela-

Effective and accountable agencies: political conditions 33

tionship between politicians and bureaucrats varies even among countries that have broadly achieved a separation of politics and administration. Hood and Lodge (2006) describe the relationship between politicians and bureaucrats in terms of a public service bargain and they distinguish between "trustee" and "agency-type" bargains. In the former, bureaucrats are expected to be independent judges of the public good; in the latter, the relationship between politician and bureaucrat is a principal–agent relation, with the agent expected to follow the wishes of the principal.

The Wilsonian/Weberian perspective on the separation of politics and administration can also produce an inaccurate portrait of the extent to which administrators are involved in policymaking. According to the classic cross-national study of Aberbach et al. (1981), both bureaucrats and politicians are engaged in policymaking, though they tend to take on different roles in the policymaking process. Politicians play the role of "energizers," whereas bureaucrats tend to try to "equilibrate" policymaking through conflict mediation. A more recent comparative study of the E.U., France, Germany, Sweden, the U.K., and the U.S. finds that politicians are only sporadically involved in routine policymaking and their involvement in policymaking is often cued by bureaucrats (Page, 2012). However, politicians do get more involved with major policymaking efforts and when they get involved "they generally get their way" (Page, 2012, 158). This discussion suggests that while there is empirical support for the separation of politics and administration at the level of careers, the separation between policy and administration is less clear-cut.

Meritocracy, Corruption and the Administrative State

The separation of the careers of politicians and bureaucrats is generally organized through the development of meritocratic civil service systems that protect the careers of civil servants from arbitrary, personalistic or political appointment or dismissal. Meritocratic systems are generally believed to increase the effectiveness of public agencies and to reduce their tendency toward corruption (Brewer et al., 2007; Montes and Paschoal, 2016; Meyer-Sahling et al., 2018). In a study of 52 countries, for example, Dahlström et al. (2012) find strong support for the argument that meritocratic recruitment reduces corruption. A survey of civil servants in five East European democracies adds the further caveat that meritocratic recruitment reduces corruption *if* civil service laws are adequately implemented (Meyer-Sahling and Mikkelsen, 2016).

Corruption appears in all countries, but is a particularly problematic and recalcitrant challenge in some parts of the world. Starting with the observation that anti-corruption efforts are often ineffectual in countries with systemic corruption, Marquette and Peiffer (2018) compare "principal–agent" and "collective action" perspectives on corruption, showing how they make different assumptions about corruption and point to different potential solutions. However, they share the view that effective monitoring and sanctioning is important for reducing corruption and there is significant support for this perspective. In a study of 100 countries, for example, Gustavson and Sundström (2018) find that "good auditing"—by which they mean auditing that is independent, professional and that recognizes the people as the "principal"—reduces corruption.

Marquette and Peiffer (2018), however, argue that both principal–agent and collective action approaches to corruption have a "blind spot," which is that they do not consider how corruption is often a solution to a problem—that is, it is functional. This point suggests that there may be resistance to anti-corruption efforts because such efforts undercut the functional solutions that corruption enables. From this perspective, they draw the conclusion that "serious attempts to control corruption would have to start by trying to gain an understanding of what solutions corruption provides to those who engage in it, and then try to deal in the business of providing those solutions through other means" (2018, 509).

Persson et al. (2013, 2019) argue that corruption is not well understood as a principal–agent problem and propose instead a collective action perspective, which argues that corruption operates at a collective level and it has the qualities of what game theory calls a coordination game (where the pressures or expectations are that everyone will engage in corruption, or conversely, that everyone avoids such behavior). They reject Marquette and Peiffer's (2018) claim that they do not appreciate that corruption has problem-solving benefits for those who engage in it and argue that this perspective is implicit in why it is so hard to move away from a corrupt equilibrium.

In any case, scholars agree that it is challenging to reduce corruption when it is pervasive in a society (Peiffer and Alvarez, 2016). Even when citizens regard corruption in negative terms, they may remain tolerant of it or find it difficult to oppose. Using Afrobarometer data from 18 sub-Saharan countries, for example, Chang and Kerr (2017) find that those who are involved in clientelistic networks perceive corruption to be widespread but are also more accepting of it. Scholars have also pointed out that politicians or public officials who benefit from corruption do not have much incentive to introduce meritocratic, anti-corruption or transparency policies. In a well-known study of Brazil, Geddes (1994) described the "politician's dilemma" in which politicians must juggle the imperatives of political survival that favor the use of the bureaucracy for self-serving purposes with the longer-term goal of increasing government performance. She argues that only balanced power among political parties is likely to create the political incentives that will lead to support for merit-based administrative reform.

Pockets of Effectiveness/Islands of Excellence

Some comparative researchers stress that there is also wide variation within, as well as between, countries, with some agencies performing well even under less-than-conducive political conditions (Bersch et al., 2017). A key interest of this research is to understand "islands" or "pockets" of excellence amidst weaker institutions, a perspective that leads to insights that depart from the prevailing strategies associated with public sector reform (Roll, 2014).

Summarizing thinking about "pockets of effectiveness" in weak governance countries, Leonard (2010) catalogues 62 different hypotheses culled from prior case study research and groups them together as five "meta-hypotheses" paraphrased here:

(1) Agency productivity depends as much on management and leadership as it does political context;
(2) An agency's "function" shapes its structure and personnel in ways that influence its performance;
(3) Efforts to improve organizational performance can partially counterbalance the more negative influences of the political context;
(4) The impacts of political institutions, however, are not necessarily negative and they may have an interest in promoting effective agencies;
(5) The underlying political economy of an agency will create both constraints on and opportunities for agency productivity.

His overall point is that we must avoid either extreme of assuming political determinism or of assuming that politics is not relevant.

McDonnell (2017) introduces the concept of "interstitial bureaucracy" to explain pockets of effectiveness in Ghana. She argues that although agencies often lack formal autonomy with respect to personnel, interstitial bureaucracies strive for "quasi-autonomy over personnel through a combination of strategic choices and leveraging political capital" (2017, 488). These agencies achieve effectiveness by upholding hiring standards, informally vetting candidates and reassigning employees with weak performance. To overcome the salary deficiencies that are typical for civil services in developing countries, interstitial bureaucracies attract and retain high-performing employees by giving them experience, career exposure and pride in their work. Interstitial bureaucracies also build personnel redundancy that allows them to meet changing conditions and external pressures.

To secure externally controlled resources, interstitial bureaucracies mobilize their own networks and social capital. They also try to shape their environments in a productive fashion by disciplining and coopting elements of their external environments. In sum, McDonnell (2017, 494) argues that "[b]ureaucratic interstices foster socially innovative or deviant values, practices, and cultural tools by clustering a critical mass of proto-bureaucratic human, cognitive, and material resources." She interprets this as a Weberian bureaucratic "ethos" and suggests that interstitial bureaucracies are likely to emerge in situations where neither bureaucratic nor neopatrimonial (political patronage) pressures are hegemonic.

Politicization

While a separation of politics and administration and a meritocratic civil service are seen as key ingredients of effective and accountable public organizations, clientelism and patronage are generally seen as unfavorable. A somewhat broader way of stating this is that bureaucracies tend to become less effective and less accountable when they become politicized. To some degree, politicization is the opposite of creating a meritocratic civil service. For example, Peters and Pierre (2004, 2) associate politicization of the bureaucracy with "the substitution of political criteria for merit-based criteria in the selection, retention, promotion, rewards, and disciplining of members of the public service." They hypothesize that politicization of the bureaucracy may not be worthwhile for political parties if politics is more consensual but becomes more attractive as party politics becomes more adversarial or polarized.

Politicization is generally seen as having negative consequences for effectiveness and accountability. Meier et al. (2019, 1577), for example, argue that "our failures of governance are failures of politics, not failures of bureaucracy" and Bersch et al. (2017, 118) conclude that "increasing levels of politicization of the bureaucracy has detrimental effects on governance." Using data from a large-scale executive survey conducted in Europe, Kim et al. (2022) found that senior public officials exhibit negative work attitudes when there is political intervention in civil service staffing, when they have little policy influence, and when political actors interfere in their managerial activities. Politicians' disrespect for bureaucratic expertise had the largest negative effect on work attitudes. Policy learning becomes challenging when agencies are politicized and may drive out agency professionals and undermine problem-solving skills and procedures (Richardson, 2019).

While politicization is generally seen as undermining agency effectiveness, scholars have begun to distinguish different dimensions of politicization (Hustedt and Salomonsen, 2014). *Formal politicization* refers to the limits on rules that safeguard meritocratic recruitment and careers, instead allowing appointment according to more political criteria. While the tendency is to see this as negative, it can also increase bureaucratic responsiveness and bring in needed expertise through the appointment of political advisors. *Functional politicization* refers to the incorporation of politically responsive tasks into the public organizations. An example is where the bureaucracy provides political-tactical advice to ministers. *Administrative politicization* refers to a situation where the advice coming from the civil service gets politicized, typically by ministerial advisors. In a comparative analysis of four European countries, Hustedt and Salomonsen (2014) find a complex mix of these forms of politicization.

Populism is seen as leading to the politicization of public agencies. Peters and Pierre (2019) observe that populists try to occupy the state and engage in mass clientielism. They predict that populist control of government will lead to an increase in the use of patronage that stresses party loyalty as a criterion for employment. Employees who are not loyal to the party may be sidelined. However, Peters and Pierre (2019) add that some forms of patronage, such as party professionals and programmatic technocrats, may be more effective than others. Bauer and Becker (2020) describe several strategies that populists may use that lead to greater politicization, including capture, dismantling, sabotage, and reform.

Autonomy, Reputation and Political Support

In addition to the separation of politics and administration and the development of a meritocratic civil service, politicization may be curtailed by giving public organizations a degree of autonomy. In addition to limiting politicization, scholars argue that autonomy—within limits—can enhance effectiveness. Fukuyama (2013) suggests that both bureaucratic autonomy and bureaucratic capacity contribute to effective governance and that they also interact such that higher levels of capacity (in terms of professionalization) merit higher degrees of autonomy (discretion). The comparative politics literature generally views high-performing bureaucracies as having both autonomy (from partisan competition and dominance) and capacity. A study of variations in Brazilian agencies found that low capacity and low autonomy is generally associated with higher corruption (Bersch et al., 2017).

Bureaucratic autonomy has been theorized from several different perspectives. From the perspective of public choice theory, the independence of regulatory agencies is important for establishing their long-term credibility (credible commitment) to regulate in a way that is not partisan or subject to regulatory capture by interest groups (Majone, 2001). Thus, effective regulatory agencies are those able to establish a degree of autonomy. A study of 100 regulatory agencies in 16 Western European countries between 1996 and 2013 finds, however, that as agency independence increases, political parties also make a greater effort to place their political allies in positions within these agencies (Ennser-Jedenastik, 2016).

The creation of autonomous agencies is also a hallmark of New Public Management (Yesilkagit and Van Thiel, 2008). The idea is basically to carve out agencies that can operate at arms length from more political ministries, thus allowing them to operate in a more business-like manner. A key adage of NPM is "let the managers manage." However, this process of "agencification" has also raised a concern about depoliticization, a form of politics that shifts decision-making power into "indirect" (independent) decision-making arenas in a way that buffers politicians from public criticism. Flinders and Buller (2006) point to the way that delegation to agencies is used by politicians to avoid blame.

While public choice discussions of independent regulatory agencies and New Public Management perspectives on autonomous agencies have stressed the value of autonomy, other theoretical perspectives also stress the theme of autonomy. J. Q. Wilson's (1989) classic, *Bureaucracy: What Government Agencies Do and Why They Do It*, stresses the harm caused by political micro-management of agencies. However, autonomy is not the same thing as neglect. In a meta-analysis of prior research on the effectiveness of U.S. federal agencies, Wolf (1993) found that political autonomy combined with strong external political support contributes significantly to government effectiveness. Some types of support may matter more than others. Moynihan and Pandey (2005) find that client group support is less important than media and public support for encouraging effectiveness and Lee and Whitford (2013) found that presidential attention was a key political resource for improving performance.

Research on administrative state-building has also been concerned with bureaucratic autonomy. The best-known statement of this argument is Carpenter's (2001) influential book on the historical development of the American administrative state. Carpenter (2001) argued that public agencies can develop a relative degree of autonomy by developing reputations for effectively serving the public or powerful constituency groups. In their study of U.S. federal agency performance, Lee and Whitford (2013) find support for Carpenter's idea that a positive reputation can improve performance, though Roberts's (2006) study of the American disaster management agency, FEMA, finds that reputation and autonomy are sensitive to political dynamics and can be easily lost.

Bureaucratic autonomy may be shaped by many factors. In addition to reputation, Roberts (2009) notes that in some cases—like the CIA or FBI—agencies gain autonomy due to the nature of their executive function, which may require secrecy or rapid response. High salience issues can lead to less autonomy and greater demands for political accountability (Koop, 2011; Maggetti and Verhoest, 2014). Agency design—such as the tenures of agency directors—also contributes to autonomy (Selin, 2015). Autonomy may be

Effective and accountable agencies: political conditions 39

formal and established by statute, or it can be de facto and established through precedent. Studies of Dutch and European agencies, however, have found that formal autonomy is not necessarily a good predictor of de facto autonomy (Yesilkagit and Van Thiel, 2008; Groenleer, 2014).

Huber and Shipan (2002) argue that legislators use statutes to make deliberate choices about how much discretion to delegate to the administration. They can write very specific and detailed legislation that purposefully limits administrative discretion or they can write vague statutes that grant greater discretion. They argue that variation in the design of discretion can be explained by the level of conflict among legislators (with more conflict generally leading to more detailed statutes), the capacity of legislators to draft detailed statutes, the ability of other political actors to limit the drafting of detailed statues (as shaped by broad national political institutions like bicameralism), and whether there are other opportunities or institutions for exercising oversight. They demonstrate support for this theory in comparative research on U.S. states and 19 parliamentary countries.

Political Control and Principal–Agent Theory

While bureaucratic autonomy is seen as a positive factor for organizational effectiveness, no scholar recommends complete autonomy because administrative agencies must ultimately be responsive to democratic control. Thus, political control is valued alongside bureaucratic autonomy and the challenge is how to strike the right balance between them. Indeed, the debate about control versus autonomy is an old one in public administration and often referred to as the Friedrich–Finer debate (Stewart, 1985).

The issue of political control over the bureaucracy has been a major issue in political science and research has examined the various means used to establish this control. A study of seven U.S. agencies, for example, found that the ability to appoint agency leadership is the most important factor in producing agency responsiveness to political oversight, while budgets, reorganizations and congressional oversight are of lesser importance (Wood and Waterman, 1991). A substantial body of research conceives of political control of the bureaucracy through the lens of principal–agent theory, which examines situations where a "principal" is concerned with controlling the behavior of an "agent" to whom discretion has been delegated. This body of theory is extensive and sophisticated and can apply to a wide variety of different relationships operating at different scales (citizens–representatives, congress–bureaucracy, boss–employee, purchaser–provider; Gailmard, 2012).

Principal–agent theory investigates control issues through the lens of the tension that can arise in the relations between the principal and agent. A first key tension is goal conflict that arises because the principal and agent have

40 *Rethinking theories of governance*

different agendas. This tension is potentially compounded by "asymmetric information" between the principal and the agent, where the agent may have privileged information that allows them to act opportunistically and that can result in generic problems like agent "shirking" or "pretending" (Lane, 2020). Problems of information asymmetry can be corrected through incentive design and through monitoring, but these measures are understood by principal–agent theory to have a cost that must be factored into the design of the relationship. Thus, the expectation is that political control over the bureaucracy will be high where: goal consensus between politicians and bureaucrats is high; where bureaucratic discretion is low; or where information asymmetries favor political principals over bureaucratic agents (Waterman and Meier, 1998).

One of the most famous political science discussions of political control over the bureaucracy draws a distinction between "fire alarm" and "police patrol" types of oversight (McCubbins and Schwartz, 1984). Police patrol oversight refers to situations where the overseer (typically, though not always, the legislature) directly investigates, monitors and sanctions bureaucratic actions, whereas fire alarm oversight establishes a set of rules that allow citizens or interest groups to investigate, monitor and sanction the bureaucracy (typically, via the courts). McCubbins and Schwartz argue that fire alarm oversight is generally more effective in achieving compliance because it tends to generate more specific as well as more comprehensive feedback.

Although not explicitly framed as a principal–agent model, the McCubbins and Schwartz article provides insight into how political overseers can respond to the challenge of information asymmetry. Framing the issue more explicitly as a principal–agent challenge, McCubbins et al. (1987) argue that monitoring and sanctions are costly and that incentives have a limited effectiveness in solving bureaucratic control challenges. They suggest that administrative procedures that allow broader publics to monitor bureaucratic behavior in a decentralized fashion offer a less costly mechanism for addressing information asymmetry problems.

One issue that has vexed the principal–agent literature is how to understand bureaucracies as political actors in their own right. Moe (2006) argues that the principal–agent literature has not fully accounted for the political power of bureaucracies and their ability to act like interest groups in pursuing their own policy interests. He uses the power of teachers' unions in California educational policy as an example of the ability of bureaucracies to exercise political power. In a comparative study of the role of politicians and bureaucrats in policymaking, however, Page (2012) finds that the "shirking" model of political–bureaucratic relations is misleading. Bureaucrats often take the lead in policymaking, he finds, but also often take the initiative to inform their political overseers of the political issues at stake in policymaking. Moreover, Page finds that bureaucrats' role in policymaking is better characterized as

Effective and accountable agencies: political conditions 41

"conformity with precedent" and as "avoiding political vetoes" than as efforts to advance their own personal interests,

Although principal–agent theory was traditionally concerned with the relationship between a single principal and an agent or agents, it is now well appreciated that agents often have "multiple principals," particularly in political and bureaucratic settings (Waterman and Meier, 1998). The relationship between Presidents, Congress and the bureaucracy is considered an archetype of this multiple-principals problem. Collective action problems among these (or comparable) principals can reduce control over agents, even when the principals broadly share objectives (Gailmard, 2009).

Meier and O'Toole (2006, 42) argue that the principal–agent perspective is "seriously flawed" but note that public administration has not offered a satisfactory alternative. They observe that this perspective ignores the networked character of contemporary governance, which can reduce the effectiveness of political oversight (Wood and Waterman, 1991; Whitford, 2002). While institutional design can improve bureaucratic responsiveness, it cannot fundamentally fix the challenge of bureaucratic discretion, particularly in highly networked contexts. This conclusion leads them to insist that "bureaucratic values" should be at the center of our understanding of how bureaucratic discretion is exercised.

A more pluralist "stakeholder" model may be one way to begin to reimagine the idea of political control (Andersen et al., 2016). Behn argues for thinking about accountability in terms of a "Compact of Mutual Collective Responsibility," that binds both political overseers and public organizations. This "compact" is a legally non-binding agreement between overseers and organizations in which the parties to the compact agree on a set of responsibilities that are freely and collectively adopted and that bind them in a form of mutual obligation. As Behn (2001, 125) notes, "accountability is imposed on you unilaterally; responsibility is assumed by you voluntarily." Such a compact holds both overseers and the organizations they oversee mutually responsible for outcomes. Overseers are responsible for not creating rules or demands that force public organizations to violate their responsibilities (for example, for fairness or financial probity).

ACCOUNTABILITY

The issue of democratic control over public organizations can also be thought about in terms of accountability. However, accountability is a more general-purpose concept than political control, in the sense that accountability is exercised at all levels of organization. It is not just about how political overseers hold a public organization accountable, but also about how employees are held accountable to their managers. The concept of accountability is an old one that refers to being called to provide an account of one's actions to an authoritative body, but the meaning of accountability has greatly expanded in the last several decades to encompass issues related to transparency, liability, controllability, responsibility, and responsiveness (Mulgan, 2000; Behn, 2001; Koppell, 2005).

In an influential public administration discussion, Bovens (2007, 450) defines accountability as "a relationship between an actor and a forum, in which the actor has an obligation to explain and to justify his or her conduct, the forum can pose questions and pass judgement, and the actor may face consequences." The accountability forum could be an individual person or an office or an organization (an agency) or institution (like a court or parliament). Accountability implies the obligation (formal or informal) to give an account to the forum, which implies informing the forum about the actors' actions. The forum, in turn, must be able to interrogate relevant actors and may pass judgement on their actions, with the actors potentially facing consequences as a result.

Bovens shows that this basic understanding of accountability can be extensively elaborated with the respect to the type of forum, the nature of the actor, the nature of the conduct, and the nature of the obligation entailed, and thus covers a wide range of specific forms of accountability. Another important distinction in the accountability literature is between ex ante and ex post accountability, because as Behn (2001) notes, accountability is often as much about deterrence of undesirable behaviors as it is about holding people or organizations accountable after an inappropriate action. While clear in theory, it is not always easy to distinguish ex ante and ex post accountability in practice (Bovens, 2007).

Principal–agent models are also the dominant contemporary framework for studying accountability, but here too they confront some limitations (Schillemans and Busuioc, 2015). In practice, principals may not actually care about agent performance, their preferences may shift, they may not take advantage of information relevant to accountability, and they may not take actions to correct agent behavior. While principal–agent models expect "agent drift" to lead to accountability failures, Schillemans and Busuioc (2015) suggest that "forum drift" actually leads to many accountability problems. They point out that a forum is analogous in many respects to a principal, but differs in important ways that suggest the limits of principal–agent theory.

Behavioral studies of accountability generally come to quite positive conclusions about the effects of accountability. Summarizing behavioral accountability experiments, Aleksovska et al. (2019) find that these experiments demonstrate that accountability pressures on decision-makers lead them to search for and remember more information, engage in deeper information processing and more analytical and integrative decision-making than those who did not face such pressures. Accountability pressures can improve decision quality, judgement consistency and task performance, particularly when expectations for decision performance are set before decisions are made. However, accountability pressures can also produce defensive behavior and risk avoidance, which is generally seen as negative, though these behaviors may appear as cautiousness, self-insight, and cooperative behavior in some contexts. Although these results were not developed in public agency contexts, Schillemans (2016) builds a model for public sector accountability based on them.

Accountability is often perceived to be a "golden concept" that "no one can be against" (Bovens, 2007, 448). But more is not always better. One theme in the accountability literature is that "multiple accountabilities" are often brought to bear in governance (Hupe and Hill, 2007; Dubnick and Frederickson, 2014; Thomann et al., 2018). A now classic account by Romzek and Dubnick (1987) identifies four different types of public sector accountability: *bureaucratic accountability* refers to the accountability of an employee to a supervisor; *legal accountability* refers to accountability to external bodies (e.g., courts) who can impose legal sanctions on the public organization; *professional accountability* refers to accountability exercised by experts; and finally, *political accountability* refers to the accountability pressures that come from elected officials or other external constituencies. A key point of their argument is that it is possible to hold an organization or individual accountable via an inappropriate form of accountability, which is then likely to lead to poor results that undermine performance.

Multiple forms and standards of accountability can also create cross-pressures that may push decision-makers in unexpected and unproductive directions (Romzek and Ingraham, 2000), possibly producing what Koppell (2005) calls "multiple accountabilities disorder." A multiple accountabilities approach suggests that accountability must be designed contextually (Hupe and Hill, 2007). The worst thing you can do from this perspective is simply layer on new forms of accountability. As a number of scholars point out, accountability has costs for organizations that can have negative consequences for organizational effectiveness (Behn, 2001). Understanding the character of the tasks that agency employees carry out is critical for designing effective accountability strategies (Wilson, 1989).

Transparency

One prominent strategy for increasing the accountability of public agencies is to promote their transparency. The idea that "sunlight is the most powerful of all disinfectants" is, according to Chhotray and Stoker (2009, 242), "one of the great truisms of governance thought." Governance by transparency

44 *Rethinking theories of governance*

works through the mechanism of making information proactively available, unleashing what Fung et al. (2007) call an "action cycle" where action taken by information users can incentivize improvements in performance (public or private). They note, however, that especially where information is complex, information disclosure can also create "transparency gaps" that demobilize action.

Reviewing 18 U.S. transparency efforts between 1996 and 2005, Fung et al. (2007) identify two general factors that produce successful transparency efforts. First, successful efforts are sensitive to the needs of information users, though it can be quite challenging to produce useful, actionable information and relevant information is often missing, distorted or undermined. Second, successful efforts demonstrate improvements in the use and accuracy of information over time. Transparency efforts, however, may degrade over time due the asymmetric power of information disclosers versus information users.

A review of research on transparency by Cucciniello et al. (2017) finds that the results of transparency are generally positive when it comes to its effect on reducing corruption, enhancing citizen participation and improving organizational performance. However, the results are decidedly more mixed when it comes to the question of whether transparency enhances accountability. A review of experimental results by Kosack and Fung (2014) also found that the effects of transparency on accountability were mixed. They tentatively conclude that transparent information is more likely to facilitate a successful action cycle when it reports: (1) inputs rather than outputs; (2) beneficiary/ citizen rights; (3) comparative performance information; (4) subjective as well as objective indicators; and when it (5) recommends or implies clear lines of action.

Social Accountability

"Social accountability" is a form of citizen monitoring of public programs that may contribute to government effectiveness and accountability. In a four-country study, Brinkerhoff and Wetterberg (2016) found that social accountability contributed to more effective governance, though this depended on a reinforcing alignment between state and citizen capacities and incentives. Fox (2015, 355) outlines a "sandwich strategy" for social accountability where "opening from above meets mobilization from below"—an idea he traces back to the "state–society synergy" strategy he associates with the work of Peter Evans.

Social accountability can take different forms. Joshi and Houtzager (2012) argue that social accountability research has focused too much on "widgets"— that is, on specific techniques of accountability like citizen report cards, which miss the overall social and political context in which social accountability

Effective and accountable agencies: political conditions 45

takes place. In a review of studies of social accountability building on this perspective, Hickey and King (2016) find that political support within government for citizen engagement is a critical factor shaping the success of social accountability. The capacity and mobilization of civil society organizations and citizen access to high-quality information are also critical factors.

Scholars have drawn a distinction between "tactical" and "strategic" social accountability. Tactical social accountability includes the use of specific tools that narrowly seek to advance citizen voice. Strategic social accountability deploys multiple tools and coordinates them with other public accountability efforts. In a review of the evidence on the effectiveness of these strategies, Fox (2015) found that tactical social accountability had limited or mixed effectiveness, whereas strategic social accountability had greater potential for impact. Several constraints on the effectiveness of social accountability can be observed, including insufficient information and bottom-up monitoring and elite capture of community programs.

Reviewing relevant studies, Fox (2015, 350) concludes that "exclusively localized, information-led 'demandside' interventions" are often unrealistic. He draws the following conclusions about necessary conditions for a more strategic approach: first, relevant information needs to be "user-centered" if it is to be perceived as useful for change; second, effective citizen voice must be organizationally mobilized and represented and, where civil society is weak, interlocutors may be critical; third, exercising their voice is often costly to citizens, especially if they fear reprisals; fourth, it is useful to distinguish between backward-facing and forward-oriented accountability; fifth, it is useful to look for reinforcing synergies between different forms of accountability, between "voice and teeth," and between top-down and bottom-up support for accountability.

CONCLUSION

The chapter addresses some of the political conditions for effective and accountable public organizations. At a macro level, there is broad theoretical and empirical support for the Weberian/Wilsonian idea that a degree of separation between politics and administration, established through the development of a meritocratic civil service, is important for achieving the twin goals of effectiveness and accountability. Meritocratic systems are likely to professionalize public employees and reduce corruption, thereby increasing both effectiveness and accountability. The politicization of bureaucracies associated with clientelist and populist politics, by contrast, is likely to reduce effectiveness and accountability.

While the Wilsonian/Weberian position has considerable empirical support at the cross-national level, the nature of the relationship between politics and administration becomes more nuanced and disputed the closer one looks at it. Corruption remains endemic in many countries and there remains a fundamental theoretical debate about how to move away from a system dominated by it. Even in countries with generally ineffective and corrupt public sectors, however, some public organizations may stand out for their effective and accountable administration. Some degree of bureaucratic autonomy is generally regarded as a positive feature of effective administration, though this autonomy also raises concerns about the democratic responsiveness of public administration. Political scientists have made important contributions to our understanding of political control over the bureaucracy from a principal–agent and public choice perspective, though this research has been centered on the United States.

Demands for accountability are a common refrain in contemporary politics. Theory has helped to make clear what accountability is and how it works or does not work in public organizations. What is clear is that there are a wide variety of institutional and political mechanisms that can be used to try to achieve accountability. A principal–agent perspective on accountability has been prominent, particularly in the political science literature, and it has led to useful insights into how to design incentives to increase accountability. Experimental psychological studies of accountability have also produced important insights and generally reach positive conclusions about the impacts of accountability. Public administration scholars, however, have called attention to the variety of institutional mechanisms used to achieve accountability and have raised concerns about the potential costs or dysfunctions of applying multiple forms of accountability.

Some accountability mechanisms—like transparency and social accountability—try to generate accountability through more indirect or distributed forms of control. While such mechanisms have attracted much attention, they are often difficult to achieve in practice. This research has developed diagnostic insights on the conditions that make them challenging and into how they might be designed and supported to make them more successful. The quality of user-centered information is critical for both transparency and social accountability.

4. Effective and accountable agencies: administrative conditions

While Chapter 3 investigated the political conditions that support the effectiveness and accountability of public agencies, this chapter turns to an investigation of relevant administrative factors—that is, to those factors internal to public agencies that influence how well they function. The chapter does this by contrasting two broad perspectives on the organizational conditions contributing to effectiveness and accountability, each of which contains several moving parts. The first perspective is New Public Management, which has dominated the reform agenda for the past 30 years. It is a perspective strongly influenced by economic and public choice theories of organization and it is often seen as an expression of neoliberalism. The second perspective is less theoretically cohesive and less well-recognized as a distinctive reform agenda, but it has deep roots in the field of public administration. Referred to here as an "institutionalist" approach, it is more easily understood as a version of "old" institutionalism than as a variant of "new" institutionalism (Chisholm, 1995). In very broad brushstrokes, New Public Management and institutionalist perspectives can be distinguished in terms of their emphasis on a logic of consequences versus a logic of appropriateness (March and Olsen, 1996).

NEW PUBLIC MANAGEMENT

The so-called "New Public Management" (NPM) is no longer new, having shaped waves of administrative reform around the world over the last 30 years (Pollitt and Bouckaert, 2017). One of the landmark statements of NPM was the book *Reinventing Government* by David Osborne and Ted Gaebler (1993), who argued for a shift from centralized, hierarchical and bureaucratic government to a more decentralized, entrepreneurial and community-based government that would "steer" rather than "row." This new government would break down government monopolies and introduce more competition into the delivery of services, leading public organizations to become mission-, results-, customer- and market-oriented. Although NPM is still alive and well, scholars now distinguish NPM and post-NPM reform trends, with the latter adopting a more "joined up" or "whole-of-government" approach (Christensen and Lægreid, 2011). The focus here is only on NPM.

In an important early article describing NPM, Hood (1991, 4–5) argued that it has seven "doctrinal components": (1) "hands-on professional management"; (2) "explicit standards and measures of performance"; (3) "greater emphasis on output controls" (management by results rather than procedures); (4) "shift to disaggregation of units"; (5) "shift to greater competition in the public sector"; (6) "stress on private sector styles of management" and (7) "stress on greater discipline and parsimony in resource use." Other scholars have developed slightly different characterizations (Dunleavy et al., 2006; Osborne, 2006).

Many scholars see NPM as exemplifying the wider international movement of "neoliberalism," in that it applies the idea of market-like discipline to government. In *The Logic of Discipline*, Alasdair Roberts (2011) chronicles the neoliberal move to create disciplined, technocratic agencies (like central banks) that are autonomous from democratic control. NPM created a tremendous wave of administrative reform, but also produced fragmentation and coordination problems that have in many cases produced "rollbacks" or compensating reforms (Dunleavy et al., 2006).

One way to interpret New Public Management is through the lens of principal–agent theory. A key characteristic of NPM is that it views organizations "as a chain of low-trust principal/agent relationships (rather than fiduciary or trustee–beneficiary ones)" (Dunleavy and Hood, 1994, 9). Indeed, the principal–agent model provides a framework for thinking about a range of key elements in the NPM model, including agencification, managerial autonomy, employee motivation, contracting and competition.

Overall reviews of NPM are mixed. Reviewing the effects of NPM reforms in the U.K. after 30 years, Hood and Dixon (2015, 266) conclude that the result is government that works a bit worse and costs a bit more. In a meta-analysis of NPM reforms in European countries, Pollitt and Dan (2011) found mixed results. Approximately half the studies they reviewed found improvements in outcomes, outputs or processes, while the remainder of the studies found that the reforms led to worse performance or to unchanged or uncertain results (Pollitt and Dan, 2011, 31, table 8). Verhoest (2005) arrives at a more positive conclusion. In a careful in-depth case study of the performance of two divisions of a Belgium employment agency, he concludes that results-oriented controls (managerial autonomy, performance management, financial incentives and competition) can enhance performance if they are used in a well-balanced fashion. In a review of NPM reform in Eastern Europe, Dan and Pollitt (2015) come to a cautiously optimistic conclusion. More than half of the studies they evaluate (18 out of 32) conclude that these reforms could have positive effects, though they faced challenges associated with weak capacity or lack of contextual support.

Effective and accountable agencies: administrative conditions 49

Mixed results were also found in a survey of perceptions of performance improvement from over 7000 public officials from 20 European countries (Hammerschmid et al., 2019). The survey finds that public sector downsizing, contracting out and the creation of autonomous agencies are generally unrelated to performance improvement, though downsizing and contracting are perceived as having positive effects on costs and efficiency and downsizing is perceived as having negative effects on service quality. Customer-orientation and flexible employment practices, however, were perceived as having more positive effects across a range of performance criteria.

Delegation and Agencification

Overman (2016) identifies four forms of delegation associated with NPM—decentralization, agencification, contracting out and privatization. In a meta-review of 250 articles on delegation, he finds mixed results with respect to NPM expectations about gains in efficiency, political control and organizational management. He proposes that contextual conditions are critical for understanding these mixed effects, with positive effects depending on skills, budgets and politics.

As discussed above, agencification is a form of delegation from executive branch ministries or departments to relatively autonomous single-purpose "agencies" (Cingolani and Fazekas, 2020; Waluyo, 2021). It is hypothesized to improve government performance by creating more business-like conditions that focus managers on achieving clear objectives, and it is sometimes referred to as "corporatization" (Nelson and Nikolakis, 2012). Vining et al. (2015, 197) provide a concise statement of how agencification is expected to improve agency efficiency and performance: "clearer incentives and targets for the CE [Chief Executive] and employees, increased transparency around managerial behaviour and performance and greater pressure on CEs to deliver results—should lead to improved performance if it is not overwhelmed by the countervailing effects of more self-interested behaviour flowing from increased agency autonomy."

As with the overall evaluation of New Public Management, studies of the performance benefits of agencification receive mixed marks. In a study of six Australian state forestry agencies, Nelson and Nikolakis (2012) found that agencification improved government performance by increasing operational efficiency, and Vining et al. (2015) found sustained labor productivity over time in a study of 13 Canadian agencies. Evaluating the effects of agencification on performance on value for money in Germany, Spain and the U.K. between 2006 and 2016, Cingolani and Fazekas (2020) find that agencification does improve value for money, producing significant savings. They find older agencies are more productive and they infer that the development of

50   *Rethinking theories of governance*

professionalism in these agencies takes some time to achieve. On the negative side, Christensen and Lægreid (2007) argue that regulatory "agencification" in Norway has tended to create fragmentation and confusion as opposed to higher performance and they call attention to the tensions that occur through the relaxing of political control. Overman and Van Thiel (2016) found that agencification did not produce gains in efficiency or value for money in a study of 20 European countries.

Managerialism

The NPM literature stresses that "management matters" (Moynihan and Pandey, 2005, 422). Although this claim certainly applies more broadly than to NPM, the value of good management—and by extension, good managers—is a central NPM precept (the "management-quality hypothesis"). NPM places a particular stress on the idea of "letting the managers manage." This idea of managerial autonomy can be seen as a kind of "deregulation" of managerial action that frees managers (and employees, for that matter) from excessive procedural rules. Critics of NPM observe that such rules are often designed to safeguard fairness and financial regularity.

Studies of Texas school districts and English local government have provided substantial support for the argument that management matters (Meier and O'Toole, 2002; Meier et al., 2007). Favero et al. (2016) identify four managerial actions that positively influence employee behavior: managers can set and communicate clear and feasible goals; they can engage in actions that build trust with employees that establish manager credibility; they can encourage participation of employees in decision-making (to elicit valuable information); and they need to provide feedback to employees on how well they are contributing to organizational goals. In their study of New York public schools, they find that managers have a significant positive effect on educational outcomes. In a study of the performance of U.S. agencies, Moynihan and Pandey (2005) find that agencies perform more poorly when managers do not feel they have the discretion to perform better, which they suggest supports the NPM argument for giving more discretion to managers.

Strategic Planning and Management

While strategic planning and strategic management are also not the sole domain of NPM, they assume a prominent role and are often linked to performance management and measurement (Moynihan, 2006). Reviews of studies on the "strategy–performance" link generally find strong support for the positive effects on strategic planning on performance (Boyne and Walker, 2010; George et al., 2019).

Effective and accountable agencies: administrative conditions 51

The terms "strategic planning" and "strategic management" are often used interchangeably, but Poister (2010) distinguishes them, pointing out that strategic management goes beyond the episodic formulation of plans to encompass the ongoing implementation of these plans. Still, the two processes are closely connected. In a study of the effects of formal strategic planning on strategy implementation in 150 Canadian public organizations, Elbanna et al. (2016) find that both formal planning and managerial involvement enhance strategy implementation and in a study of the implementation of strategic plans in Flemish municipalities, George (2021) boils down the success factors to the importance of connecting people, process and plan.

While strategic planning and strategy management are in the wheelhouse of NPM, Favoreu et al. (2016) distinguish between rational, political and collaborative approaches to strategic planning and found that the collaborative model best characterized strategic planning in a local French agency. Bryson's (2018) model of strategic planning also clearly emphasizes the importance of collaboration and deliberation, a departure from the rational model more closely associated with NPM.

One of the best-known concepts in public sector strategic management is Mark Moore's (1995) concept of public value. Emphasizing that managers are strategists and not simply technicians, he argues that they cannot be satisfied with simply responding to direction from politicians and must engage in innovation and initiative. He conceives this strategic role as working with what he calls the "strategic triangle," which calls for public managers to triangulate between substantive judgements about what is useful and valued by the public, what political overseers (and the political context) want and expect, and what is feasible. Moore argues that this model of strategic management is normative in that it prescribes what managers should do. At the core of this perspective lies the claim that public organizations are creators of public value, a claim in some tension with the Wilsonian/Weberian idea of neutral competence.

Competition, Contracting and the Hollow State

Perhaps one of the most impactful ideas associated with NPM is that greater efficiencies can be achieved by contracting out services and production to private and non-profit contractors. This idea is commonly referred to as the "purchaser–provider split," because government becomes the purchaser of goods and services from private or non-profit providers. The fundamental idea is that contracting out increases efficiency because it subjects producers to the competitive discipline of the market. Contracting is expected to produce cost savings by encouraging competition among providers and by reducing the size of the public sector.

Research on whether contracting does indeed produce such cost savings or does reduce the size of government again reaches mixed conclusions. Petersen et al. (2018) conduct a systematic review of research on contracting produced between 2000 and 2014 and find that of the 37 articles reporting on the relationship between contracting and cost savings, the results are roughly split on whether contracting produces cost savings or not. Evaluating data on 15 EU countries between 1983 and 2011, Alonso et al. (2015) find that contracting out has not led to a reduction of the size of government.

Researchers have sought to identify when governments contract out and to specify the conditions under which contracting out is an appropriate and desirable strategy. While many factors have been debated for why governments contract out–including ideology, partisan competition and interest group behavior–cost savings have been a particularly prominent factor (Amirkhanyan et al., 2007). Generally, the expectation is that contracting is more attractive as an option when markets are well developed, when there is a low degree of asset specificity (i.e., the degree to which service provision requires specific knowledge or skills developed through providing that service) and when outcomes are easy to measure (Brown et al., 2006).

Contracting out has led to significant concern that government will lose the competence to direct public affairs, becoming a "headless chicken" (Dunleavy and Hood, 1994) or a "hollow state" (Peters, 1994; Milward and Provan, 2000). Effective contracting clearly requires that public agencies must at least have the competence and capacity to effectively write and monitor contracts (Amirkhanyan et al., 2007; Kettl, 2011). Contracting out can stimulate efficiencies, but can also create "multiple principal–agent" problems that generate challenges for steering and monitoring (Voorn et al., 2019).

Complex and interdependent networks of contractors operating in market-like (competitive) environments often pose significant accountability challenges for contract administrators and politics can intervene to undermine effective sanctioning of contractors. Formal contract specification is critical for achieving accountability but is often insufficient in complex contracting networks (Romzek and Johnston, 2005). In such networks, Romzek et al. (2012) theorize that shared norms of trust, reciprocity and respect can help parties exert informal rewards and sanctions that encourage accountable behavior. Frequent and sustained communication, following through on commitments, information-sharing, extending favors and acknowledging mistakes can facilitate informal accountability, while competition, staff turnover and fiscal pressures can work against it (2012, 445–446).

Performance-Based Management

Another central plank of NPM is the focus on "managing by results," which is typically operationalized through performance management. Performance is a general term, but as Van Dooren et al. (2015) point out, it has a specific meaning in the NPM world: it is associated with performance as results, which tends to emphasize the quality of achievement over the quality of input actions. Moynihan (2006) outlines what he refers to as the "performance management doctrine," which assumes that hidebound government can be made more efficient, accountable and rational through the development of performance management. To achieve these positive gains, it is necessary to build a performance information system and managers must have the capacity (clear goals and authority) to act on this performance information. Based on this doctrine, the adoption of performance management is expected to lead to performance improvements.

Boyne (2014, 209) argues that performance management has three components: "selecting indicators, setting targets, and taking action to influence scores on the indicators." He provides a detailed examination of how this strategy is expected to lead to improvements in organizational performance and reviews the limited evidence on the impact of performance management on organizational performance. He concludes that, on balance, the evidence generally supports the view that performance management encourages improved performance. A meta-analysis of 49 studies of the impact of performance management on performance also finds a small but positive effect (Gerrish, 2016). This review also finds that when performance management is combined with effective management, the positive impact is more substantial.

At the heart of performance management is performance measurement, which Behn (2003, 586) notes can be used for many different purposes ("evaluate, control, budget, motivate, promote, celebrate, learn, and improve"). He notes that these different purposes make various demands on performance measurement and effective performance measurement effectively depends on being clear about the implications of these purposes for selecting and using measurement. Van Dooren et al. (2015) point to five steps in performance measurement: (1) decide what will be measured; (2) identify indicators that capture these performance concepts; (3) collect data on these indicators; (4) analyze this data; and (5) report the analyzed data. While this sounds like a straightforward process, it can be quite challenging to identify measures that capture the underlying desired performance.

The challenges of performance management are commonly pointed out. In a book-length critique, Radin (2006) argues that performance management tends to underestimate the uniqueness of programs, to disenfranchise professionals and to bury the reality of competing values. Performance information is also subject to "motivated reasoning"—that is, to interpretations of performance measurement that validate one's prior knowledge and perspective (Baekgaard and Serritzlew, 2016). A wide range of factors contributing to inappropriate performance measurement, and potential corrective actions, have been identified (Van Dooren et al., 2015).

Moynihan and Pandey (2010) develop a model of how performance information use is fostered by certain organizational characteristics. They find that organizational cultures that are open, innovative and risk-taking are more likely to use performance information. Analyzing data on U.S. public schools, Destler (2016) found that organizational cultures characterized by trust and psychological safety where frontline workers felt supported were more likely to use performance information and that these factors were more important than external incentives.

A common puzzle is that public organizations that engage in performance management often collect information that they do not ultimately use to improve performance (Moynihan, 2006). Performance management is often politically mandated and merely of symbolic importance, and performance information is often ambiguous and subject to conflicting interpretations. Actual use of performance information often depends on whether public managers embrace the value of performance management. Learning forums can help actors with different perspectives and interests to engage in dialogue with one another about what lessons to draw from available performance information. Moynihan and Kroll (2016) argue that such dialogues must be routinized and hypothesize that the use of performance information will increase when agency personnel experience these learning routines. Analysis of data on performance from U.S. agencies supports their argument.

Accountability for Results

The NPM emphasis on market discipline and performance management leads to a particular understanding of accountability that stands in some tension with more traditional notions of accountability stressing fairness and financial probity (Behn, 2001). NPM prioritizes holding organizations, managers and employees accountable for "results" rather than to hierarchical or legal rules or professional standards.

Dubnick (2005) challenges NPM's assumption of a relationship between accountability and performance, pointing out that it is equally possible to conclude that accountability may reduce performance. This paradox occurs because the time and energy invested in account-giving can come at the expense of time and energy invested in improving performance. Dubnick argues that, at the very least, there is a need to better specify the link between accountability and performance. He observes that "we found nothing in the

Effective and accountable agencies: administrative conditions 55

existing literature ... that would provide a logical (let alone a theoretical or empirical) link between account giving and performance" (2005, 403).

Several recent studies have tried to evaluate the link between results-oriented accountability and performance. In a study of U.S. Federal Agencies, Han and Hong (2019) find that results-based accountability enhances organizational performance, particularly when management autonomy is high. In a study of Korean local government, Ji (2022) finds that performance accountability increases local government attention to performance in low-performing cases. The study also finds that performance accountability is complementary rather than competitive with political accountability.

PUBLIC ORGANIZATIONS AS VALUE-BASED INSTITUTIONS

As this review suggests, NPM is controversial among public administration and governance scholars and the evidence for its success or failure is mixed. Although many point to negative effects of NPM and suggest that we have moved on to post-NPM or New Public Governance, the evidence presented here suggests that it is difficult to dismiss NPM outright. At the very least, NPM provides a framework for thinking about a range of important issues, from managerial autonomy, to contracting, to performance management and results-based accountability.

The economic model that underpins NPM is not the only game in town when it comes to understanding public organization effectiveness and accountability. The alternatives to NPM, however, come from a more disparate range of sources. Nevertheless, it is possible to pull together an equally comprehensive theoretical perspective that stresses the *institutional* nature of public organizations. There are many variants of institutionalism, of course, so it is worth noting that this perspective harkens back as much to an "old institutionalism" as it does to a "new institutionalism" (Chisholm, 1995; Selznick, 1996; Stinchcombe, 1997; Heclo, 2011). This institutionalism is not only concerned with how values are collectively and publicly formed, expressed, inculcated and protected, but also how the organization is able to create a positive and motivating work environment and how it is able to institutionalize the skills and capacity for analysis and action. From this perspective, effectiveness and accountability are achieved by successfully harnessing collective commitments to public-serving values.

Leadership and Mission Orientation

An alternative to NPM and principal–agent models starts with the view that high-performing government institutions are driven by a strong mission orientation (Selznick, 1958; Kaufman, 1967; Tendler, 1997; Goodsell, 2010; Ansell, 2011). In *Leadership in Administration*, Selznick (1958) built on prior organization theory to stress the importance of leadership in transforming an organization into an institution. He stressed the importance of "mission" as a leadership tool for transforming organizations and described how organizational cultures could be built around supporting this mission. Selznick's approach emphasized the importance of informal culture and the internalization of missions through socialization. Selznick referred to organizations that have built a sense of value and purpose around a common mission and shared culture as "institutions."

Building on an analysis of six high-performing U.S. Federal Agencies, Goodsell (2010) elaborates on the importance of what he calls "mission mystique" to agency effectiveness and greatly nuances the ways that an organization's "mission" plays a critical linking role between internal employee motivation and external agency support. Research on the effectiveness of public organizations in developing countries has drawn similar conclusions. In a study of public organizational performance in six developing countries, Grindle and Hilderbrand (1995, 456) concluded that "[w]ithout exception, the organizations that performed well were able to inculcate a sense of mission and commitment to organizational goals among staff, while those that were poor performers did not provide the same sense of mission."

Summarizing a range of prior research, Rainey and Steinbauer (1999) develop a theory of effective government organizations. Briefly, effective government organizations will have supportive external relations with overseers, client interest groups and the public, and they will enjoy (to a point) significant autonomy. They will also have a positive "mission valence"—that is, a mission that appears positive to both external stakeholders and to employees—and a strong organizational culture linked to this mission. Leadership of effective government organizations will be stable, committed to the mission and capable of setting goals and coping with external challenges. Employees will be professionalized, their work ("task design") will produce intrinsic and extrinsic rewards, and they will be highly motivated to serve the public and to complete their mission and tasks.

The important flipside of this argument—and it might be thought of as a scope condition—is that organizations that have unattractive missions or who serve unimportant or unloved clientele will face "impossible jobs" (Hargrove and Glidewell, 1990). In addition, performance will suffer in agencies that have "multiple, conflicting, and ambiguous goals" (Moynihan and Pandey, 2005, 433). Brewer and Selden (2000) develop an empirical analysis of a modified Rainey and Steinbauer theory using survey data of U.S. government employees and find considerable support for it but give it a new twist. They observe that the common denominator of variables that have

Effective and accountable agencies: administrative conditions 57

a positive relationship to organizational performance is that they all support a "high-involvement workplace strategy" that empowers employees, clients and stakeholders (2000, 706).

Boin and Christensen (2008, 277) set out a developmental model of public institutions in the sense described above. They argue that an institution begins to form when an "effective practice gives rise to a norm of practice." This norm must then become widely accepted in the organization, which can occur through processes of "escalating commitment." However, employees must believe that the norm itself (as an abstraction) is functional and it must be relatively aligned with the political context in which it is put forth. If it survives, it must become embedded into the different symbolic, social and material dimensions of the organization—that is, it must be "firmly anchored in the organization's structure and culture" (2008, 279). Ultimately, such normative practices must then establish their legitimacy with both employees and the wider publics that the organization serves. Once created, however, an institution also supports the conditions under which good leadership can prevail (Boin, 2001).

Styles of Leadership: Transactional versus Transformational Leadership and Beyond

There are a variety of theories of administrative leadership and no single best theory (Van Wart, 2013). However, perhaps the dominant theoretical approach to public sector leadership is inspired by the distinction between transactional and transformational leadership (Burns, 1978). Transactional leadership fits well with NPM's incentive-based, results-oriented approach because it views the relationship between leader and follower as an exchange, with leaders providing rewards or sanctions in exchange for performance. Transformational leaders, by contrast, exercise leadership by both understanding and supporting their followers and by changing how followers think about their work and their purpose.

As a value-based form of leadership, transformational leadership is complementary with an emphasis on the importance of organizational missions (Denhardt and Campbell, 2006). There is a significant body of research supporting these linkages. In a survey of U.S. local government public managers, Pandey et al. (2016) find empirical support for the hypothesis that transformational leadership directly and indirectly influences employee embrace of normative public values. Transformational leadership also contributes to both mission valence and public service motivation (Wright et al., 2012), and in a survey of state departments of transportation in the U.S., Pasha et al. (2017) find that transformational leadership enhances mission valence. In a survey study of Danish teachers, Jensen and Bro (2018) find that transformational leadership enhances employee work motivation by helping to fulfill basic psychological needs for autonomy, competence and relatedness. Sun and Wang (2017) find that transformational leadership reduces employee turnover and Caillier (2016) found that this effect is mediated by the effect that transformational leadership has on mission valence.

Although NPM emphasizes more transactional modes of leadership, transformational leadership is not necessarily at odds with effective performance management (Behn, 2009; Moynihan and Pandey, 2010). In a study of New York public schools, Sun and Henderson (2017) found that transformational leadership of school principals improved student test scores, in part, by improving the use of performance information. Van der Voet et al. (2016) found that transformational leadership (by direct supervisors) helps to explain the affective commitment of employees to change efforts. However, Van der Voet (2014) found that transformational leadership matters more for emergent than for planned organizational change. While there is relatively strong empirical support for claims that transformational leadership has both direct and indirect effects that improve organizational performance (Moynihan et al., 2014), Van Knippenberg and Sitkin (2013) also point to various problems with its conceptualization and operationalization.

Bernard Bass and colleagues have reinterpreted transactional and transformational leadership as complementary rather than as strict alternatives (Bass and Avolio, 1993). Transactional leadership operates through contingent rewards and sanctions and by intervening when performance deviates from expectations ("management by exception"). Transformational leadership inspires by providing a sense of mission and instilling pride, communicating high expectations, promoting effective problem-solving, and giving individualized consideration. Both styles may be used to improve performance and they may be used effectively in combination, though Bass (1990) suggests that greater weight on transformational leadership will yield dividends in terms of superior performance.

Finding support for Bass's argument that transactional and transformational leadership can be complementary, Park and Rainey's (2008) analysis of U.S. survey data finds that both transformational leadership and public service motivation enhance employee satisfaction and perceived performance and work quality, while transactional leadership has a smaller but still positive benefit for these outcomes. Transformational leadership also has a positive impact on public service motivation. Park and Rainey point to what they see as the broader message of their research, which is that incentive systems that primarily reward "extrinsic motivation" need to be cautious to avoid crowding out the "intrinsic motivation" associated with public service.

Personnel Matters and Public Service Motivation

There is a long tradition in public administration that interprets the behavior of civil servants in terms of their commitment to public service. In a landmark article, Perry and Wise (1990) examined what has come to be known as "public service motivation (PSM)," clarifying that this has both rational (policy or self-interest driven), norm-based (desire to serve public or general public values) or affective (patriotic, etc.) components. A key point of their classification is to make it clear that public service motivation is not solely altruistic, an interpretation that has dogged the public service literature (Ritz et al., 2016).

Perry and Wise (1990) framed three hypotheses about the implications of PSM: first, people who are motivated to serve the public will be more likely to pursue employment in public organizations; second, public service motivation will shape, in a positive way, work behavior ("individual performance"); and third, public organizations that recruit employees with high public service motivation will not have to rely on "utilitarian incentives" to achieve effective organizational performance. The broader implication of PSM, Perry and Wise suggest, is that public management is different than private management.

As noted, the research literature on PSM that followed Perry and Wise is prolific (Perry and Vandenabeele, 2015). In a review, Ritz et al. (2016) find several important themes and management recommendations that have grown out of this research. Frequent management recommendations include: (1) assessing the public service motivation of job candidates and using this information to recruit civil servants; (2) taking management actions that enhance the public service motivation of public employees; and (3) tailoring specific management strategies that align with public service motivation (e.g., reinforce employee experiences of making significant contributions to public service). Their review finds that research confirms positive relationships between public service motivation and positive organizational outcomes like job satisfaction, low turnover, individual and organizational performance and job commitment. They observe, however, that these relationships have been primarily studied using cross-sectional data that does not permit strong causal identification.

Moynihan and Pandey (2007) find that organizations shape PSM, with the notable finding that increasing red tape (i.e., bureaucratic rules) can reduce public service motivation. In findings similar to those of Ritz et al. (2016), Christensen et al.'s (2017) review of management tactics with respect to public service motivation identify a number of lessons. Organizations can recruit employees with high public service motivation, which they can do in part by fashioning an attractive organizational mission. They can also avoid "crowd[ing] out intrinsic or prosocial orientations" (2017, 533) and can design work environments that reinforce PSM and give public service meaning to work.

In a broad-based theoretical and empirical analysis of the work of U.S. bureaucrats (at the local, state and federal levels), Brehm and Gates (1999) found that supervisors in public bureaucracies were highly constrained in their ability to incentivize the work performance of public employees. The surprise in their research was that despite these constraints on supervisors, both supervisors and employees viewed themselves as hardworking and "functional" (a sense of accomplishment), and "solidary" (recognition from others) reasons for this perceived hard work were preeminent. Counterintuitively, they found that police officers who were more observable and more in contact with supervisors were more likely to shirk, a finding that led them to conclude that professionalism and organizational culture (as opposed to supervision) are the key to reducing shirking. They conclude that although supervision matters, professionalism and organizational culture are more fundamental in shaping how bureaucrats behave.

Professionalism

The view that employee professionalism will increase organizational performance is a longstanding one. Professionalism is understood to provide both the mastery of skills and the accountability that allow employees to operate in a discretionary way (Verkuil, 2017). Systematic training and institutionalized standards of competence are expected to translate into high performance. While there is limited research to support this claim, Wolf's (1993) meta-analysis of the effectiveness of U.S. cabinet agencies found that a combination of public leadership, political autonomy, professionalism, and sense of mission are significant predictors of effectiveness—a model of effectiveness he attributes to the work of J.Q. Wilson. In a more recent study of U.S. federal agency performance, Lee and Whitford (2013) also found that employee professionalism is an important positive factor.

Professionalism is often seen as a key mechanism for allowing employee discretion over complex tasks. However, a tension between organizational (managerial) and occupational (professional) control has long been recognized in organization theory and public administration (Schott et al., 2016). Noordegraaf (2016), however, argues that challenges to professional autonomy and work have been overly focused on this organization–professional tension and that the challenges of professionalism need to be understood within a wider perspective that includes societal and professional tensions that occur outside of organizations. Noordegraaf (2016, 801) stresses the fragmentation of professional fields and describes professions as an "unstable category."

Professionalism and performance management are also seen as in tension. Kerpershoek et al. (2016) find that the motivations of professionals can be at odds with performance management assumptions because professionals are motivated by more value-based concerns related to professional standards and autonomy. The authors also find that performance measurement is not flexible enough to capture the dynamic nature of professional work. In a study of the Swedish National Audit Office, Öberg and Bringselius (2015) point out that where NPM has reduced professional autonomy, it has also reduced organizational performance.

CONCLUSION

This chapter has organized theoretical discussions of public organization effectiveness around two broad overarching theoretical perspectives—New Public Management and value-based institutionalism. NPM conceptualizes organizations through the lens of principal–agent relations and stresses the importance of incentive design and management by results. Markets or quasi-markets can discipline employees, managers and organizations, which leads to support for contracting and performance management. NPM stresses "extrinsic motivation" and the transactional nature of leadership. It often conceives of performance in terms of efficiency and envisions accountability in terms of results. The institutionalist perspective sketched here, by contrast, conceptualizes public organizations as communities centered around common missions that instill a sense of public service. The emphasis is on "intrinsic motivation" and the transformational nature of leadership. It is less concerned about efficiency and more concerned about whether organizations have sufficient capacity and professional skill to effectively carry out their mission. Accountability is achieved by the inculcation of public-regarding values and by professional standards.

Each of these broad theoretical perspectives identifies different recipes for successful public administration and management. Both are multi-dimensional and both—implicitly at least—provide criteria and perspective for diagnosing why public organizations may not be sufficiently effective and accountable. The NPM model suggests that input-oriented rules are an inefficient way to motivate and control employees and that a results-oriented accountability and quasi-market discipline can remedy this problem. The institutionalist model suggests that public organizations will be less effective and accountable when they fail to motivate and focus employees on public and professional missions and that agencies can be made more effective and accountable through professionalization and transformational leadership.

The empirical warrants for these contrasting theoretical perspectives are mixed. Whether NPM actually produces more efficient or accountable organizations is not really convincingly demonstrated. However, the evidence is stronger that certain components of the NPM model, such as performance management, can produce positive results. Empirical support for the institutionalist perspective is less mixed, but the evidence base itself may not be as strong or comprehensive. There is little attempt to evaluate them relative to one another and, with the exception of Bass's "full range leadership model," little explicit attention to how they might work together. One point of commonality between them is that they both regard organizational and managerial autonomy as an asset for effectiveness.

5. Building effective and accountable governance

While the effectiveness and accountability of individual public organizations is a core component of effective and accountable governance, governance shifts the lens from organizational to interorganizational dynamics, from the role of individual public agencies to the wider role of the state, and from a focus on government to a consideration of state–society interactions. As we widen the aperture, our theoretical expectations about what produces effective and accountable governance tend to shift as well. Basically, this chapter will start with a more state-centric perspective and then move on to a more society-centric perspective, examining theoretical claims made by governance scholars about what makes governance effective and accountable.

GOVERNANCE AND THE STATE

State Capacity

There is a common belief that state capacity is essential for public sector performance. Indeed, this belief is often axiomatic or definitional. Grindle and Hilderbrand (1995, 445), for instance, define capacity as "the ability to perform appropriate tasks effectively, efficiently and sustainably." In the broadest sense, state capacity refers to the capability "to create and maintain order over a sovereign territory, which in turn entails the capacity to enact measures to protect its sovereignty such as raising taxes, declaring war, and administering legal justice" (Matthews, 2012, 281).

The discussion of state capacity can be traced back to discussions in the 1970s and 1980s about "bringing the state back in," which argued that the state had been neglected by social science (Evans et al., 1985). Theorists suggested that the state's ability to intervene in the market and in society depended on its ability to police its territory, extract taxes, and deliver public goods. Michael Mann (1984) made a key contribution to this discussion of state capacity by drawing a distinction between the state's despotic and infrastructural power, with the former referring to the state's ability to act without consulting civil society, and the latter referring to the state's capacity to administratively penetrate society. Infrastructural power is considered particularly significant for modern governance.

States have historically had more despotic than infrastructural power and infrastructural power still varies significantly from nation to nation. Elaborating on Mann's concept of infrastructural power, Soifer (2008) identifies three different approaches to infrastructural power. The first he calls a "national capabilities" approach, which refers to the resources that the central state can deploy. The second he calls the "weight of the state" approach, which focuses on whether the state's penetration of society actually transforms society. He calls the third approach the "subnational variation" approach because it investigates the state's uneven institutional development across its territory.

A voluminous body of research on state-building investigates the development of modern state capacity. In a comparison of two depression-era American agencies, for example, Skocpol and Finegold (1982) found that the capacity to effectively intervene in the market depends on building institutional capacity over time. While this research goes far beyond the scope of this book, Dincecco (2015) concludes that there were two key conditions in the development of effective European states—the centralization of fiscal capacity and the development of parliamentary oversight over the budget. The capacity of the state to extract taxes is particularly important for long-term economic growth and has been a particular point of interest for comparative political economy perspectives (Dincecco and Katz, 2016). Reviewing research on state capacity, Berwick and Christia (2018) distinguish between extractive, coordination and compliance capacity.

Strong state capacity is regarded as important for effective governance. In a cross-national analysis, for example, Lin (2015) finds that greater state capacity reduces disaster losses, particularly in democratic countries. Yen et al. (2022) argue that the response of Asia states to COVID-19 depended on state capacity, with higher capacity states responding more quickly and utilizing a wider variety of tools than lower capacity states. Capano et al. (2020) have argued that the different responses of governments to the COVID-19 pandemic can be understood in terms of their policy capacities to learn from prior pandemics and to develop, build support for, and implement a repertoire of specific response policies.

While comparative politics research has been concerned about state capacity on a macro-structural level, the disciplines of public administration and public policy studies have focused more on meso-level governing capabilities (Lodge and Wegrich, 2014; Wu et al., 2015; Ansell et al., 2021). The public policy literature, for example, argues that effective governing depends on the government's policy capacity, which is "the ability to marshal the necessary resources to make intelligent collective choices about and set strategic directions for the allocation of scarce resources to public ends" (Painter and Pierre, 2004, 2). Effective policymaking depends on investment in what Wu et al. (2018, 11) call "analytical capacity," which they argue "can be measured by the extent and quality of system-wide data collection; the availability, speed and ease of access generally across different stakeholders involved in the policy process; and the level of competition and diversity in the production of policy knowledge." Policy capacities also vary within and across nations and in his analysis of Canadian policy-analytic capacity, Howlett (2009) found significant variation across different departments, governments and fiscal situations.

The emergence of new forms of governance is sometimes seen as an indicator of the weakening of state capacity, particularly if it is understood to be associated with the "hollowing out" of the state. For example, as Rhodes (2007, 1248) writes: "The 'hollowing out of the state' means simply that the growth of governance reduced the ability of the core executive to act effectively, making it less reliant on a command operating code and more reliant on diplomacy." Tosun et al. (2016) suggest that when state capacity is low and delivery costs are high, they would expect the formation of cooperative patterns of co-governance. Conversely, when capacity is high and delivery costs are low, they expect more of a competitive pattern of co-governance between the state and private actors. This competitive pattern may prove to be more cooperative or conflictual depending on the congruence of goals between the public and private sector, with incongruent goals producing conflict.

Governance, as distinct from government, is considered to be particularly challenging in areas of limited statehood. Börzel and Risse (2010) identify a spectrum of forms of governance based on the relative involvement of the state, ranging from "governance without government" to "governance by government." They note that the state's "shadow of hierarchy" can produce strong incentives for non-state actors to cooperate, but the state's incentive to cooperate with non-state actors may decline as it becomes stronger vis-à-vis these actors. They argue that that problem-solving governance is likely to be strongest somewhere in the middle where non-state actors have an incentive to cooperate, and the state has an incentive to cooperate with them. Given this analysis, they argue that limited statehood poses a dilemma, because the "shadow of hierarchy" is too weak to incentivize non-governmental actors to cooperate.

Centralization and Decentralization

Given the importance of state capacity, the issue of the decentralization of the state has played a central role in discussions of governance. Faguet (2014, 2) argues that "[t]he strongest theoretical argument in favor of decentralization is that ... it will improve the accountability and responsiveness of government by altering its structure so as to increase citizen voice and change the deep incentives that public officials face." However, a broad review of empirical research on decentralization confronts mixed results, with some research finding improvements in policy outcomes and other research finding worsening outcomes (Faguet, 2014). Decentralization also takes highly varied forms, both in terms of how it is structured and how it is implemented (Faguet, 2012; Kuhlmann and Wayenberg, 2016).

In a broad overview of claims for both the good and bad of decentralization, Treisman (2007) concludes that it is very difficult to draw any robust theoretical or empirical generalizations. Faguet (2012, 5) writes that "[d]espite four decades of policy experimentation all over the world, it is ultimately unclear what [decentralization] reform has or has not achieved." In a comparative quantitative study, Doorenspleet and Pellikaan (2013) find that centralization has more positive effects on good governance indicators (voice and accountability, political stability, government effectiveness, government regulatory quality, rule of law and corruption) in more homogeneous countries, while decentralization has more positive effects in more heterogenous countries.

Even detailed single-country studies find relatively mixed findings. Linder (2010), for example, finds mixed results in a case study of the effects of decentralization in Mozambique, but finds that it does contribute to the improvement of local public services. In an extensive case study of the Bolivian experience, Faguet (2012) finds significant local variation in the success of their decentralization reform. Based on his empirical analysis, he develops a theoretical model to explain why the results of decentralization might vary. His fundamental insight is that heterogeneity in local markets (and hence interests) and civil society organizations will generate "substantive electoral competition" that produces both responsive and accountable local government.

These findings suggest that it may be useful to more closely examine the conditions under which decentralization proves more effective. Werlin (2003) developed an overlooked theory of "political elasticity" to explain effective governance, arguing that we must understand the reasons that decentralization works in some countries but not others. He argues that effective decentralization marries strong formal government institutions with an extensive pattern of public–private consultation and interaction. These conditions allow government to be responsive to changing social and economic needs and demands.

Kuhlmann and Wayenberg (2016) argue that the effect of decentralization will depend on the nature of the task being decentralized. They hypothesize that "[w]herever horizontal coordination becomes a significant aspect accompanying the discharge of those tasks, and economies of scale feature as less important, decentralization could be expected ... to lead to real performance improvements" (2016, 246). Arguing that many theoretical treatments of decentralization are overly simplified and pointing to the complex findings on the decentralization of natural resource governance, Bartley et al. (2008, 171) draw on different versions of institutional theory to argue that decentralization will only improve natural resource governance "where the policies resonate with decision-making structures in other arenas (institutional complementarities), where the responsibilities and capacities of actors at different levels are not radically contradictory, and where incentives for local politicians are aligned with broader objectives of environmental management."

An extensive literature on fiscal federalism envisions subnational jurisdictions in competition to provide efficient public services—a perspective known by political economists as the Tiebout model (Tiebout, 1956; Oates, 1972). Although competition between jurisdictions is generally seen in a positive light in this literature, it also notes constraints and tradeoffs. One such tradeoff is that central governments typically enjoy more economies of scale than local governments. Moreover, decentralization is regarded as less efficient when public goods provided by one jurisdiction spill over into other jurisdictions.

The assumptions of the Tiebout model are not always easily met. Reviewing theoretical and empirical work on decentralization in developing countries, Bardhan (2002) finds that successful decentralization depends on local governments having the accountability and capacity to produce effective and efficient public services. A review of decentralization of natural resource governance comes to similar conclusions, noting that local governments often lack motivation to take on local resource management responsibilities (Larson and Soto, 2008).

A key issue in the decentralization debate concerns whether decentralization increases or decreases corruption. One view is that local governments are closer to citizens and this closeness facilitates accountability. An alternative view is that local governments are more easily "captured" by local elites. In a study of 64 nations, Altunbaş and Thornton (2012) conclude that fiscal decentralization reduces corruption. However, they also find that the autonomy of local governments (vis-à-vis central governments) reduces the positive corruption-reducing effects of fiscal decentralization. By contrast, in a study of U.S. states, Shon and Cho (2020) found that fiscal decentralization increases corruption, which they attribute to more direct interest group influence and weaker monitoring at the local level.

General conclusions about the relationship between decentralization and corruption are difficult to draw, as Fan et al. (2009, 32) point out: "Given the complicated, interacting effects that theorists have posited, it seems quite unlikely a priori that there exists a simple, general relationship between decentralization and corruption that holds in different contexts and geographical settings." However, these authors do draw several conclusions based on a business survey of corruption in 80 countries. They find that developing countries with more tiers of government are more likely to extract significant bribes. Higher subnational public employment also increases corruption, particularly in developed countries. Lessmann and Markwardt (2010) find that effective monitoring of local officials is necessary for reducing corruption in decentralized systems.

One perspective suggested by this review is that centralization and decentralization are not necessarily starkly opposing choices and their virtues may be combined in various ways. Gerring et al. (2005, 567), for example, develop a "centripetal" theory of good governance that combines desirable features of centralization (unity) and decentralization (inclusion). They argue that good governance arises not where the center monopolizes power, but when distributed power flows toward the center and leads to collective decision-making. They identify four institutions that support centripetal governance: strong political parties, corporatist-style interest representation, collegial decision-making, and authoritative public administration. In a cross-national analysis, they find significant empirical support for the centripetal argument, though their optimism is somewhat tempered by other research (Bernauer et al., 2016).

Multi-level Governance

The multi-level governance literature has called attention to both the challenges and opportunities of working across levels of governing. This literature was first developed to describe the dynamics of European integration and the specific relationships it created between subnational, national and European-level institutions (Marks, 1996; Piattoni, 2010; Tortola, 2017). However, researchers eventually extended the discussion beyond the EU, as it was recognized that multi-level governance dynamics characterized many different policy areas (for example, see Betsill and Bulkeley, 2006, on climate change). The literature also distinguishes between two different types of multi-level governance (Hooghe and Marks, 2003). Type 1 systems are federal in character in that they are represented by a nested set of general-purpose governments. Type 2 systems are, by contrast, polycentric in character and organized around task-specific institutions with overlapping jurisdictions that operate at multiple scales (for a useful critical discussion of this dichotomy, see Bache et al., 2016).

In addition to stressing the intensification of governing relationships across governance levels, the multi-level governance literature has challenged conventional notions of state sovereignty and stressed the disaggregation of the state. Piattoni (2010) argues that the concept implies more than just governing across levels and she summarizes three broad claims associated with multi-level governance: (1) as much political mobilization takes place across levels of governance as it does within them; (2) neither policymakers and policytakers nor public and private actors are as distinct as they once were;

Building effective and accountable governance 69

and (3) states are not the only polities making important policy decisions. As she summarizes, multi-level governance is distinctive in that it connects three ideas: "the blurring of the center–periphery divide, the trespassing of the states–society boundaries, and the overcoming of the domestic–international distinction" (Piattoni, 2010, 252).

Tortola (2017), however, has sought to distinguish this "state transformation" version of multi-level governance from a version that is more narrowly focused on explaining public policy outcomes. A more public policy-oriented perspective focuses on how actors interact across different levels (subnational, national, regional, global), and the opportunities and challenges they face in making and shaping policy. From this perspective, multi-level governance can be interpreted as a solution to the challenge of governing across different scales and levels (Homsy et al., 2019). However, Maggetti and Trein (2019, 358) argue multi-level governance also creates its own problems, which arise from the "increased complexity, opacity, informality, selectivity and unresponsiveness" associated with operating across levels—an argument that echoes Wildavsky's (1979) claim that large-scale policy solutions create their own problems.

Mobilization in multi-level contexts often takes the form of networks, which Papadopoulos (2010) has argued raise significant accountability problems. Governance networks often lack visibility and are decoupled from conventional democratic accountability arrangements, blurring responsibility. These challenges are common to governance networks of all sorts but are amplified by multi-level arrangements because accountability problems at any one level are multiplied by networks that straddle governing levels. Furthermore, incentives to find consensus across levels can exacerbate accountability issues on any one level. Multi-level governance networks, Papadopoulos writes, accentuate "peer accountability" (accountability to others in the network) over "home accountability." Indeed, multi-level governance does not reflect so much the absence of accountability as it does the multiplication of forms of accountability. The paradoxical result, he writes, is more accountability but less democracy.

Some theoretical effort has been given to thinking about constructive responses to multi-level accountability concerns. Harlow and Rawlings (2007) propose that multi-level accountability issues can be addressed by creating "accountability networks"—networks of specialized accountability institutions. They sketch out how courts can play this role and provide the example of the European ombudsman system as an emerging form of accountability network.

NETWORK GOVERNANCE

An extensive body of theory has now grown up around the concept of network governance (Kickert et al., 1997; Rhodes, 1997; Koppenjan and Klijn, 2004; Provan and Kenis, 2008; Sørensen and Torfing, 2016; Koliba et al., 2017). Indeed, Rhodes (2007, 1246) equates governance with networks: "governance refers to governing with and through networks." Ideas about the importance of networks in contemporary governance have converged from a wide variety of sources, including complexity theory, the study of policy subsystems, theories of intergovernmental and interorganizational coordination, and social network analysis. Governance networks embody the shift toward what Torfing et al. (2012) call "interactive governance" and Osborne (2006) dubs "New Public Governance."

Klijn and Koppenjan (2012, 591) argue that the theory of network governance has a number of basic conceptual components, including the propositions that (1) "[p]olicy and service delivery are formed and implemented in a network of interdependent actors," that (2) outcomes are "a consequence of the interaction of many actors," which (3) results in the "institutionalisation of relationships between actors" and (4) "requires guidance and management" to succeed. Sørensen and Torfing (2009) argue that while traditional measures of effectiveness can be ill-suited to studying network governance, networks can still be evaluated in terms of whether they improve the understanding of problems, generate innovative policy options, achieve negotiated outcomes that go beyond the lowest common denominator, smooth the path to and enhance the legitimacy of policy implementation, allow flexible adjustment as conditions change, and spur future collaboration.

Network Effectiveness

Provan and Kenis (2008, 230) define network effectiveness as "the attainment of positive network level outcomes that could not normally be achieved by individual organizational participants acting independently." In a study of community mental health services in four U.S. cities, Provan and Milward (1995) developed an important "preliminary" theory of network effectiveness. Their research led them to propose that service networks will be more effective when they are integrated via a core agency (network centralization), when control by external funders is direct and consolidated, when the overall system is stable (rather than in the midst of reform), and when they have adequate resources (resource munificence).

Research provides general support for Provan and Milward's (1995) theory, but with some mixed findings. In a study of 12 Swiss public service deliv-

Building effective and accountable governance 71

ery networks, Cristofoli and Markovic (2016) use Qualitative Comparative Analysis (QCA) to analyze the influence of centralization, resource munificence, formalization and management on network effectiveness. They find that adequate resources (resource munificence) is essential for network effectiveness. However, they find that both centralized and decentralized networks can be effective but depend on different combinations of factors. Centralized networks become effective in combination with network management. For decentralized networks, by contrast, formalized coordination mechanisms are important and appear to substitute for centralized control and network management (formalized coordination refers here to formal contracts, procedures and rules structuring the interaction between networks participants). Studying the effectiveness of Beijing neighborhood housing reform networks with a low degree of formalization, Wang (2016) finds that network centralization is not a necessary ingredient of network effectiveness, but that network stability and resource munificence are critical factors.

Raab et al. (2015) analyze 39 crime prevention networks in the Netherlands using QCA. They find that network age (networks take time to form and consolidate), system stability, and centralized integration are necessary but not sufficient conditions for network effectiveness. It is worth quoting their overall conclusions:

> The results further demonstrate that to generate sustainable positive results, networks for the implementation of healthcare and social services require a long time horizon, long-term commitment, and investment in the network by managers and policymakers alike. Networks might provide a solution for the complex or even wicked problems in society, but they are unlikely to succeed in policy areas that are subject to short-term considerations and frequent changes in policy, funding, and political and managerial personnel. (Raab et al., 2015, 506)

Although resource munificence did not prove to be a necessary condition for network effectiveness in this analysis, they interpret these overall findings as providing support for Provan and Milward's (1995) theory of network effectiveness.

Building on Provan and Milward's theory of network effectiveness, Provan and Kenis (2008) describe three different types of governance networks: a participant-governed network, which leads to a model of shared governance by participants; a lead organization-governed network, which is sponsored, hosted or administered by a single lead organization (which may also be a network member); and a network administrative organization (NAO)-governed network, which is led by a separate secretariat or facilitator (which is not a network member). They describe both the lead organization and NAO models as "brokered" and argue that as the number of network members increases, as trust among members declines, as goal consensus at the network level declines, and as the need for distinctive network-level competencies increases, these brokered models will lead to more effective network governance than the shared-governance model. They further hypothesize that the lead organization model is likely to be more effective than the NAO model in low trust and low consensus settings.

All three network types identified by Provan and Kenis have to deal with similar tensions, but they are expected to address them in different ways. With respect to a tension between efficiency and inclusiveness, the participant-governed model will tend to come down in favor of inclusiveness, while the NAO and lead organization models will come down on the side of efficiency (with NAO somewhat more balanced). With respect to a tension between internal and external legitimacy, the participant-governance model will favor internal legitimacy and the lead organization will prioritize external legitimacy, while the NAO model will balance them sequentially. With respect to a tension between flexibility and stability, participant-governed networks will favor the former, while the brokered (NAO and lead organization) models will come down on the side of stability.

In a comparative study of the continuum of care networks organized to address chronic homelessness, Mosley and Park (2022) found that participant-governed networks were associated with greater reductions in chronic homelessness than NAO networks, and government-led networks were associated with increases in homelessness. The key mechanism for the success of participant-governed networks was that they did a better job of soliciting real and meaningful participation in decision-making by service providers. The study of Swiss service delivery networks described above concluded from interviews that participant-governed networks depend on "equal status, transparency, reliability and fairness among major network participants .... [to produce] uniform, coherent action and ultimately for successful service delivery (Cristofoli and Markovic, 2016, 104).

Noting that there can be no single metric for capturing network performance, Cepiku et al., (2021, 1482) distinguish between intermediate network-level outcomes from final community and organization-level outcomes. Focusing on community outcomes in networks around UNESCO World Heritage Sites in Italy, they also use QCA to evaluate a "multidimensional model of network performance." Selectively drawing on a wider range of possible factors, they hypothesize that reduced network complexity (number of actors, their heterogeneity and their maturity), internal trust, external resources (including external political support) and effective network management are four critical conditions for effective network performance. They found two important configurations of these variables produce network effectiveness: the first combined good network management and low network complexity to produce effectiveness without the need for trust or external resources; the second

Building effective and accountable governance 73

combined sufficient resources, high trust, and good network management. In general, these context-specific findings suggest that specific configurations of factors are important, with some factors substituting for or reinforcing other factors.

Network Management and Accountability

Effective network management is important for successful governance network outcomes (Kickert et al., 1997; Koppenjan and Klijn, 2004; Klijn et al., 2010). Network managers help to manage competing pulls that networks experience between unity and diversity (Ospina and Saz-Carranza, 2010). This can be done by cultivating relationships among network members and maintaining an open process of participation. Network managers, however, not only have to promote cooperation among network members, but they must engage externally as well, making efforts to promote the external credibility of the network and brokering between different levels of government and action. Given the complexity of networks, there may be several network managers and to some extent they may be in competition (Rethemeyer and Hatmaker, 2008).

Agranoff and McGuire (2001) distinguish four key network management behaviors. *Activation* is about selectively engaging the relevant and necessary people and resources in the collaborative process; *framing* is about setting the rules of interaction within the network and shaping the values, purposes and ideas associated with it; *mobilizing* is about motivating and supporting action within the network; and *synthesizing* is about helping to integrate efforts and ideas. Smith (2020) reviews the extensive literature on network effectiveness and points to the importance of structure, management, process and context.

Governance networks can reduce accountability if they are not easily visible and not anchored in representative institutions, conditions that may be more likely as governance becomes more multi-level in nature (Papadopoulos, 2010). Alternatively, multi-level governance may also increase the number of accountability controls, as networks spanning institutional levels are often held accountable in a range of ways. Ironically, governance networks, particularly in multi-level systems, may be subject to "more accountability, but less democracy" (Papadopoulos, 2010, 1044). Koliba et al. (2011) elaborate the many different types of accountabilities brought to bear on governance networks and argue that, as a result, accountability in such networks is likely to be a hybrid arrangement.

Public–Private Partnerships

Public–private partnerships (PPPs) are one distinctive type of network governance. They have been defined as "durable complex cooperation between public and private sectors aiming to supply infrastructure and public service" where "public and private sectors should share their risks and benefits to achieve their mutual goals" (Wang et al., 2018, 302). PPPs have a very wide range of objectives and motivations ranging from narrowly financial to broadly political and symbolic, making it a challenge to evaluate their performance. Hodge and Greve (2017) find that there have been a limited number of rigorous and independent public assessments of "value for money" for long-term infrastructure contracts, one of the most common forms of public–private partnership.

While PPPs are often governed contractually, their complexity and open-ended nature often make it difficult to regard them as simply a version of contracting out (Van Ham and Koppenjan, 2001). They often create a "joint product" that builds on the combined functionalities and mutual goals of public and private actors, rather than operating as garden-variety purchaser–provider relationships. This focus on jointness creates a number of risks, barriers and threats to effective PPPs that must be shared in the case of risks and collectively overcome in the case of barriers and threats.

Klijn and Koppenjan (2016) investigate the character of contracts for public–private partnerships in the Netherlands, examining which characteristics have positive consequences for performance. Long-term contracts are often seen as valuable for encouraging quality service provision and innovation. Contractual provisions that allow negative and positive sanctions to be imposed are also claimed to lead to higher performance, while greater contract complexity is expected to reduce performance. However, contracts that build in flexibility and negotiation (e.g., relational contracts) are likely to allow more innovation.

Based on a survey of Dutch participants in these PPPs, Klijn and Koppenjan found that none of these contract characteristics (length of contract, sanctions, complexity, flexibility or negotiation) had positive impacts on contract performance or innovation, but sanctions had a negative impact on performance. They conclude that the formal characteristics of contracts—judged in isolation from other factors, such as managerial effectiveness—are not the critical factors in explaining PPP contract performance and innovation. Subsequent research using this data found that both trust and network management were significantly associated with PPP performance (Warsen et al., 2018). Kort et al. (2016) find that network management strategies were critical for producing successful public–private partnerships in urban regeneration in the Netherlands.

In a review of the public–private partnership literature, Wang et al. (2018) identify a wide range of factors that may influence the success of partnerships. Very broadly speaking, these factors are related to the nature of the contract or to the management of the partnership. Effective risk-sharing and monitoring are also found to be critical for the success of partnerships. Research on Belgian PPPs stresses the value of contracting authorities having clear objectives and the importance of ensuring that all parties reap benefits from the partnership (Willems et al., 2017). The wider public must support the PPP and government must make a conscious role shift from being the "executor" to being a "producer." This research also finds that it is important to manage the complexity of PPPs and valuable to simplify PPP contracts.

COLLABORATIVE GOVERNANCE

The concept of network governance overlaps significantly with the idea of "collaborative governance," which also converged out of many parallel studies on interorganizational and intergovernmental coordination, alternative dispute resolution, network governance, natural resource management, collective action, negotiation, deliberative democracy, leadership and planning (Agranoff, 1986; Susskind and Cruikshank, 1987; Gray, 1989; Rhodes, 1996; Freeman, 1997; Innes and Booher, 1999; Wondolleck and Yaffee, 2000; Fung and Wright, 2003; Healey, 2003; Vangen and Huxham, 2003; Bingham et al., 2005; Crosby and Bryson, 2005). What all these studies share is the idea that public policy, planning and management operate in a multi-organizational or multi-stakeholder world that necessitates improved communication and negotiation in order to achieve more cooperative and less adversarial outcomes. Collaboration operates on a model of shared power that requires the mutual consent of participating stakeholders (Gray, 1989).

Defining collaborative governance as "[a] governing arrangement where one or more public agencies directly engage non-state stakeholders in a collective decision-making process that is formal, consensus-oriented, and deliberative and that aims to make or implement public policy or manage public programs or assets," Ansell and Gash (2008, 544) synthesize much of the prior case study literature into a "contingency" framework. Their model distinguishes "starting conditions" (power–resource–knowledge asymmetries, incentives to participate, and the prehistory of conflict and cooperation) from the "collaborative process" (with its cycle of face-to-face dialogue, trust-building, commitment to process, shared understanding, and intermediate outcomes), which is in turn shaped by both institutional design and facilitative leadership. Collaborative outcomes are expected to be more successful when these contingent factors are favorable.

Emerson, Nabatchi and Balogh (2012) build on but extend this model. They define collaborative governance as "the processes and structures of public policy decision making and management that engage people constructively across the boundaries of public agencies, levels of government, and/or the public, private and civic spheres in order to carry out a public purpose that could not otherwise be accomplished" (2012, 2). Their "integrative framework" distinguishes the "system context" for collaboration, which in turn shapes the "drivers" of collaboration. These drivers produce collaborative dynamics characterized by principled engagement, shared motivation and capacity for joint action, which produces both outputs and outcomes that may lead the collaboration to adapt the context or dynamics. A key contribution of this model is to describe what they call a "collaborative governance regime," which refers to "the particular mode of, or system for, public decision making in which cross-boundary collaboration represents the prevailing pattern of behavior and activity" (2012, 6).

Emerson and Nabatchi's (2015) subsequent work demonstrates the important implications of understanding how collaborative governance regimes are formed and sponsored, which fundamentally shapes the collaborative dynamics that ensue. *Self-initiated regimes* are created by relational processes among the eventual participants and reflect their interests and perspectives. Leadership is particularly important for the success of self-initiated collaborative efforts. *Independently convened regimes* are facilitated by third parties, but depend on good faith participation by stakeholders. Building shared knowledge is often critical for success. *Externally directed regimes* are mandated or organized, which typically creates preset conditions that influence collaboration. The procedures and resources established for the collaboration can be expected to have an important influence on collaborative dynamics. An important implication of this typology is that it calls attention to the potential drawbacks of mandating collaboration.

Collaborative governance raises specific challenges for leadership, requiring "integrative" or "facilitative" strategies (Mandell and Keast, 2009; Crosby and Bryson, 2010; Ansell and Gash, 2012). Collaboration across organizations and sectors leads to greater emphasis on relational, shared, and collectivist models of leadership (Ospina, 2017; Quick, 2017; Crosby and Bryson, 2018). However, Torfing and Ansell (2017) and Sørensen (2020) also turn the relationship between leadership and collaboration around, arguing that collaboration is a strategy that can be used to support leaders.

In evaluating the theory of collaborative governance, it is important to put it into proper perspective. The conditions that create a demand for collaborative governance—complexity, interdependence, conflict, and fragmentation—often mean that a collaborative approach is called for when and where governance challenges are most difficult. Society often "fails into collaboration." But the ability to align and reconcile stakeholders who have their own interests, authority and perspectives is itself a challenging proposition no matter how favorable the starting conditions. Collaboration, according to Vangen (2017), is inherently "paradoxical" because it requires both respecting and transforming difference. Thus, collaboration often faces a "double whammy": tackling a challenging and perhaps intractable problem by aligning stakeholders with different perspectives, interests and values. As a result, as

Crosby and Bryson (2010, 227) hypothesize, the "normal expectation ought to be that success will be very difficult to achieve" in cross-sector collaborations. If it is easier, less costly, and equally legitimate and effective to proceed in a non-collaborative fashion, then taking a non-collaborative direction may be desirable (Sher-Hadar et al., 2021).

If collaborative governance is challenging, why would public managers ever invest in or commit to such strategies? Scott and Thomas (2017) hypothesize a number of possible reasons, including to shore up agency legitimacy, to respond to problems operating at different geographical and functional scales than they are prepared to operate, to expand their policy tool kit, to access external resources, to manage the costs of controversy or litigation, or to serve a brokerage role.

While there is a mountain of work on collaborative governance, there is a relative dearth of systematic research comparing the outputs and outcomes of collaborative and non-collaborative processes. One important study by Doberstein (2016) compares the outputs of collaborative and more tradition-ally bureaucratic processes of decision-making about homelessness funding in Vancouver, Canada. In contrast with more bureaucratic decision-making, he found that collaboration diversified the knowledge and perspectives brought to bear in funding discussions and created an opportunity for meaningful deliberation and learning among participants, which ultimately produced more integrated policy priorities.

Other collaborative governance studies have evaluated environmental out-comes. A study comparing the outcomes of collaborative and hierarchical strategies for making U.S. hydropower regulatory policy found that a collab-orative strategy was more effective at introducing and integrating environ-mental considerations into regulatory regimes (Ulibarri, 2015). A study of U.S. watershed management found that watersheds governed collaboratively achieve environmental improvements in the watershed, particularly if they are focused on management activities rather than coordination or planning (Scott, 2015).

As with network governance, accountability is a challenging topic for collaborative governance because it raises concerns about democratic rep-resentation, procedural legitimacy and the production of valued outcomes (Page et al., 2015). By bringing multiple stakeholders together, collaboration can create a "tangled web" of accountability (Lee, 2022). Tensions often arise between accountability to a stakeholder's home institution and accountability to the collaboration (Waardenburg et al., 2020). Working through accountabil-ity tensions in a mission-oriented way can advance the accountability of the overall collaborative network (Lee, 2022). Although accountability is typically seen as a challenge for collaborative governance, Sørensen and Torfing (2021) describe a nested model in which collaborative governance enhances government accountability, while social accountability enhances the accountability of collaborative governance.

Participatory Governance

While network and collaborative governance have generally been more concerned with organized stakeholders, these literatures often overlap with discussions of citizen participation. We can distinguish governance that emphasizes the role of citizen participation by referring to it as "participatory governance," while recognizing that it builds on a long history of research on citizen participation that precedes much of the contemporary discussion about governance. Most famously, Arnstein's (1969) "ladder of participation" identifies a range of types of participation and the challenges that citizens may encounter as they try to move "up" the ladder toward more empowered engagement.

A variety of different modes of participatory governance are possible and Fung (2006) distinguishes them along three dimensions: communication, authority and power, and the inclusiveness of participation. Taking these three dimensions together, he shows that specific strategies of participatory governance tend to occupy different spaces within what he calls the "democracy cube." Where participatory governance falls within the democracy cube depends on whether the purpose is to enhance legitimacy, to achieve justice or to increase the effectiveness of governance. Reviewing developments in participatory governance since his 2006 article, Fung (2015) examines the different ways that participation can enhance governance effectiveness by improving collective and individual problem-solving and preventing social injustice. He notes that while the number of participatory governance efforts have expanded significantly in recent years, they often face a problem of "triviality" (participation in projects of limited scope or importance)—a limitation that can undermine the value of participatory governance (Fung, 2015, 521).

Participatory governance strategies depend in part on whether they attract participation. Van der Does (2022) observes that participation is often limited and conducts an experiment to determine whether "low stakes" lead to low participation. However, the results of the experiment reject this finding and he concludes that this is because participants have a variety of reasons for participating, a finding supported by the research of Gustafson and Hertting (2017), who found that the motivations for participating in a Swedish urban renewal project ranged from self-interest to the desire to contribute to the common good. In a study of U.S. local governments, Olsen and Feeney (2022) find that positive manager perceptions of the value of citizen participation are more important than legal mandates in encouraging participation. Earlier research on managers by Huang and Feeney (2016) found that managers with strong public service motivation are likely to encourage citizen participation.

Building effective and accountable governance   79

Many citizen participation or citizen engagement strategies are organized in a top-down way, but Edelenbos et al. (2018) point out that they can also have a "self-organizing" quality. Examining the interaction between official participatory strategies and self-organizing, they suggest that it is important to examine the attitudes and behaviors of the actors involved, which can be negative or positive. Comparing three cases of citizen self-organization in the Netherlands, U.K., and U.S., they find that citizen self-organization is often motivated by dissatisfaction. They also note that the representativeness of self-organizing efforts often becomes an issue and they observe that boundary spanners are important for bridging between community and government. Overall, they stress that such self-organizing efforts still operate within and are distinctly shaped by their governmental context.

Some governance genres display a particular interest in participatory governance. Urban governance, for example, places a strong emphasis on citizen participation (Da Cruz et al., 2019). Wagenaar (2007) argues that participatory and deliberative governance are better able to handle the complexity of contemporary urban problems than top-down, expert-dominated governance, an argument he illustrates in a study of neighborhood regeneration in the Netherlands. Other urban governance scholars are more critical, arguing that citizen participation schemes support neoliberalism. Lombard (2013) acknowledges this critique in a study of citizen participation in Mexico, but also finds that participation has slowly contributed to improved local governance.

Environmental governance is another genre that has taken participatory governance very seriously. Newig et al. (2018), for example, summarize the range of theoretical reasons advanced for why participatory governance may contribute positively to environmental outcomes. These reasons include opening up the decision-making process to environmental concerns, contributing relevant knowledge, improving the quality of deliberation and negotiation, providing downstream support for decisions, and contributing to governance capacity (note that these five clusters of reasons are further broken down by the authors into 19 causal mechanisms, as well as a number of conditioning variables).

Development studies is a third genre of research with a special concern for public participation. Gaventa and Barrett (2012) review the arguments for and against citizen engagement in development studies and analyze evidence from a sample of 100 cases from over 20 countries. They find that citizen engagement has generally produced positive effects, but a significant number of studies also find more negative outcomes. Their research finds that local associations and social movements are an important vehicle for mobilizing citizen participation and that formal participation not backed up by collective action can lead to tokenistic participatory responses. They find that positive citizen participation outcomes are not limited to fully institutionalized democratic regimes, though local associations are particularly important for civic mobilization in less democratized countries.

Co-production

Another way that the governance literature has thought about citizen participation is in term of what has been called "co-production," which refers to the joint production of public services by governments and citizens. It has been argued that "co-production"—the joint production of services by producers and consumers—can increase the effectiveness and efficiency of government when technical and institutional conditions are favorable (Parks et al., 1981). Case study evidence has generally been positive, but scholars also warn that co-production is not a panacea and that "context matters" (Bovaird et al., 2019). Co-production has been found to operate in many different public services, but it is often perceived as a risky endeavor for politicians and public professionals (Loeffler and Bovaird, 2016; Kleinhans, 2017).

As is the case for many concepts, the term "co-production" is elastic, but Osborne et al. (2016, 640) define it as "the voluntary or involuntary involvement of public service users in any of the design, management, delivery and/ or evaluation of public services." Alford (2014) notes that it is possible that products as well as services are co-produced and that co-production can be conceptualized as including joint production with partners as well as with clients. Bovaird and Loeffler (2012) also expand the concept, noting that it can include a wide range of functions, including co-commissioning, co-design, co-delivery and co-assessment. Osborne et al. (2016) discuss the possibility of using co-innovation to improve service systems and Sorrentino et al. (2018) examine how information technology can expand the role of co-production.

Governance scholars distinguish a range of different types of co-production. Brandsen and Honingh (2016) distinguish types of co-production along two dimensions: the extent to which citizens participate in the design or the implementation of public services and the degree to which citizens co-produce core services or remain limited to co-producing complementary services. Nabatchi et al. (2017) elaborate a 3×4 typology with one dimension referring to whether the level of co-production is individual, group, or collective and another dimension referring to the "phase" of co-production (co-commissioning, co-design, co-delivery or co-assessment). They argue that distinguishing these 12 types of co-production can facilitate subsequent research and help practitioners to select and design co-production strategies.

What motivates citizens to engage in co-production? Much like the case of participatory governance discussed above, researchers find that a range of motivations—from self-interest to altruism—are possible drivers of co-production and it is important to understand how they interact and mix

(Verschuere et al., 2012; Alford, 2014; Van Eijk and Steen, 2014). It is also important to recognize that co-production may produce individual, group and public value (Alford, 2014). In a survey of five European nations, Parrado et al. (2013) find that "self-efficacy"—i.e., the belief that citizens can make a difference—is an important factor shaping citizen engagement. Fledderus et al. (2014) also theorize that participation in co-production can enhance self-efficacy. In a study of Dutch activation policy, Fledderus and Honingh (2016) find that citizens who participate in co-production have higher levels of trust and they suggest that trust be considered a precondition for participation in co-production.

Researchers have also focused on the conditions that make co-production effective. In their review of a decade of research on co-production, Verschuere et al. (2012) observe that it is important that both citizens and governments understand and appreciate their reciprocal goals for pursuing co-production. Successful co-production also depends on an appreciation of the capacity that citizens have to engage in co-production. In a systematic review of factors that facilitate co-production, Sicilia et al. (2019) identify two overarching factors— *organizational factors* that include conducive organizational arrangements, supportive professional roles and provision of useful managerial tools; and *procedural factors* that include active citizen recruitment, adequate preparation of participants, and effective process design.

A range of barriers to co-production have been identified, including risk-aversion and the professional fear of loss of control (Bovaird and Loeffler, 2012). In a systematic review, Voorberg et al. (2015) find that the key influences identified on the government side include the compatibility, openness, and risk-aversion of the public organization with regard to citizen participation and the incentives they face for engaging in co-production. With respect to citizens, personal characteristics (e.g., education) and values are key factors, and it is often noted that a sense of ownership and responsibility are influential. Social capital is noted as a positive influence, while citizen risk-aversion is cited as a negative factor.

Co-creation

Although the term "co-creation" is often used interchangeably with the concept of co-production (Voorberg et al., 2015), scholars have begun to distinguish them more sharply. With a focus on the provision of public services, Osborne (2018, 225) observes that the concept of co-production is too closely connected to a linear "goods-dominated" (as opposed to a service-oriented) logic and by contrast co-creation "assumes an interactive and dynamic relationship where value is created at the nexus of interaction." Torfing et al. (2019) argue that co-creation implies a government–citizen engagement that entails a broader creation of public value than suggested by co-production. This interpretation, however, also brings the concept into the realm of discussions of collaborative governance. Ansell and Torfing (2021a) point out that the concept of co-creation overlaps with the concept of collaborative governance but is distinctive in that it addresses the distributed nature of social innovation.

Scholars have begun to investigate the drivers and barriers of co-creation. Torfing et al. (2019) emphasize that "sedimented roles" associated with public administration (citizens as subjects or customers; politicians and political officials as sovereign) are a major barrier to advancing co-creation, but they note that these roles are limiting in ways that can encourage role-breaking. Ansell and Torfing (2021b, 91) argue that given its distributed, open-ended and emergent nature, co-creation should be thought of in terms of "generativity"—that is, as a mode of governance that "facilitates and enables the emergence of productive interaction among distributed users." They identify four important types of generativity: generative interaction (e.g., trust, synergy, mutual respect), generative tools (e.g., technologies that give participants creative leverage), generative processes (e.g., structured procedures to facilitate problem-solving and joint action), and generative institutions (e.g., platforms and arenas to promote co-creation). Leadership is typically understood to be critical for co-creation (Sørensen et al., 2021; Hofstad et al., 2022).

The concept of co-creation has been linked to the idea of public value creation (Sørensen et al., 2021). Williams et al. (2016) point out, however, that if it is possible for co-production or co-creation to create public value, it is also possible for it to destroy public value. They suggest that this co-destruction of value can arise from the misuse of resources.

META-GOVERNANCE AND THE SHADOW OF HIERARCHY

Meta-governance is a conception of how governance can be steered. Jessop (2002b) noted that all forms of governance can fail and introduced the idea of meta-governance as setting the overarching conditions for governance—that is, meta-governance refers to the "governance of governance." He further suggests that meta-governance is responsible for aligning and coordinating basic types of governance (markets, hierarchies, and reflective self-governance). Governments play the key role in meta-governance, which they can achieve through institutional design and what Jessop (2002b) calls culture governance (the shaping of the subjects of governance). Based on a recent review of the meta-governance literature, Gjaltema et al. (2020, 1771) define meta-governance as "a practice by (mainly) public authorities that entails the coordination of one or more governance modes by using different instruments, methods, and strategies to overcome governance failures."

Building effective and accountable governance 83

A similar, but slightly different concept grew up around the idea of "the shadow of hierarchy" or the "shadow of the state." The argument, as developed by Fritz Scharpf and Renate Mayntz, is that the self-organization that takes place in networks (or other delegated or decentered forms of governance) is often influenced by the potential exercise of hierarchical or state control (Scharpf, 1994; Héritier and Lehmkuhl, 2008). In a study comparing two local Dutch networks, Nederhand et al. (2016) find that the "shadow of hierarchy" does indeed shape self-governing processes, but note that there are different "shadows" depending on the character of trust inherent in self-governing relationships. A general finding of their study is that meta-governance strategies will tend to be "softer" and less oriented toward provoking the participants to organize in cases where self-organizing cooperation is already developed.

Meta-governance is critical for governing networks and other forms of interactive governance and can help to contribute to the effectiveness and democratic legitimacy of network governance (Sørensen and Torfing, 2005; Torfing et al., 2012). In his study of homelessness collaboration, for example, Doberstein (2016) finds that effective meta-governance of collaboration to set homelessness policy was critical for producing "collaborative advantage" and finds that meta-governance constrained, channeled and targeted deliberations in ways that produced effective and meaningful collaborative outputs.

Sørensen and Torfing (2005) suggest that there are three different ways that meta-governance by elected politicians can contribute to the democratic legitimacy of network governance. First, through network design, politicians can shape who participates and on what terms. Second, by framing the goals and objectives of networks via the use of narrative and storytelling, politicians can help to steer their direction. Third, politicians can directly participate in networks, influencing the dynamics of network processes via their direct engagement. In a subsequent paper, Sørensen and Torfing (2009) add network management as a fourth meta-governance strategy.

Torfing et al. (2012) also distinguish between "hands-off" and "hands-on" meta-governance and argue that effective network governance depends on a mix of the two. These strategies must be deployed, however, without undermining the self-organizing character of networks. Network design is an example of a hands-off strategy, while network management is a hands-on strategy (Sørensen and Torfing, 2009). Extending the idea of meta-governance to the issue of collaborative innovation, Sørensen and Torfing (2017) argue that meta-governance can shape who is included in collaborative innovation and how they pool and exchange resources and it can help to align and integrate policies and programs in order to achieve innovation.

CONCLUSION

This chapter travels from a state-centric to a society-centric view of governance. At the state-centric beginning of the trip, there is a general expectation in the political economy, comparative politics, public administration and public policy literatures that state capacity matters for effective governance. Different types of capacity have been distinguished and studies of how this capacity matters in specific policy domains have been conducted.

Extensive research has also been conducted on how the centralization and decentralization of the state impact both governance effectiveness and accountability. One key expectation often associated with the good governance perspective is that decentralization will bring government closer to citizens, enhancing both effectiveness and accountability. Empirical support for such a claim is mixed and scholars have begun to develop more nuanced arguments that can help diagnose when and where decentralization will have positive or negative effects. While empirical support for decentralization is mixed, a general prescription in favor of decentralization is not warranted.

While the centralization–decentralization debate focuses on the level at which state resources and authority are primarily organized, research on "multi-level" governance shifts attention to the way that governance operates across subnational, national and international levels. The multi-level governance literature emphasizes the importance of governance networks in linking decision-making and action across levels, which in turn raises significant concerns about accountability. This debate ties into a wider discussion of network governance, which is often portrayed as an alternative to both hierarchical (traditional Weberian administration) and market-oriented (NPM) governance.

An important theoretical perspective on network governance is that effectiveness is enhanced when networks are centrally led and funded, stable and well-resourced. This perspective is generally supported, but the empirical literature suggests that different configurations of factors are possible. Network scholars have also clearly established that network management is important for effective network governance and have identified some of the key principles of a network management approach. While governance networks are viewed by many as a necessary response to the complex and cross-cutting nature of contemporary political problems, critics sometimes associate networks with neoliberalism or governmentality or with problems of democratic accountability.

While network governance stresses the mobilization and coordination of both public and private institutions and stakeholders, a closely related body of research examines how the state interacts with both citizens and private stakeholders. Although not necessarily distinct from network governance, collaborative governance tends to focus more on the process than on the structure of interaction. This process is negotiated and consensus-oriented rather than adversarial or managerial. While collaboration is never for the faint of heart, the collaborative governance literature has diagnosed some of the specific challenges that arise in the course of collaboration. However, there is limited empirical research demonstrating its inherent superiority over other modes of governance.

While both network and collaborative governance literatures tend to focus on the cooperation and coordination of organizations and stakeholders, related research explores how the state engages with citizens, either for purposes of representation and policymaking (e.g., participatory governance), joint production of services (e.g., co-production) or for innovating solutions to public problems (e.g., co-creation). These theoretical perspectives have begun to identify many of the drivers and barriers of effective cooperation between state and society.

Having arrived at the society-centric governance terminus of our voyage, what do we say about the continuing role of the state? The governance literature has theorized that even when governance networks can be characterized as self-governing, the state still plays a significant leadership and accountability role through either direct or indirect means. Governance theorists have identified different types of meta-governance and argued that meta-governance is important for achieving both effective and accountable governance. These arguments remain fairly abstract in nature but point to significant possibilities for empirical research.

6. Enhancing democratic legitimacy and managing political conflict

This chapter investigates whether theories of governance contribute to our understanding of how to improve democracy and manage political conflict. Clearly, the relationship is bidirectional. There is good reason to believe that effective and accountable governance is harmed by low political legitimacy and high political conflict, but also that effective and accountable governance can enhance legitimacy and ameliorate conflict. The focus in this chapter is primarily on the latter relationship—that is, on whether and how governance influences and shapes democratic legitimacy and societal conflict management.

The chapter begins by considering the relationship between governance and state legitimacy, with a focus on what governance theories tell us about the production of legitimacy. It also investigates some of the democratic critiques of new modes of governance. The second section of the chapter explores some of the ways that governance may contribute to the "deepening" of democracy, with an emphasis on the production of social and civic capital and the expansion of opportunities for public participation and deliberation. The chapter then turns to the issue of conflict management and examines what governance theories—broadly construed—contribute to our understanding of how to ameliorate societal conflicts. This section considers how collaborative governance and similar governance mechanisms might mediate conflict and build trust. It then focuses on the relationship between governance and violent conflict and concludes with a discussion of power-sharing.

GOVERNANCE AS POLITICS

Governance and Legitimacy

A key question for democratic theory and political sociology is when will citizens regard the democratic state as "rightfully holding and exercising political power" (Gilley, 2006, 48)? That is, when do citizens regard the state as legitimate? While many factors may be relevant, the quality and mode of governance very likely plays an important role. Cross-national analysis of surveys of citizen beliefs about state legitimacy (72 countries) find that a "general governance" variable (which combines rule of law, government effectiveness, and corruption control) has a large impact on citizen evaluations of state legitimacy (Gilley, 2006). Effective governance is also hypothesized to enhance citizen support for democracy (Magalhães, 2014) and a comparative study of 32 countries finds that impartial and professional public institutions matter a great deal for citizen satisfaction with democracy (Dahlberg and Holmberg, 2014).

While this evidence supports a positive association between effective governance and democratic legitimacy, development scholars have raised concerns about how this relationship might work in areas of limited statehood. Schmelzle and Stollenwerk (2018) scrutinize the conditions necessary for producing a "virtuous cycle" between governance effectiveness and legitimacy. They identify four conditions that may be necessary for translating governance effectiveness into legitimacy: first, the audience in question must judge legitimacy in terms of governance performance; second, governance effectiveness must be judged by this audience in terms of shared goals and values; third, audiences must be able to attribute positive governance outcomes to those providing the governance; and fourth, audience support for specific governance actions must translate into diffuse support for governance.

Reciprocally, for governance legitimacy to support governance effectiveness, three conditions are important: first, an increase in legitimacy should lead to greater compliance and cooperation by the governed; second, this greater compliance and cooperation leads to greater governance effectiveness; and third, governance actors have the capacity to deliver outputs based on enhanced compliance and cooperation. They argue that these conditions are difficult to meet in conditions of limited statehood because of the plurality of audiences and governance actors and the limits on state capacity.

The project of European integration has spawned an extensive literature on the relationship between governance and legitimacy. A key source of this discussion was Scharpf's (1999, 6) distinction between input and output legitimacy. Input legitimacy is based on the "will of the people"—that is, on the inputs citizens have over the government that rules them. Output legitimacy is based on "government for the people"—that is, on the outputs of government and their impact on the welfare of citizens. His purpose in drawing this distinction was to point out the weakness of input legitimacy in the European Union (the idea of a "democratic deficit"), while calling attention to the various ways that the EU could avail itself of "output legitimacy." Applying these ideas to the EU, he argues that the Union maintains legitimacy if it acts on consensus and avoids conflictual policy, if it adopts judicial over political modes of decision-making, and if it relies on multi-level networks to facilitate agreement.

To Scharpf's distinction between input and output legitimacy, Schmidt (2013) added "throughput legitimacy," which refers to "the efficacy, accountability, openness and inclusiveness of the governance processes" (2013, 3).

She suggests that throughput legitimacy is distinctive in that it faces an asymmetry: it does not add much to perceptions of overall EU legitimacy when it is positive, but it has significant negative effects on legitimacy perceptions when throughput safeguards are violated. Steffek (2019) argues that the concept of throughput legitimacy reflects a growing "proceduralism" that seeks to accommodate societal pluralism and value conflict without resorting to substantive values. However, Schmidt and Wood (2019) argue that throughtput legitimacy should be understood as a complement rather than as a substitute for input and output democracy. A study of legitimacy in public transportation in eight European cities found all three types of legitimacy mattered to citizens (Strebel et al., 2019).

Sørensen (2020) argues that political leadership has the potential to enhance input, throughput and output legitimacy and she sets out a broad theoretical account of what she calls "interactive leadership" for the "age of governance." Interactive leaders engage with an active citizenry and a mobilized society and they lead through a "systematic involvement and mobilization of relevant and affected members of the political community" (2020, 3). Interactive leadership can produce "robust political authorization" by enhancing "account-giving" and thereby reducing the resistance of relevant and affected actors to policy implementation. However, interactive leadership is not without its challenges. The multi-level nature of politics and the mediatization of politics create significant challenges for interactive leadership, though Sørensen points out that these challenges are themselves best met by interactive leadership.

Soft governance mechanisms—those that are not legally binding—may raise issues of democratic legitimacy (Borrás and Conzelmann, 2007). A common view is that informal governance—read "old boys networks"—erodes legitimacy. Kleine (2018), however, argues that a wider interpretation of informal governance leads to more varied interpretations, and she draws on the distinction between input, throughput and output legitimacy to argue that in many cases informal governance is quite inclusive and may enhance input legitimacy. While informal governance can be manipulative, it can also create dialogue that enhances throughput legitimacy, and by promoting cooperation, it can improve output legitimacy.

In one of the few studies to compare the legitimacy of different governance arrangements, Hui and Smith (2022) found that U.S. citizens view "collaborative governance" as having higher input legitimacy than "traditional government," but found no difference in terms of their view of the output legitimacy of these different governance arrangements. A survey experiment with U.S. citizens found that respondents perceived the legitimacy of collaborative governance to be driven by considerations of how representative it is (input legitimacy) and by perceptions of its performance (output legitimacy) (Lee and Esteve, 2022). In a study of Canadian homelessness networks, Doberstein and Millar (2014) found that input and output legitimacy were partially substitutable for one another, but throughput legitimacy was a necessary imperative.

Democratic Critiques of New Governance

While effective and accountable governance may enhance democratic legitimacy, there are various democratic critiques of governance. One such argument is that governance that leads to depoliticization and technocracy can encourage "anti-politics" and populism in response. The concept of "anti-politics" has multiple origins. One key inspiration was Bernard Crick's (1962) book *In Defence of Politics*, which led to an investigation of how citizens become alienated from politics, leading in some cases to the rise of populism. Another key source was James Ferguson's (1994) critique of the idea of international development aid. He argued that the unintended consequences of the discourse of development was an expansion of state bureaucratic power and a depoliticization of society, an outcome he called the "anti-politics" machine. It is often used to refer to the substitution of technocracy for politics (as in the critique that neoliberalism places economic rationality above democracy). Clarke et al. (2018, 21) identify three versions of anti-politics, which refer respectively to citizen "negativity" toward politics, populist "denigration" of politics and to strategies of depoliticization.

Some scholars have argued that governance may potentially lead to a "depoliticization" that plays into anti-politics (Walters, 2004; Fawcett et al., 2017). Specifically, Flinders and Wood (2014) argue that "delegated governance"— by which they primarily mean the agencification associated with NPM—can contribute to anti-politics. Durose et al. (2015), however, challenge the idea that arms-length governance institutions necessarily lead to a "democratic deficit," noting that some arms-length bodies institutionalize protections for minorities.

New modes of governance are particularly in tension with populist politics. Stoker (2019) has raised the question of whether rising populism undercuts the governance paradigm because populism challenges the assumption of pluralism that underpins much of the governance literature. Populism is also negative toward the assumptions of complex interdependence, self-organization and compromise that motivate the concept of governance. For populists, "networks" are unaccountable and elitist. Stoker argues that governance needs to avoid simply arguing that governance can get the job done and must focus more on how it can engage directly with politics.

New modes of governance also raise challenges for conventional conceptions of representative democracy (Bevir, 2010). Klijn and Skelcher (2007) examine arguments about whether networks are incompatible or complementary with representative democracy. Arguments for their incompatibility tend to focus on their closed and private nature and on how they make decisions without the sanction of representative democracy. Arguments for their complementarity, by contrast, tend to stress that networks connect the state to civil society and tend to enlarge opportunities for democratic participation. They point out that assessments of whether networks add or subtract from democracy ultimately depends on how democracy is understood. From a perspective that regards all democratic authority as lodged in elected representatives, networks appear to be a derogation of power to unelected powerholders. By contrast, complementary perspectives tend to start from a deliberative democracy position that regards societal communication about policy and programs as contributing to democracy.

In a study of Swiss drug governance, Wälti et al. (2004, 84) ask "how democratic is governance?" They suggest two possible criticisms of the relationship between governance and democracy. A "deliberative criticism" suggests that governance is really a form of technocracy that moves issues out of the public sphere. A "participatory criticism" suggests that governance supplants opportunities for public participation. Their study focuses on interagency and interorganizational networks developed to deal with a rising drug problem in the early 1990s. They conclude that this mode of governance did reduce public deliberation by encouraging a technocratic style of decision-making and did not promote wide participation. Elected representatives could participate in these networks, but more extreme voices on both sides of the issue were excluded. Nevertheless, the authors found little support for the view that these networks undermined the democratic legitimacy of network decisions.

GOVERNANCE AS THE DEEPENING OF DEMOCRACY

Social Capital

Theoretical discussions of governance often make appeal to the concept of social capital, which Adler and Kwon (2002, 23) define as follows:

> Social capital is the goodwill available to individuals or groups. Its source lies in the structure and content of the actor's social relations. Its effects flow from the information, influence, and solidarity it makes available to the actor.

Building on a Tocquevillian tradition that emphasizes the importance of a strong civil society, Putnam et al.'s (2001) comparative regional study of Italy found that social capital could contribute to the effectiveness of governance. Subsequent studies of U.S. cities and towns provided additional support and nuance for this claim (Rice, 2001; Pierce et al., 2002; Goldfinger and Ferguson, 2009). Cross-national analysis of the relationship between social

Democratic legitimacy and managing political conflict   91

capital and the quality of government (measured as government effectiveness, rule of law, impartiality, professionalism, and a governmental quality index) finds a positive, statistically significant relationship (Doh, 2014).

Putnam's (2000) subsequent research distinguished between bonding, bridging and linking social capital. Bonding capital is similar to what social network theorists have called "strong ties" that deepen connections within a given community or organization, whereas bridging ties are similar to "weak ties" that bridge between social groups or make connections between otherwise weakly connected groups. Linking ties are connections across hierarchical levels. Governance scholars have used these distinctions to investigate how different types of social capital affect governance. Grafton (2005), for example, argues that each of these three types of social capital is important for fisheries governance, which depends on trust and cooperation within and between fishing communities and between these communities and the state.

While this research demonstrates positive correlations between social capital and effective governance, the social mechanisms that translate social capital into improved governance are not always obvious. Boix and Posner (1998) distinguish five mechanisms. First, social capital could work by helping to make voters more knowledgeable, which in turn allows them to hold officials accountable through elections. Second, social capital might also enhance the compliance of citizens with government rules and programs, thus adding to the efficiency of governments. A third possibility is that social capital shifts citizens away from a focus on narrow distributional issues toward broader public-interest concerns. Fourth, social capital may contribute to the dedication and cooperativeness of public officials, encouraging them to cooperate more fully. Finally, social capital may help to overcome deep social conflicts (like ethnic cleavages) that make government performance difficult.

Tavits (2006) identifies two broad mechanisms translating social capital into improved government performance: one is that social capital increases the political sophistication of citizens and enhances their ability to collectively hold government accountable, which Tavits dubs "policy activism"; the other mechanism is that social capital improves government performance through its positive effects on government elites, encouraging hard work and cooperation, which Tavits dubs "bureaucratic efficiency." Using data on local governments in Germany and the U.S., Tavits finds that social capital does explain policy activism but does less well in explaining bureaucratic efficiency.

Not all forms of social capital necessarily have positive effects. In their comparison of urban regeneration programs in Bristol (UK) and Naples (Italy), Cento Bull and Jones (2006, 782) conclude that "uncritical advocacy of pluralistic participation tends to underestimate the many different forms that social capital can exhibit, not all of which necessarily lead to more inclusive and democratic practices." In a cross-national statistical study, Young (2014) found, counterintuitively, that greater corruption control was associated with less social capital. She speculated that one possible explanation might be that corruption control reduces "bad" forms of social capital (forms of social solidarity that contribute to corruption).

Social capital is often produced by informal community and societal relations (ethnicity, religion, local community), so it is not self-evident that governance per se has any direct effect on the formation of social capital. Fukuyama (2001), however, has argued that the state does have some levers that it can pull to promote social capital, primarily through education and the effective delivery of public goods. The state can also undermine social capital by intervening in areas understood to be the domain of private actors or civil society. In an analysis of Swedish survey data, Kumlin and Rothstein (2005) find that a universalistic (as opposed to targeted) welfare state is more conducive to the development of social capital (see Chapter 8 for more discussion of the distinction between targeted and universalistic welfare policies).

Lowndes and Wilson (2001) argue that local government can promote social capital through institutional design and through how they interact with citizens and voluntary associations. One key dimension of institutional design is whether local governments promote an instrumental (i.e., service delivery) or democratic (i.e., partnership for community problem-solving) relationship with voluntary associations, with the latter more conducive to cultivating social capital. Another important design factor relates to how citizen participation in local governance is organized and promoted and to how local governments respond to these political inputs.

Other research also suggests that the institutional design of governance can affect the production of social capital. In a study of 11 Nepalese community forestry groups, McDougall and Banjade (2015) found that all groups had conflicts related to power and access to decision-making, disputes over rights and resources, and ethnic or inter-group conflicts. Initially, elites had much higher social capital than marginalized social groups. Over the course of their study, however, decision-making was decentralized to the hamlet level and shifted from a more hierarchical to a more collaborative mode of decision-making. They found that this shift encouraged the building of social capital among marginalized groups, as well as between elite and marginalized groups, which resulted in greater capacity to constructively manage forestry conflicts. As this example suggests, collaborative governance may both depend on social capital and produce it (Ansell and Gash, 2008; Oh and Bush, 2016).

Governments can not only engage constructively with communities, but they can also directly promote civil society. Government can be a "civic enabler" (Sirianni, 2010). Brandsen et al. (2017), however, caution that we should not let the pendulum swing too far in the direction of the top-down manufacturing of civil society and we must explore ways to balance top-down and bottom-up

Democratic legitimacy and managing political conflict   93

production of civil society. They suggest that this balance lies in the creation of intermediary institutions and processes that link governments and citizens in problem-solving communities. In a study of natural resource management conflicts in Uganda, Sanginga et al. (2007) found that social capital was likely to be most effective in contributing to conflict resolution when it was combined in a synergistic way with local policies: "Formal policy and informal social capital mechanisms work best when, through redistributive, integrative and capacity building measures, they strengthen the capabilities of stakeholders to enter into voluntary negotiation and mutually beneficial collective action to resolve conflicts" (2007, 16).

Trust

Interest in the relationship between trust and government has a long history in political theory (Braithwaite and Levi, 1998). The trustworthiness of government is regarded as a necessary condition for citizens to grant "contingent consent," which in turn leads to their compliance with policies they may not favor (Levi, 1998). Trustworthy government is generally viewed as being enhanced by fair, universalistic and impartial institutions.

While trust is typically viewed as a foundation for democratic legitimacy, Russell Hardin has raised an important challenge to this claim. Reasoning from what he calls an "interest-encapsulated" understanding of trust rather than a moral conception, Hardin (1998, 10–11) argues that "[a]ny claim that government requires citizen trust is conspicuously false." "Interest-encapsulated" trust means that my trust in you is based on my expectation that you have an interest in fulfilling my trust. Hardin argues that for most people, citizen expectations about government functioning do not amount to interest-encapsulated trust, but merely to inductive expectations (like expecting the sun to rise each day). Hardin does not rule out that some citizens (those most knowledgeable about the behavior of government institutions) may find government trustworthy, but the relationship of most citizens to government cannot be considered a relationship of trust.

In a range of studies, however, Tyler (1998) finds that trust is a critical factor in understanding citizen compliance with authority. He argues that there are two basic kinds of trust—instrumental and social trust. Instrumental trust refers to expectations about achieving positive outcomes from interactions with public authorities and is essentially equivalent to what Hardin calls an "interest-encapsulated" view. Social trust is "relational" and is linked to the nature of social connections and to identity derived from those connections, particularly pride and respect. This distinction leads Tyler and his colleagues to an important finding. When people identify with public authorities, trust is more likely to depend on social judgements about "character," whereas when they do not identify, they will base their trust on more instrumental calculations about how they expect to win or lose from the relation to authority.

Braithwaite (1998) also argues that there are different kinds of trust that depend on different value systems. Exchange-based trust basically follows Hardin's depiction of interest-encapsulated trust and is rooted in what she calls "security values." By contrast, she argues that communal-based trust emphasizes "perceptions of need and feelings of responsibility for others" and "harmony in social relationships" (Braithwaite, 1998, 54). Her empirical work finds that exchange and communal trust co-exist but are operative to different degrees in different kinds of institutional contexts. A key implication of this perspective is that understanding citizen trust in democracy requires consideration of both types of trust.

Governance institutions can, in part, moderate the factors affecting trust between state and society (Peters, 2010). Goodsell (2014) argues that bureaucracy can play a central role in building trust in government and can counter some of the negative consequences of political polarization on citizen trust. In a study of a Swedish e-petitioning initiative, however, Åström et al. (2017) find that it is important to discern how governance initiatives differentially affect different kinds of citizens. They found that the e-petitioning initiative held in the city of Malmo attracted more critical citizens and did not reinforce their trust in government.

Civic Capacity and Public Participation

In a book on urban school reform, Stone et al. (2001) distinguish the term "civic capacity" from "social capital." They suggest that while "social capital" refers to relations that are "interpersonal and private," "civic capacity" stresses the public nature of social action and engages major community stakeholders and the public sector. Civic capacity thus refers to the capacity to widely mobilize a community around common reform and problem-solving agendas. Briggs (2008) has argued that deepening democracy requires building civic capacity, which means helping different community groups in the community to work together to engage in problem-solving. He argues that this entails a broader understanding of democracy than one that merely seeks to create more opportunities for the public to participate.

A key lesson, Briggs argues, is that civic capacity is not merely a historical legacy—something that communities either have or do not have; it can be built. Civic capacity can take the form of creating broad-based coalitions, with non-governmental and civic organizations playing a key intermediary role. This civic capacity should be structured around learning and effective negotiation, enabled by multiple forms of vertical and horizontal accountability connecting public and private efforts and encouraged by leadership and initiative coming from above or below. This analysis leads Briggs to argue that deepening democracy entails building the capacity for communities to collectively solve problems.

In a comparative analysis of urban planning in the Seattle region, Page (2016) introduces a framework for analyzing how civic capacity is built in urban politics. He suggests that efforts of urban actors to frame common agendas, bridge between network divisions, and construct purpose-built governance institutions are of critical importance. By giving rise to effective learning and negotiation, these strategies can build the civic capacity necessary to address challenging urban problems. By contrast, diffuse policy networks and fragmented governance institutions will limit civic capacity. He also finds that common or shared values must first be identified or generated before stakeholders can engage in designing solutions to problems and that policy transparency is an important ingredient for fostering the learning needed to generate shared values and commitments. (See the discussion of "collective impact" in Chapter 8 for related ideas.)

Public participation is also seen as a way of enhancing civic engagement. In their evaluation of case research on citizen participation in over 20 countries, Gaventa and Barrett (2012) found that participation goes beyond affecting instrumental policy outcomes to also influence the development of democratic citizenship. However, fostering citizen participation is clearly a challenge. In a 10-year study of a neighborhood democracy effort in Los Angeles, Musso et al. (2011) drew six important lessons from the effort: (1) citizen participation efforts are politically vulnerable because political support for them waxes and wanes; (2) achieving descriptive representation is challenging; (3) capacity-building efforts are important for aligning citizen and administrator knowledge and skills; (4) strong leadership is necessary for effective initiation and management of participation; (5) foundations and universities can play an important role in promoting citizen participation, but can also encounter resistance; and (6) citizen participation efforts can cultivate social capital.

In a study of citizen participation in two Dutch cities, Michels and De Graaf (2010, 481) found that citizen participation did not really change the vertical relationship between government and citizens, and that while citizens contributed information to government, they did not play a significant role in policymaking. Despite these significant limitations, they observed that citizen participation did have positive effects for local democracy, including an increased sense of citizen responsibility for public policy, a greater citizen openness to the ideas of others, and increased legitimacy of decisions. Michels (2011) found similar results at an aggregate level in a study of 120 "democratic innovations" involving citizen participation in Western nations. These innovations contributed to the development of citizen skills and virtues and to the legitimacy of policy choices. Revisiting their 2010 article, Michels and De Graaf (2017, 877) write that

> [f]rom more recent research, we now know that the conclusion that the influence of citizen participation on policy mainly remains limited to providing ideas and suggestions is still valid in most cases but that at the same time the role of citizens and their impact depends on the specifics of the design of the participatory process.

Governance theorists have identified many kinds of citizen engagement and participation (Fung, 2006; Chhotray and Stoker, 2009, 246). Hendriks and Dzur (2021) distinguish between "invited" and "claimed" spaces of citizen participation. In the latter, which they call "citizen governance spaces," citizens may initiate innovative, experimental and disruptive strategies of governance that may address neglected or unresolved problems. Such collective efforts can enhance citizens' agency and sense of efficacy, develop their knowledge and skills with respect to certain issues, and allow them to reframe existing problem definitions and work across institutional boundaries.

Scholars have also analyzed the reasons why citizens participate. In a study of participatory governance in an urban renewal program in Stockholm, for example, Gustafson and Hertting (2017) find that participants have a mix of motives for participating, ranging from self-interest to the desire to contribute to the common good. They also find that this program created opportunities for both marginalized groups and more privileged groups to participate. A range of research suggests that a citizen's sense of efficacy for making a difference is important for motivating participation, and recent research points to how government responsiveness to citizen participation can shape this sense of efficacy (Sjoberg et al., 2017). The importance of knowledge and expertise in policymaking is often seen as a barrier to greater citizen participation.

Deliberation, Participation and Governance

While there are concerns that new modes of governance depoliticize issues and foster a technocratic approach to politics, many governance theorists might counter that a "conveyor-belt model" of political representation—participation via elections—is also a limited form of citizen engagement (Chhotray and Stoker, 2009). Taking a more positive view of the democratic potential of new modes of governance, Dryzek with Niemeyer (2010, 124–125) point out that governance networks are by nature deliberative because "their medium of coordination is language." While acknowledging that networks may also operate in an exclusive fashion, they observe that the deliberative nature of networks may contribute to the wider system of democratic deliberation.

Democratic legitimacy and managing political conflict 97

A critical note has been sounded with respect to the deliberative potential of new modes of environmental governance. Summarizing theory and case study research, Bäckstrand et al. (2010) find that deliberative rationality in environmental policymaking mostly takes place in hierarchical settings. They also conclude that deliberative forms of governance do not necessarily improve environmental problem-solving (i.e., output legitimacy) and do not always meet a high standard of deliberation. They conclude that: "The most significant and obvious finding is that the win–win rhetoric of new modes [of environmental governance] fails to translate into practice. Not surprisingly, the promise to deliver more legitimate and effective environmental policies seems too ambitious" (2010, 231).

Not all governance scholars reach such conclusions. Fung (2001) describes two successful efforts to develop participatory and deliberative governance in the areas of education and policing in the city of Chicago. He argues that the key ingredient for the success of these efforts was "accountable autonomy." On the one hand, these efforts gave local bureaucrats significant discretion to develop strategies with the public (autonomy). On the other hand, these efforts were centrally supported, monitored and, if necessary, sanctioned (accountability). Fung and Wright (2003) elaborate on this model of accountable autonomy, which they call "empowered participatory governance," and identify three design principles that support it. The first is *devolution*, by which they mean the localization of governance around specific problems and geographies. However, local strategies do not operate in isolation, but are guided by the second design principle—*centralized supervision and coordination*. Empowered participatory governance also calls for a third design principle, which is to *transform the administrative state into a group of deliberative bodies*.

One prominent line of argument in the governance literature is that processes of governing can themselves be democratized by creating governance mechanisms that allow public deliberation and participation. The concept of mini-publics is a notable example (Niemeyer, 2011). Farrell and Curato (2021, 3) define deliberative mini-publics as "carefully designed forums where a representative subset of the wider population come together to engage in open, inclusive, informed and consequential discussions on one or more issues." These include specific formats for engaging citizens, such as citizen juries, consensus conferences, deliberative polls, citizen assemblies, townhall meetings and issue forums (Goodin and Dryzek, 2006; Farrell and Curato, 2021). They argue that random selection of members is a key design principle for mini-publics.

An extensive body of research and debate has grown up around the idea of mini-publics. Curato and Böker (2016) review optimistic and pessimistic perspectives and they find that these perspectives depend on how mini-publics are linked to the broader system of deliberation. It is not sufficient, they argue, for mini-publics to generate high-quality deliberation among the participants of the mini-public ("internal" deliberation). They must also foster deliberation, legitimacy and capacity beyond these internal processes with wider (non-participating) publics ("external" deliberation). Finding that internal and external dimensions of deliberation are not always mutually supportive in the case of actual mini-publics, they suggest the importance of the "co-development" of internal and external features of deliberative systems.

Similar in some respect to the idea of mini-publics, governance scholars have recently explored the democratic potential of the concept of "co-creation" (Ansell et al., 2021). While the concept developed out of the idea of "co-production," the joint production of services by the state and citizens, it has recently been used to describe collaborative innovation and problem-solving (Ansell and Torfing, 2021a; Sørensen et al., 2021). Chapter 5 examined the role of co-creation in contributing to governance effectiveness, but scholars have also begun to point to its democratic potential to bring citizens into a new relationship with the state and with one another (Ansell and Torfing, 2021b; Ansell et al., 2021).

Røiseland (2022) argues that co-creation is an example of what Warren (2009) called "governance-driven democratization." Building on the ideas of input and output legitimacy, he distinguishes between input-based and output-based co-creation, where the former provides input into the policy and planning process and the latter assists in the improved production of public services. In a comparison of case studies from Denmark and Norway, he shows how these two types of co-creation have the "potential" to enhance democratic legitimacy, though they also encounter "pitfalls" that may detract from or act as barriers to enhancing democratic legitimacy.

GOVERNANCE AS THE MANAGEMENT OF CONFLICT

In addition to its role in contributing to or detracting from democracy and state legitimacy, governance has an underappreciated role to play in the management of conflict. Governance is often thought about as "getting things done" and societal conflict is often viewed as a barrier that must be overcome to do that. However, given that many societies are politically polarized, it is useful to examine the more direct role that governance might play in managing conflict. While the governance literature, narrowly construed, has not been focused on conflict management per se (with some important exceptions), this topic has been a central theme for political science. This section of the chapter examines some of the ways that governance and conflict management may intersect.

Trust and Conflict Mediation

It is useful to begin by returning to the topic of trust, which plays a central role in discussions of conflict management. The relation between trust and conflict is interactive in that conflict can breed distrust and lack of trust can deepen conflict (Di Nucci et al., 2021). As a result, trust-building at the individual level is an important ingredient for reducing conflict and promoting collaboration (Getha-Taylor et al., 2019). Following the discussion in the previous section, trust research distinguishes between calculus-based and identification-based trust and draws a distinction between trust and distrust (Lewicki and Wiethoff, 2000). These distinctions yield insights into the conditions for the repair of trust. For instance, calculus-based trust is generally an important first step in building trust, but identification-based trust is likely to deepen trust and be more resistant to the loss of trust.

Kelman (2005) has argued that "building trust among enemies" is a key strategy for international conflict resolution. In high-conflict situations, however, trust-building must confront a number of dilemmas, the most fundamental of which is that to begin the process of trust-building, one must engage in an act of trust. He suggests that parties can address this dilemma by starting out with low commitment activities in problem-solving workshops and then gradually building up to higher commitment activities. Yet even this strategy of gradually building mutual commitments is problematic in situations of antagonism and mutual distrust. Thus, he proposes that third parties serve as the repositories of trust, particularly in earlier phases of interactive problem-solving. In high-conflict situations, he suggests that the goal is to establish "working trust," which is based on the interests of the respective parties (what Lewicki and Wiethoff call calculative rather than identification-based trust). Overcoming the initial barriers to trust-building can be facilitated through "mutual reassurances" from negotiating parties that signal to other parties their goodwill, seriousness and appreciation of the other parties' fears.

Collaborative governance is one strategy for mediating conflicts that stresses the important role of trust-building, and it has been particularly important for understanding how to manage ubiquitous resource conflicts (Wondolleck and Yaffee, 2000; Ansell and Gash, 2008). In a study of collaborative governance to manage resource conflicts in the Amazon, Fisher et al. (2020) found that deepening the joint understanding of the sources and causes of conflict allowed for the customized development of collaborative capacity to manage conflict. In a study of community forestry in Nepal, collaborative governance actually mobilized latent conflicts in the short term but ameliorated them in the long term (McDougall and Banjade, 2015). Urban planning is another area rife with conflict. In a study of urban regeneration in Shanghai, Wang et al. (2022) found that collaborative governance was effective in addressing "street-level" conflicts about regeneration. However, given the dilemma of needing trust to begin trust-building, it should not be too surprising that collaborative governance may also fail to resolve fundamental conflicts (Vihma and Toikka, 2021; Bennett et al., 2022).

The Advocacy Coalition Framework, a policy process model, distinguishes between collaborative and adversarial policy subsystems and examines the factors that may explain transitions between them (Weible, 2008). An adversarial subsystem is expected to transition to a collaborative subsystem when there is a "hurting stalemate"—that is, where opposing coalitions have exhausted their options and where the status quo is unacceptable (Weible, 2008, 629). Weible and Sabatier (2009) draw on the management of Lake Tahoe to provide some empirical support for this proposition. Reciprocally, a collaborative subsystem can transition to an adversarial subsystem when new actors enter the scene or where events shift the balance of power between coalitions (Weible, 2008, 629). In a study of EU biofuels policy, Rietig (2018) found that a shift from a collaborative to an adversarial policy process was caused by new scientific evidence that changed the beliefs in one coalition.

Violent Conflict

While politics is nearly by definition about conflict, scholars often distinguish between non-violent and violent conflict. While collaborative governance and dispute resolution may be useful after people pick up arms to settle their conflicts, we are arguably in a qualitatively different world. As a result, there is a different type of discussion about the relationship between conflict and governance.

One issue is about the general relationship between governance and conflict. Weak or poor governance is often seen as contributing to intrastate conflict (Brinkerhoff, 2011). There is a vicious cycle implied here, however, because weak states are not seen as having the capacity or will for "good" or "effective" governance. Analyzing the relationship between democracy, governance and peace, Norris (2012) finds that "bureaucratic governance" reduces internal conflict, while the legal and security capacity of the state reduces civil rebellion and the capacity of states to administer and deliver public good reduces societal grievances (recall the discussion of state infrastructural capacity at the beginning of Chapter 5).

Cortright et al. (2017) argue that good governance enhances peace and reduces armed conflict. It does so, they argue, in two fundamental ways—by ameliorating the conditions that make people fight and by providing conditions to mediate and transform disputes. They theorize that three key features of good governance are responsible for such effects: governance must be *inclusive* of different social and political groups; it must be *participatory*, allowing individuals and groups to express their concerns and interests; and governance must be *accountable*, and thus perceived as fair and legitimate, In addition, states must be able to ensure security and provide public goods.

Although they find significant evidence for these claims, they observe that there are some tradeoffs that arise in building good governance. Greater inclusion and participation are important, but in some circumstances they create fundamental challenges to governance institutions. For example, empowerment of women and girls is an important and often successful strategy for supporting inclusion, participation and accountability, but it can also lead to political conflict. International aid to countries with weaker governance institutions is also essential, but it can heighten conflict between winners and losers. Cortright et al. stress that efforts to build good governance must recognize the interconnected nature of governance efforts and the importance of fitting them to context.

Some scholars, however, challenge the "weak state" view of political violence and argue that state capacity is not the primary issue. Kleinfeld and Barham (2018) identify a group of states with higher capacity and higher levels of political violence and isolate a common pattern of governance. These states have high levels of corruption, weak court systems, poorly served rural populations and marginalized minorities. They refer to the pattern of political violence they observe in these states as "privilege violence," because it is characterized by elites utilizing non-state violence to secure their privileges.

One important argument is that the prevailing development and security discourse about weak, fragile or failing states imposes a Western "Weberian" notion of the state that often undermines customary forms of governance. When Weberian institutions are combined with various forms of political and economic mobilization that arise in response to state weakness and globalization, they produce "contradictory and dialectic co-existence of forms of sociopolitical organization that have their roots in both non-state indigenous societal structures and introduced state structures" (Boege et al., 2009, 17). The problem with the failed state narrative, according to these authors, is that introducing central state institutions to correct the problem of weak states can disrupt the forms of governance that are providing services, order or security.

One line of thinking about the relationship between governance and conflict in civil war and armed conflict situations has also begun to point to informality as a source of order—a position that flies under the banner of "governance without government" or "hybrid governance." Meagher (2012, 1076) describes this changing perspective as a "gestalt shift," one that shifts attention away from the Weberian rationality of good governance prescriptions and the security focus on "failed states" toward finding order in non-state institutions and processes that are often informal in character.

Constructing a "good governance" index from several formal and informal indicators of "good governance," Hegre and Nygård (2015) find that good governance significantly reduces the risk that conflict will reoccur. Parsing the separate impacts of the formal and informal aspect of governance, these authors conclude that formal governance is not sufficient to significantly reduce the risk of conflict relapse, which leads them to the conclusion that informal governance must support formal governance. Meagher (2012), however, warns that we need to be cautious in erecting informal governance as a new paradigm that replaces attention to government and formal institutions. She argues that informal security arrangements are highly problematic for producing legitimate governance.

Consociationalism and Power-Sharing

There is a longstanding discussion in political science about societal conflict management. A key question is how societies can hold together politically despite deep social cleavages. Political scientist Arend Lijphart (1969) initially investigated the stability of small, but culturally diverse European democracies like the Netherlands, Belgium, Austria and Switzerland. Describing the cultural and institutional features that allowed stability despite diversity as "consociationalism," he identified the "grand coalition" cabinet as one of its most prominent mechanisms, describing it as a cartel that allows for stable negotiations across cultural and political divides. He initially argued that consociationalism came about in these countries due to external (international) threats and that stability depended on a balance of power between subgroups.

A key feature of consociational power-sharing, as developed by Lijphart, is the use of non-majoritarian institutions to manage elite conflicts, an idea he eventually elaborated in his important distinction between consensus and majoritarian democracies (Lijphart, 2012). His later work also settled on four key principles of consociationalism: grand coalitions, proportionality, segmental autonomy, and mutual veto. Quantitative evidence supports the claim that consociationalism fosters stability through inclusive coalitions and minority veto rights, but that segmental autonomy or proportional representation do not necessarily promote stability (Kelly, 2019).

Lijphart's theory has been influential and extended far beyond its original focus on small European democracies (Bogaards et al., 2019). As it moved from explanation to prescription, however, nearly every aspect of the theory has been intensely scrutinized and criticized (Lustick, 1997; Andeweg, 2000). Recent research finds that the role of external actors (i.e., outside of the nation in question) and the management of security arrangements are particularly important to the success of consociationalism (McGarry, 2019). Other research suggests that constructing politics around group difference can intensify rather

Democratic legitimacy and managing political conflict   103

than ameliorate inter-group conflict and institutionalizing these social groupings can have negative unintended consequences (O'Flynn and Russell, 2005). Instead of advocating consociational arrangements, this approach argues for more "integrative" political institutions, particularly those that incentivize post-election cooperation. This perspective, however, grants that integrative strategies are likely to be less efficacious in situations where group conflicts are already sharply defined.

Governance reform at the subnational level is argued to be particularly central to conflict resolution (Brinkerhoff, 2011). Federalism and decentralizing reforms are seen as mitigating ethnic conflict by giving minority ethnic groups a voice and a stake in federal or national governments. However, the devil is often in the details when it comes to whether federalism and decentralization mitigate or exacerbate conflict. Distinguishing between several different dimensions of decentralization—including accountability mechanisms (local elections), service delivery and fiscal transfers—Pierskalla and Sacks (2017) find that local elections reduce routine forms of violence, but that, surprisingly, improved local service delivery increases it. They suggest that this is because the increasing quality of local services can create distributive conflicts between different groups competing for access to these resources. Conflict is reduced, however, as services become equitably distributed across groups.

Other research finds that federalism increases low-intensity ethnic conflict but reduces high-intensity conflict. By fragmenting and decentralizing power, federalism reduces the intensity of inter-ethnic tensions at the central government level. Proportional representation operates in a similar manner, reducing high-intensity conflicts (though not necessarily increasing low-intensity conflicts) (Cohen, 1997). In an empirical study of 62 Asian and African nations, Linder and Bächtiger (2005) find that a "power-sharing index" based on Lijphart's consociational theory is a strong predictor of democratization.

A key theoretical debate in the literature on the democratic management of political conflict is around the concept of "power-sharing," which Norris (2018, 23) describes as updating Lijphart's theory of consociationalism. A key point she draws from Lijphart's model is that majoritarian systems will tend to exacerbate conflict in multi-ethnic nations, or in nations with strong civic cleavages. Norris identifies four basic dimensions of power-sharing: proportional representation, federalism or decentralization, significant checks and balances on government, and an independent and pluralist news media. Her research supports the importance of power-sharing institutions and finds strong support for federal over unitary systems. Critics of power-sharing (of which Horowitz is the key figure) suggest that power-sharing arrangements can institutionalize ethnic divisions.

CONCLUSION

A very broad theoretical expectation of the governance literature is that more effective governance will lead to more legitimate governance. There is considerable cross-national support for this expectation, though both the informal and technocratic aspects of governance raise legitimacy concerns. Governance theories have usefully distinguished different kinds of legitimacy (input, throughput and output), and there is some preliminary theorization and empirical research linking different aspects of governance to these different sources of legitimacy. An unresolved point of tension in the governance literature is related to the "depoliticization" or "anti-politics" aspects of governance. These criticisms have mostly been leveled at good governance and NPM ideas, but they raise concerns about the ways that new forms of governance may subordinate the democratic will to the functional needs of governance.

Research generally supports the idea that social capital and trust are important assets for effective governance and democratic legitimacy, though several caveats have been made to this argument. A few governance scholars have also turned this idea around and suggested that the state and various governance designs are in a position to cultivate social capital and trust. The relationships between social capital, trust, governance and democracy are complex and we still lack a more general theoretical framework to analyze these relations.

Governance scholars have been very interested in how new modes of governance create opportunities for civic engagement. At the urban level, research on "civic capacity" picks up on many of the themes of social capital research, but stresses that capacity-building is more of an active political process than a social-structural resource. But building civic engagement is no picnic and it is clear from research that achieving authentic citizen participation is not easy. On balance, governance theorists are favorable toward the idea that citizen participation is valuable for citizens and democratic citizenship and they have provided some empirical support for this optimism.

Ideas about governance arose roughly alongside democratic theory discussions of deliberation. The combination of new modes of governance and traditional ideas about citizen participation have been interpreted as creating new possibilities for a more deliberative democracy. One important strand of governance theory that explores these possibilities is the research on "empowered participatory governance," which has theorized the institutional conditions supporting deliberative citizen participation and has provided case study evidence supporting their plausibility. A closely related body of work on "mini-publics" describes how forums can be created that allow citizens to deliberate about public issues and an emerging body of research about "co-creation" has theorized the conditions under which citizens and stakeholders can come together with state institutions to address public problems.

A range of theoretical perspectives have been put forth to understand how societal conflicts can be managed and resolved. Within the governance literature, collaborative governance offers one prominent perspective on conflict mediation. By bringing together groups of relevant and affected actors, collaborative governance offers one important model of conflict mediation, one that has been particularly relevant for addressing natural resource conflicts. This model stresses the value of face-to-face deliberation and facilitated conflict mediation. While conflict is a central issue for collaborative governance models, it seems fair to say that it has mostly seen conflict management as a necessary step for achieving "collaborative advantage" rather than as a valuable end in itself.

Political scientists have been attentive to the broad institutional conditions that prevent violent conflict. Weak governance is widely regarded as one contributing factor that leads to violent intrastate conflicts and there has been some effort to identify the specific mechanisms that link weak governance to violence. However, the precise relationship between "weak states" and violence remains a point of significant debate. Some researchers argue that the "Weberian" assumptions embodied in the analysis of "weak states" may lead to state-building that inadvertently undermines more informal mechanisms of conflict management.

Political scientists have also extensively explored the role of consociationalism, federalism and power-sharing to manage intense societal conflicts related to ethnicity, religion and regionalism. While there is considerable debate about the warrants of specific institutional arrangements, and concern that these arrangements can reinforce rather than ameliorate societal conflicts, there is general support for the view that power-sharing arrangements are a necessary if imperfect strategy for managing intense conflict.

7. Improving global cooperation and coordination

The topic of international cooperation and coordination is vast and deep and this chapter cannot cover it in any comprehensive sense. What this chapter will do, more selectively, is examine how theories of governance are adopted and developed at the global level and consider where and how these perspectives contribute to our understanding of global cooperation and coordination. To begin, the very term "global governance" often signifies a shift away from the traditional international relations focus on inter-state politics toward a concern with interactions among a wider group of actors and institutions (Dingwerth and Pattberg, 2006; Biermann and Pattberg, 2008). Weiss and Wilkinson (2014, 213) argue that global governance is a "halfway house between the international anarchy underlying realist analysis and a world state" and Willetts (2010, 148) defines global governance as consisting of "policy-making and policy implementation in global political systems, through the collaboration of governments with actors from civil society and the private sector."

The challenge of global governance, Zürn (2018b) writes, is that it is highly contested, both politicized and polarized. Institutional authority is fragmented, and contestation often takes the form of "counter-institutionalization," which means that those who oppose existing institutions create their own institutions to advance their objectives. In general, the more authority bestowed on an international or transnational institution, the more that that authority can become politicized and the more likely that others will attempt to delegitimate it. This process can lead to either a decline of global governance or to significant reforms that eventually strengthen it.

Global governance is frequently described as "fragmented" (Kim, 2020) and Biermann and Pattberg (2008, 284) describe global environmental governance as:

> characterized by an increasing segmentation of different layers and clusters of rule making and rule implementing, fragmented both vertically between supranational, international, national, and subnational layers of authority (multilevel governance) and horizontally between different parallel rule-making systems maintained by different groups of actors (multipolar governance).

Improving global cooperation and coordination 107

A resulting challenge is "gridlock," which is attributed to a number of factors, including the rise of new powers with more heterogeneous interests (Hale et al., 2013). Global problems have become more intractable and existing international institutions place limits on problem-solving. The result is a "governance gap" (Hale et al., 2013, 3) or a "global governance deficit" (Haas, 2017). Gridlock, however, must also be understood as an outgrowth of the very success of postwar global governance, which created the conditions for new powers to take their place in the global order. The growing economic and political interdependence made possible by this system also produced new problems that existing institutions were ill-prepared to address. Although new institutions were created to deal with these problems, these institutions contributed to the growing fragmentation of the global order. Hale et al. (2013) refer to this pattern of success leading to new and more intractable problems as "self-reinforcing interdependence."

Kahler (2018) sketches out three possible futures for global governance. The first is a trend toward greater regionalism, where emerging economies create their own regional institutions for managing the economy and security in lieu of multilateral institutions. The second is a trend toward the rise of populist and nationalist forces that oppose the existing multilateral order, leading to political stagnation. The third possibility is the increasing complexification of the existing system of international organizations, complemented or challenged by a wide range of public–private and private schemes to address specific issues (i.e., by various forms of "new governance"). None of these options is pretty, but this last possibility highlights the importance of understanding mechanisms of governance.

GLOBAL GOVERNANCE AS GOVERNANCE

Perhaps the most general theoretical account of global governance is provided by Zürn (2018a), who argues that "world politics is now embedded in a normative and institutional structure that contains hierarchies and power inequalities and thus endogenously produces contestation, resistance, and distributional struggles" (2018a, 3). A central concept of his theory is what he calls the "authority–legitimation" link. His argument is that we can expect resistance to global authorities to the extent that they have not established legitimacy. Such conflicts can lead to either a strengthening or weakening of the global governance system.

A leading global governance scholar, Oran Young (2021), identifies five types of governance at the global level: *rules-based governance* is often the standard view of governance. Constitutive ("rules of the game") and operational or regulatory rules are prescriptive and enforced through sanctions. He distinguishes rules-based governance from *principles-based governance*.

Principles are codes of conduct that specify appropriate behavior, but they are implemented through processes of socialization and enforced through peer processes. *Pledge-based governance* entails voluntary commitments and typically uses periodic review processes to evaluate whether pledges are met and to expand future commitments. *Goal-based governance* operates by setting priority goals and allocating resources to meet those goals. Finally, *standards-based governance* sets performance benchmarks and typically uses certification to evaluate whether participants have achieved those standards. He argues that each of these strategies of governance has strengths and drawbacks, and we are better off not thinking of one as better than the other, but rather evaluating how they "fit" with the problem context.

Abbott and Snidal (2009) distinguish "old" and "new" governance at the national and international or transnational levels. At the national level, old governance was state-centric, bureaucratic and rule-oriented, while new governance is decentralized, characterized by state orchestration (as opposed to control) and oriented toward non-binding "soft law." Applying this distinction to the international level requires some modification. Old international governance was expressed through the agency of intergovernmental organizations, which lacked state-like authority and could not set mandatory rules for their member-states. These international organizations were designed to complement but not replace or challenge state-centric governance. New transnational governance is also decentralized, has dispersed expertise and relies on voluntary codes. It also relies on orchestration, though international organizations do not bring as much authority or capacity to bear on orchestration as do states. As a result, new transnational governance is often created from the bottom up, often through the initiative of non-governmental organizations (NGOs).

THE BASIC STRUCTURE OF GLOBAL GOVERNANCE

International Organizations

International organizations (IOs) are a key feature of global governance—both old and new. However, they encounter many challenges in fulfilling their leading role. IOs are typically intergovernmental organizations whose members are nation-states. The political tensions between these member-states create significant constraints on IO action, which is often experienced as internal fragmentation and contested legitimacy (Graham, 2014; Dingwerth et al., 2019; Hurd, 2019). IOs are asked to adapt to many emerging issues and demands but are structurally hamstrung in terms of their ability to adapt. Dingwerth et al. (2019) find that IOs must meet a lengthening list of legitimacy standards and respond to wider and more diverse constituencies. New standards and demands do not so much replace earlier standards and expecta-

Improving global cooperation and coordination

tions but are rather layered on top of them. This layering expands procedural contestation in IOs, leading to more attention to inclusion, transparency and participation.

Two leading scholars of international organizations, Michael Barnett and Martha Finnemore (2012) stress that IOs must be understood as bureaucracies characterized by their emphasis on impersonal rules. Understanding their relative autonomy from states requires appreciating their bureaucratic nature. While IOs control resources and information, their power derives "not so much because they possess material and informational resources but, more fundamentally, because they use their authority to orient action and create social reality" (2012, 6). IO power, they argue, is derived from their production and control of rules and knowledge, which they can deploy in both regulative and constitutive ways. IOs regulate through their ability to set rules or control information in ways that shape the incentives for others to act. IOs, however, also have constitutive power that derives from their ability to define problems and establish moral standards. They also construct social reality by classifying the world and interpreting the meanings associated with these classifications and they act as conduits for diffusing norms.

Barnett and Finnemore (2012) also call theoretical attention to the bureaucratic dysfunctions of IOs, which they attribute to the bureaucratic emphasis on impersonal rules and specialization. Building on a Weberian analysis, they identify five mechanisms that produce bureaucratic dysfunction: (1) the iron cage of bureaucratic rules; (2) the problems of applying universal rules to specific contexts; (3) the normalization of deviance, or the way that exceptions become cognitively and normatively accepted; (4) the way bureaucracies tend to become insular; and (5) the tendency toward internal contestation between different organizational subcultures.

Regimes and Regime Complexes

A central theoretical idea in the analysis of global governance is the concept of an "international regime," which was developed to describe "multilateral agreements among states which aim to regulate national actions within an issue-area" (Haggard and Simmons, 1987, 495). Regimes are composed of formal and informal "principles, norms, rules and decision-making procedures" that can facilitate cooperation and conflict management (Krasner, 1983, xiii). Regime theory stresses that institutions matter in international relations and it examines how regimes form, their stability over time, and their conditioning effect on the behavior of states. Viewing international regimes as a distinctive form of global governance, Young (1999b, 7) describes them as having horizontal rather than vertical (hierarchical) authority and observes that they represent "governance without government."

Regime theory essentially tries to provide an answer to the question of how states can cooperate in the absence of overarching authority, and it debates whether it is the formality of rules or the convergence of expectations that fundamentally matters in producing regime effects (Young, 1999b). Levy et al. (1995) suggest that these two dimensions—formal rules and converging expectations—can be used to describe variations in regimes: regimes can be high on one dimension and low on the other. Using Arctic governance as an example, Young (2021) argues that formal governance—in the sense of legally binding agreements—is not always preferable to informal governance.

Raustiala and Victor (2004) introduced the concept of "regime complex" to describe the growing density of international institutions and to try to capture the idea that the effects of regimes are not easily decomposable into the effects of individual regimes. Using the case of plant genetic resources, they describe five distinct international institutions linked to agriculture, trade and environmental protection that developed over time to regulate property rights over these resources. Regime complexes like this arise, they argue, due to the increasing legalization of international cooperation, leading to complexes of overlapping and interactive but non-hierarchical regimes.

An important implication of regime complexes is that negotiations about how to address international issues develop in a complex institutional space that both constrains and enables subsequent institutional change ("no clean slate"; Raustiala and Victor, 2004, 296). Regime complexes also create a plurality of institutional venues and hence the possibility of forum shopping, where different actors pursue their interests in the forum that best serves their agenda. Regime complexes also foster the challenge of legal consistency and restoring or avoiding consistency becomes a key dynamic of complexes. Regime complexes also produce a dynamic in which the regimes evolve in a bottom-up fashion through experimentation and implementation.

Regime complexes arise because of a lack of global hierarchy, which means there is no appeal to higher authority to settle differences between institutional agendas (Alter and Raustiala, 2018). While it may appear desirable to form more encompassing and streamlined regimes, global actors rarely pursue this agenda when addressing global governance problems. It is much easier, in general, to add a new agreement or institution to address a specific problem than to try to order them. As these initiatives accumulate over time, global governance becomes a "crowded" space (Alter and Raustiala, 2018, 345). Some international organizations may discover greater room for maneuver in a regime complex, while others may find themselves placed in more constraining and challenging circumstances (Betts, 2013).

A key debate in the literature on regime complexes is about whether they undermine or enhance global cooperation. On the negative side, regime complexes reflect the fragmentation of global governance, as noted earlier. On

Improving global cooperation and coordination 111

the positive side, Orsini and Godet (2018) argue that regime complexes may have an "emulsifying effect" on global governance agendas, by expanding the influence of non-state actors and by expanding the opportunities for advocacy. Keohane and Victor (2011, 15–16) argue that the climate change complex has advantages over a more integrated and comprehensive regime because it provides greater "flexibility across issues" and "adaptability over time." Their position is analogous to the argument in favor of "polycentric" institutions (see Chapter 9).

INGOs

International non-governmental organizations (INGOs) play a prominent role in global governance and have pushed for and achieved a significant degree of representation and influence in international organizations and regimes. Willetts (2010) argues that NGO participation has transformed the normative structure and style of international negotiations, with particular influence in the areas of women's issues, global population growth, development, human rights, environmental protection and arms control. Often, INGOs are themselves federations, associations, or networks of NGOs, which may or may not be nationally based.

The significant role of INGOs in international organizations and regimes has come about through several mechanisms. States have promoted their participation when it serves their agendas and IOs have engaged them in order to take advantage of their experience, skills, resources, and legitimacy. INGOs have also demanded representation, particularly in UN organizations, and they are often actively involved in treaty negotiations. Their facility with using the global internet for advocacy purposes has enhanced their influence.

Despite this significant influence, INGOs are sometimes described as facing a legitimacy crisis due to concerns about whether they represent the needs and interests of those they claim to serve or the donors who fund them or the states or international organizations that sanction them. Walton et al. (2016) argue that, as a result, INGO legitimacy has tended to be approached from either a top-down or a bottom-up perspective. International law and international relations scholars tend to take a top-down view of INGOs, focusing on their legal status and on how they contribute to or ameliorate the democratic deficit at the international level (e.g., by acting in non-representative ways or by helping to hold international institutions accountable).

By contrast, development scholars tend to view legitimacy from the bottom up and focus on the difficulty that INGOs have in working with diverse national and social constituencies. Walton et al. (2016) note that the backlash against INGOs in the global south has been particularly significant, because donor states have relied on them to deliver aid, sometimes by going around governments. Development scholars note the "symbiotic functional relationship" between IOs, donor states and INGOs, who depend on one another to deliver development aid to the local level (Campbell, 2018, 95).

INGOs directly and indirectly lobby international organizations (Dellmuth and Tallberg, 2017). Like domestic interest groups, they may adopt "insider" strategies that seek to directly influence and inform IO decision-makers and/or "outsider" strategies that seek to mobilize public opinion that then indirectly influences decision-makers. Dellmuth and Tallberg (2017) hypothesize that the more NGOs prioritize their influence over IO decision-making, the more they will adopt insider strategies. Membership-based organizations, by contrast, may give greater weight to outsider strategies. Based on a large-N database of interviews with NGOs, they find that most NGOs use both insider and outsider strategies, and they find that both of their hypotheses are supported.

GLOBAL GOVERNANCE NETWORKS

In the fragmented, complex and decentered world of global governance, it is perhaps not a surprise that "networks" of various sorts play an important role in global cooperation and coordination. This section describes the range of different types of networks that have been investigated by global governance scholars.

Epistemic Communities

One of the earliest discussions of the networked character of global governance described the importance of "epistemic communities," which are networks of "knowledge-based experts with an authoritative claim to policy relevant knowledge within their domain of expertise" (Haas, 2021, 699). Haas (1992) introduced the idea of epistemic communities to international relations, arguing that our understanding of international policy coordination could be enhanced by attending to the role of experts. He stressed that complexity and uncertainty were key drivers of the turn to experts for information and policymaking guidance. Communities of experts share principled beliefs or judgements and have similar standards of knowledge validity and they tend to develop where science is extensively applied to a policy area and where experts have a measure of autonomy from funders or political supporters. Part of the goal of epistemic communities research is to show that experts play a central and often overlooked role in global governance (An and Yoo, 2019).

Focusing on the ecological epistemic community, Haas (2021) argues that epistemic community involvement has important consequences for the development of multilateral environmental agreements (MEAs). MEAs with active epistemic communities and backed by strong international organizations are more likely to demonstrate "social learning" and negotiations will be conducted within the framework of expert consensus. These MEAs are likely to develop strong and comprehensive environmental management. MEAs established without the active support of epistemic communities or strong international institutions, or both, are likely to exhibit outcomes that are not well articulated in terms of their relationship to ecological science.

Summarizing the prior literature on epistemic communities, Cross (2013) finds that they are likely to have more influence when: (1) there is uncertainty about an issue and the issue is politically salient; (2) they have access to decision-makers; (3) debate over an issue is taking shape or where technocratic issues are salient; (4) they are united by professional standards or beliefs; and (5) they have relevant quantitative data and their contribution is compatible with existing institutional frameworks. She builds on this framework to stress that the influence of epistemic communities will vary in terms of their "internal cohesion," which depends on both shared knowledge and professional socialization. She also stresses that epistemic communities are not simply composed of scientists and that professionalism is as or more important as a basis of community than science per se.

Regulatory Networks

Another type of global governance network is regulatory in nature. In an influential book, *A New World Order*, Slaughter (2004) called attention to the importance and ubiquity of transgovernmental networks of national and international regulators. Often based on informal cooperation and operating in a context of globalization, these transgovernmental regulatory networks are often used to reduce and manage interjurisdictional conflict and competition (Slaughter and Zaring, 2006). While these networks are understood to be functional solutions to global cooperation and coordination challenges, they also raise fundamental questions about their accountability.

Research on transnational regulatory governance stresses the importance of networks between national regulators, which are often mediated by international institutions. Summarizing the literature in the European Union context, Bache et al. (2016) describe three types of transnational regulatory regime: (1) the creation of transnational agencies that coordinate national agencies; (2) transnational networks of EU institutions and national agencies; and (3) global regulatory networks promoted by the EU. They describe two types of conventional explanations of these regimes: functional explanations focus on the delegation of powers to non-majoritarian institutions to achieve certain common goals; and political explanations focus on power relations between national and EU institutions and between EU institutions.

Global Public Policy Networks

Global public policy networks are "loose alliances of government agencies, international organizations, corporations, and elements of civil society such as nongovernmental organizations, professional associations, or religious groups that join together to achieve what none can accomplish on its own" (Reinicke, 1999, 44). One of the earliest observers of these networks, Wolfgang Reinicke (1999), described them as sharing knowledge, addressing market failures and enhancing participation in response to the challenges of globalization. They are conceived as helping to achieve multi-sectoral collective action that can provide public goods at the global level and characterized by their interdependence, their flexible and open form, and their emphasis on the complementarity of member interests (Benner et al., 2004). There is also a body of research that understands global networks as conduits of policy diffusion (Stone, 2004).

Global public health networks have been found to face at least four important challenges in generating support for the issues that they champion: first, members of the network must overcome their internal disagreements about how to define problems; second, the network as a whole must successfully frame these problems for external audiences ("positioning"); third, the network must go beyond its core supporters to successfully build wider coalitions; and fourth, the network must establish governance institutions that can successfully manage and orchestrate the network. In an analysis of eight global public health networks, Shiffman (2017) shows how these factors shape the strength or weakness of these networks. As with other forms of network governance, global public policy networks raise concerns about their accountability and a wide range of accountability mechanisms have been identified for these networks (Benner et al., 2004).

Global Public–Private Partnerships

Global public–private partnerships (GPPPs) began to develop in the late 1970s and early 1980s, reflecting a changing attitude toward public–private collaboration, a concern about the effectiveness of UN agencies, a growing appreciation of the interdependence of the public and private sectors, and a UN desire to harness the resources of the private sector (Buse and Walt, 2000a). International organizations, according to Andonova (2017, 3), are central to the creation of GPPPs, because they "often lead or provide the forum and normative glue for such collaboration, crafting a political space for the interface between public purpose and private practice in international relations."

GPPPs represent an innovation for global governance and, according to Andonova (2017), they have developed more through ad hoc experimentation than through explicit design. They represent a new mode of governance that brings new actors into the governance process and shifts the role of private actors from lobbying to collaboration. GPPPs rearticulate power and authority in global governance because they create decentralized networks that bring multiple types of authority and competence together and they tend to rely on softer governance instruments. They are also distinguished from traditional multilateral organizations by being coalitions of the willing.

GPPPs are created for policy development, implementation or information-sharing and their central mission tends to be focused on one of these agendas (Andonova, 2017). In a study of 323 transnational climate change partnerships, Pattberg (2010) finds that the largest group of partnerships is oriented toward knowledge dissemination (with a smaller group oriented toward knowledge production). States play the most important roles as partnership leaders and members. While GPPPs play a highly visible role in global governance, a large-n study of multi-stakeholder partnerships in the area of sustainable development comes to pessimistic conclusions about whether such partnerships can satisfactorily address what they call the regulatory, implementation and participation deficit at the global level (Biermann et al., 2007).

Andonova argues that GPPPs have some advantages over traditional multilateral organizations, in that they are more flexible and quicker to react. But their contribution is also likely to be "partial and uneven precisely because their organizational structure relies on a high degree of congruence of interests, norms and overlapping private and public benefits" (2017, 11). She concludes that "public–private partnerships represent neither a radical 'power shift' from established institutions nor a marginal governance aberration from traditional state-centered power politics" (2017, 23).

In a review of eight major global public health partnerships, Buse and Tanaka (2011) find that they have produced many important achievements but also face similar internal governance and accountability challenges. They create concerns about membership, accountability, and resource mobilization (Buse and Walt, 2000b). Buse and Harmer (2007) identify seven habits of highly effective global health partnerships, which include harmonizing their efforts with national planning processes, developing representative governing bodies, giving attention to the costs of alternative service delivery strategies, paying attention to mutual accountability, improving oversight, attending to financing gaps, and avoiding conflicts of interest. While GPPPs often advertise the importance of civil society participation, a study of health GPPPs finds little civil society involvement in high-level decision-making (Storeng and de Bengy Puyvallée, 2018).

Advocacy Networks

One of the most important global governance studies is Keck and Sikkink's *Activists beyond Borders* (1998), an analysis of transnational advocacy networks. Such networks have a long history and were important in the anti-slavery and women's suffrage movements, but they have proliferated in recent years. The book is best known for what the authors dubbed the "boomerang pattern" of advocacy where local activists or NGOs, facing political challenges in their own states, reach out for international allies, who in turn place pressure on the local activist's or NGO's home state.

Keck and Sikkink also provide a range of insights into how transnational advocacy networks work. They typologize network tactics (information, symbolic, leverage and accountability politics) and analyze the ways that networks frame issues. They observe that transnational advocacy networks generally do not engage in mass politics, but instead engage in venue shopping and provide critical information. Advocacy networks raise attention to issues and try to change the discourse around them, particularly those related to bodily harms to vulnerable people and to legal equality and opportunity. Successful advocacy campaigns, they suggest, develop powerful causal stories that attribute blame. In many respects, the logic of the book is to translate ideas that have been developed to study domestic social movements to the distinctive context of transnational governance.

THE INSTITUTIONAL MECHANISMS OF GLOBAL GOVERNANCE

Despite their imperfections, networks are clearly an important part of global governance. By linking different groups together across the globe, they create some basis for cooperation and coordinated action. What are the frameworks for cooperation and coordination that bring together the various components of global governance in concerted action? While any detailed answer to this question takes us far beyond the scope of this chapter, we can explore a few key ideas that are often characterized as forms of "new governance."

Orchestration

One of the most important ideas advanced to understand global governance is "orchestration." Abbott and Snidal (2009, 2010) introduced this concept to the global governance literature and argue that it is critical for realizing the advantages of new forms of public–private regulation at the international level. Orchestration is an indirect form of governance in that the orchestrator shapes action through intermediaries, such as NGOs or INGOs, whose help must

Improving global cooperation and coordination 117

be enlisted voluntarily (Abbott and Bernstein, 2015). Lacking control over intermediaries (as assumed in a principal–agent model), the orchestrator gains influence over intermediaries by providing them with support of various kinds or via the capacity to convene actors. Abbott and Bernstein (2015) identify two different dimensions of the orchestrator's role: first, to identify, enlist and some cases to create intermediaries, and second, to manage the relationships between them.

The authority of international organizations to organize, coordinate and direct networks of public and private actors is more circumscribed than it is for states. As a result, orchestration at the international level is necessarily more facilitative than directive. Research by Abbott et al. (2015) provides evidence that orchestration is adopted as an approach by international institutions precisely because their governance capabilities in a given area are limited. Kienzle (2019) has found that orchestration is even used in global security regime complexes, such as the weapons of mass destruction regime complex, though he finds that the success of orchestration in this domain has been limited by the unwillingness of intermediaries to share information.

While Abbott and Snidal conceived of orchestration as a recent phenomenon, their subsequent research (Abbott et al., 2015) found that it has been present for a long time at the international level. Both states and IOs can initiate orchestration and it can also be demanded by intermediaries. States initiate it when they can achieve satisfactory governance outcomes without the potential loss of sovereignty entailed by delegation to IOs. IOs, by contrast, are more likely to initiate orchestration when there is goal divergence between states and when states exercise weak oversight over them. Their research also finds that intermediaries are quite diverse and include not only NGOs, but also other IOs. States may exercise control over IOs by limiting who they may enlist as intermediaries.

In an analysis of the High-Level Forum on Sustainability as an orchestrator, Abbott and Bernstein (2015, 225) find that orchestration is a "viable" but "challenging" strategy. They note that orchestrators often have ambitious goals, but only moderate governance capacity, and they identify two conditions that they regard as important for orchestration success—legitimacy and a focal institutional position. Since an orchestrator (by definition) lacks the power to coerce or command, its influence will depend heavily on its legitimacy with intermediaries. It will also depend on occupying a central position amidst important institutions, which can lend the orchestrator "political weight." In a comparison of many cases of orchestration, however, Abbott et al. (2015) do not find support for the theoretical claim that "focality" is an important condition for orchestration.

Abbott et al. (2015), however, emphasize and find support for the argument that orchestration is more likely when IOs find suitable intermediaries that share their goals, though it is also possible for IOs to create or encourage the creation of intermediaries. In addition, international organizations must have a degree of autonomy, enthusiasm and sufficient capacity to serve as effective orchestrators (Abbott and Snidal, 2010). Although their power may be limited, these organizations do often have some degree of cognitive, normative and executive influence that can be used for orchestration, and they may be able to expand this influence by becoming effective orchestrators. As orchestrators, international organizations can promote public–private regulatory schemes, provide guidance, support and resources to aid their functioning and they can assist them in developing effective performance measurement and evaluation.

Global Regulation

Global regulation is another important form of global governance and Djelic and Sahlin-Andersson (2006) have called attention to the expansion of rules at the transnational level. These rules, however, often take the form of legally non-binding "soft" rules combined with various types of auditing and monitoring activities. Networks of different state and non-state actors are the agents of these transnational regulatory systems, which form a web of network activity that rapidly transmits ideas and practices across the globe. While extensive, global regulation is often constrained in ways that national regulation is not.

Global regulation has been a hotbed of governance innovation but has also raised many questions about its effectiveness and accountability. Abbott and Snidal (2009) describe the expansion of "regulatory standard-setting" at the global level, which is characterized by the prominence of firms or NGOs as key participants, by the voluntary nature of regulation and the reliance on "soft law" and by the use of orchestration. They further characterize variations in global regulation in terms of a "governance triangle" that distinguishes the relative contribution of states, firms, and NGOs.

Global regulation often takes the form of standards or codes, which are typically expressed as non-binding best-practice rules. Kerwer (2005) asks why standards have proliferated as a form of global governance. He suggests that it is because they embody expertise that helps encourage compliance and because standards are easier than national laws to diffuse broadly. Standards are also more adaptable than regulatory directives and do not require a centralization of authority. Thus, they are more amenable to the international system. A necessary, but not sufficient condition for standards to be effective, Kerwer argues, is that they must be based on expertise, which helps to motivate compliance. Effectiveness also depends on the degree of enforcement, which can be enhanced when third-party certifiers monitor compliance. A challenge for global standards is that they lack the sort of accountability mechanisms that operate on national regulators, particularly if standard-setting and standards-enforcement are decoupled (due to third-party enforcement). He argues that these accountability challenges can be mitigated by giving those who are subject to standards an opportunity to participate in standard-setting.

Private and Hybrid Forms of Regulation

Cashore (2002) dubbed transnational private regulation schemes "non-state market-driven governance." These private forms of regulation do not rely on state authority and their ability to create compliance rests with the market incentives that they create. He argues that these new forms of governance arose in response to globalization, the rise of boycott campaigns, and with increasing interest in voluntary market-based forms of regulation. Their viability depends on their capacity to achieve legitimacy in the market, which depends in part upon the ability to find acceptable third-party certifiers. Their design also matters: they may or may not be dominated by the same parties that the scheme regulates and they may be established to reflect either supply-side or demand-side audiences. Since these schemes cannot draw on state authority for their legitimacy, he argues that their legitimacy must have a pragmatic, moral or cognitive basis. For instance, environment groups can bestow moral legitimacy on a non-state market-driven form of environmental regulation.

Studying transnational rulemaking bodies that have grown up since the 1990s in the area of global sustainability, Dingwerth and Pattberg (2009) argue that there is a convergence on a very similar model of regulation. In terms of design, these organizations typically have a board of directors, a secretariat and a quasi-parliamentary body of stakeholders. They have a strong process-oriented rhetorical emphasis on inclusiveness, transparency, accountability and deliberation and they adopt process-oriented institutional mechanisms to facilitate participation. Dingwerth and Pattberg stress that this is somewhat surprising because it is costly to institutionalize these participatory and process-oriented features. They argue that this convergence arose through the interaction of the different initiatives, with the International Federation of Organic Agricultural Movements (IFOAM) serving as an early model. Gradually, a standard model that stressed the importance of stakeholders became institutionalized.

Can multinational corporations fill the "governance gap" (Bartley, 2018; Eberlein, 2019)? Johns et al. (2019) argue that if the U.S. steps away from its commitment to multilateralism, multinational corporations are likely to fill the global governance vacuum, with the effect of increasing the power of corporations vis-à-vis states. Eberlein (2010, 1129) argues that "[t]he consensus in the literature is that private initiatives by themselves are not sufficient to even partially fill the governance gap." However, there is a range of opinion that varies from highly pessimistic to modestly optimistic about whether corporations can productively contribute to global governance (Grabs et al., 2021).

Multinational corporations have a strong interest in rules that coordinate markets, but a more indirect and defensive stance toward those that restrict markets (Bartley, 2018). Rules that focus on products are more likely than those that focus on production processes because products are more visible and consumer-facing. Companies concerned about their reputation with consumers will therefore more readily accept market restrictions on products than on production processes. Thus, multinational corporations are more likely to invest in private regulatory regimes that are market-coordinating and product-oriented.

Global regulation may be particularly prone to regulatory capture by certain narrow interests (Mattli and Woods, 2009). Weak due process and limited information, combined with limited demand for more representative regulation, are key factors leading to capture, while due process, information about the impacts of inadequate regulation, and broad coalitions demanding change are necessary for common interest regulation. While the opening up of international organizations to wider participation can be interpreted as a way of making global regulation more transparent, it may actually increase the possibilities of capture by giving access to special interests.

A necessary but not sufficient condition for avoiding capture, according to Mattli and Woods (2009), is that information about the costs of capture must be available to wider publics. In addition, the demand for common interest regulation must be championed by a group or coalition with the motivation, resources and stamina to bring about change. Public officials (including judges) may be critical to providing the necessary demand, though they are also subject to capture. Private sector groups, including certain kinds of corporations, can also become important backers of common interest regulation under certain conditions.

Bartley (2022) argues that the concept of regulatory "capture" is less useful in understanding transnational private regulation and it is more useful to see these efforts in terms of their "saturation" with corporate power. As noted, firms are far more central to the design and operation of private regulation than in traditional state models of regulation, rendering the idea of capture somewhat misleading. Bartley identifies three patterns through which power dynamics shape transnational private regulation. First, there is the "politics of harmonization," which refers to contestation around particular standards. Second, there is the "politics of credibility," which develops where regulatory standards impose costs on private actors and often leads to ongoing contestation. Finally, there is the "politics of grounding," which occurs at the point at which transnational standards are put into practice in national and local contexts. Competition between different standard-setting bodies (e.g., producer-backed versus NGO-backed) often drives their evolution (Gulbrandsen, 2010).

Some transnational regulatory schemes are hybrid governance arrangements rather than strictly public or private, and in other cases, public and private forms of regulation may be complementary (Verbruggen, 2013). Cashore et al. (2021) have recently proposed that we think about the relationship between private authority and public policy as operating in a complementary, competitive or co-existing fashion, and they specify a range of possible arrangements for each of these categories. Similarly, Eberlein (2019) describes four different kinds of state–business relationships with respect to regulation: *substitution* occurs where the state chooses not to regulate and business steps in to develop self-regulatory schemes; *support* occurs where the state actively encourages corporate self-regulation; *shadow of hierarchy* occurs where the possibility of state intervention is a key motivator for the development of self-regulation; and *soft steering* occurs where the state meta-governs private regulation.

The varied role of states in shaping private regulation has been a topic of investigation. States can use their power to both shape and support private certification systems. However, Giessen et al. (2016) have also noted that state bureaucracies may reclaim more direct control of private regulatory schemes (which they describe as a transition "from governance to government"). In their analysis of timber regulation in Argentina and Indonesia, they find that state bureaucracies, influenced by domestic politics, exerted their power to reclaim their control over ostensibly private certification schemes.

Private and hybrid regulation often takes the form of certification systems, where third-party certifiers are deployed to monitor private or public–private standards. In an evaluation of certification systems in the fisheries and forestry sectors, Gulbrandsen (2010, 180) concluded that:

> [o]n balance, although certification seems to change some management practices and create better environmental outcomes in some cases, it does not seem to be an effective environmental institution in the sense of addressing some of the most serious environmental challenges in the forest and fisheries sectors. That said, we still know too little about the environmental impact and efficacy of certification as a problem-solving instrument.

He does find, however, that including a range of stakeholders (particularly environmental NGOs) in the standard-setting and governance process enhances the legitimacy of non-state governance.

Global Experimentalist Governance

De Búrca et al. (2014) distinguish a strategy of global cooperation and regulation they call "global experimentalist governance," which they describe as having five steps. First, groups of global stakeholders are brought together to deliberate around shared concerns. Second, these stakeholders define a framework for action that sets out a common set of open-ended goals. Third, individual stakeholders with local and contextual knowledge are granted discretion to decide how they will try to achieve these goals. Fourth, these stakeholders are then obligated to report on their experiences and progress, with this information being subject to peer-review. Finally, based on these peer evaluations, stakeholders periodically deliberate about framework goals and revise them as necessary.

De Búrca et al. (2014) argue that the experimentalist governance approach is appropriate where stakeholders know what goals they want to achieve but are uncertain of how to attain them. They observe that that the success of this mode of governance depends on the existence of a "penalty default"—that is, a penalty that occurs to those who do not participate in good faith. Peer-review is the key mechanism that helps to ensure both learning and accountability. Global experimentalist governance is likely to be less successful when key stakeholders are unwilling to cooperate because they have "veto rights over relevant decisions" or when they do not face a penalty default (2014, 484).

Several studies have explored specific examples of experimentalist governance at the global level, including the development of the Financial Action Task Force (Nance, 2018), the global response to AIDS (Goldstein and Ansell, 2018), forestry regulation (Overdevest and Zeitlin, 2014), human rights (De Búrca, 2017; O'Brien et al., 2022) and a number of cases in the EU (Sabel and Zeitlin, 2008). Other scholars have pointed to the limits on the successful functioning of global experimentalist governance—as for example in the domain of global migration and refugees (Lavenex, 2020).

Global experimentalist governance can evolve from regimes and regime complexes or from transnational networks and global public–private partnerships (De Búrca et al., 2014). Overdevest and Zeitlin (2014) identify four pathways that led a transnational regulatory regime complex for illegal logging to evolve into an experimentalist regime. These pathways include: first, an expansion of private regulatory regimes with experimentalist elements; second, the expansion of unilateral national or regional efforts to regulate international trade; third, pressure for the coordination of different national or regional regimes; and fourth, public comparison of the results from different parts of the regime complex.

Rangoni and Zeitlin (2021) expand upon this evolutionary perspective in an analysis of EU electricity regulation. Taking strategic uncertainty as a key scope condition, they argue that experimentalist regimes may evolve back toward hierarchy if the problem of strategic uncertainty is resolved, or the regime may refocus on addressing the remaining aspects of uncertainty. Strategic uncertainty may also deepen as more is known, reinforcing existing

Improving global cooperation and coordination 123

experimentalism (stumbling back into experimentalism). Finally, there may be a wider recognition of the value of experimentalism and the pervasiveness of strategic uncertainty, leading to its wider application and institutionalization. They find that in EU electricity regulation, the regime evolved toward both a focusing on certain aspects of uncertainty and on the wider application and institutionalization of uncertainty recognition of the value of experimentalism.

Goal-based Governance

Similar in many respects to experimentalism, Biermann et al. (2017) describe a shift from rule-based to goal-based governance at the international level. Rule-based governance focuses on establishing rules and developing a system of compliance with these rules. The problem with this approach is that it often gets bogged down in intractable disputes over the rules or their enforcement and gets caught in disputes between disciplines, sectors and issues (Kanie et al., 2019). Goal-based governance is an alternative approach that starts by getting actors to agree on general principles or goals rather than on the divisive features of enforceable rules. Thus, at least at the goal-setting level, goal-based governance is "detached" from the international legal system (Biermann et al., 2017). Moreover, rather than overseeing these goals through an elaborate international bureaucracy, goals are set through broad-based participation and details of goal implementation are pushed down to the national and local levels. Although the goals are "non-binding," they develop their force through the clear articulation of targets and indicators and the measurement of progress toward their attainment.

Kanie et al. (2019) suggest four steps for advancing goal-based governance. The first is to establish governance mechanisms for "cross-silo interaction" that can identify integrative goals and strategies (Kanie et al., 2019, 1747). Second, goals should be set in terms of what participants would like to achieve and then participants should "backcast" to establish baselines for measuring meaningful progress toward these goals. Third, this process and subsequent efforts should be deliberative in nature, engaging a range of actors in goal setting and attainment. Fourth, goal-based governance should enhance appreciation for the emergent nature of governing and foster flexible and agile strategies for realizing the goals.

One of the most important examples of global goal-based governance was the Millennium Development Goals (MDGs), a precursor of the even more ambitious Sustainable Development Goals (SDGs). While there is a general view that the MDGs contributed significantly to poverty reduction (Besada et al., 2017), Hickel (2016) argues that the UN's claim that the MDGs were the "most successful anti-poverty movement in history" is statistically deceptive and he comes to a decidedly less rosy view. However, statistical analysis by

Asadullah and Savoia (2018) finds that MDG adoption did matter for reducing poverty, though this effect was not uniform across countries. They find that this variation depended on whether states had the capacity to deliver on the MDG's anti-poverty agenda.

CONCLUSION

While international relations scholars debate the relative autonomy of global governance processes from states, no one really doubts that state sovereignty strongly conditions global cooperation and coordination. States are always the elephant in the room and modes of global governance strongly reflect the degree of state involvement and their degree of multilateralism—often in a negative sense. A traditional model of international cooperation is built around international organizations, such as the World Health Organization or the World Bank, and around institutions or "regimes" to govern specific policy domains. With the development of globalization and the erosion of commitments to multilateralism, these traditional arrangements have been supplemented with new modes of governance.

One feature of these new modes of governance has been the increasing role of international non-governmental organizations, which operate as both stakeholders and lobbyists in international policymaking. This increasing role has led some scholars to question the agendas and accountability of INGOs. Another important shift in the terrain for global cooperation and coordination is the rise of institutional fragmentation, which global governance scholars have theorized using the concept of "regime complexes." Theorists draw somewhat different conclusions about the impact of regime complexes on global cooperation and coordination. On the one hand, their fragmentation can be seen as undermining effective and integrated policies and programs and leading to "venue shopping." On the other hand, regime complexes may create scaffolding or opportunity structure in which new global initiatives can take root.

Another important feature of new modes of global governance is the pro-liferation of networks of various kinds. The international relations literature has long pointed to the importance of epistemic communities—networks of experts and professionals—for global policymaking and identified some of the specific conditions under which they are likely to have an influence. Governance theorists have also called attention to the important role played by networks of regulators (i.e., transnational regulatory networks), policymakers (i.e., global public policy networks), and advocacy groups (i.e., transnational advocacy networks). Global Public–Private Partnerships have also become a prominent mode of global cooperation and coordination. These various network forms raise questions about effectiveness and accountability analogous to those discussed for network governance in Chapter 5.

Governance theory has also contributed to understanding other distinctive aspects of global cooperation and coordination. Research has found that international organizations often engage in a style of governance called "orchestration," which tries to influence targets (such as states) through the mobilization of intermediaries (such as INGOs). Governance scholars have also called attention to the distinctive features of "transnational regulation," which relies more heavily state regulation on "soft law" (i.e., voluntary codes or standards). Experiments with private or hybrid (public–private) forms of regulation have also proliferated globally and research has investigated their inner workings, which often take the form of third-party certification systems. Researchers remain divided in their assessment of their efficacy.

Global governance scholars also describe two related forms of global governance. The concept of "global experimentalist governance" describes how global cooperation and coordination can be advanced by giving decentralized actors discretion over how to achieve common framework goals. The relative success of these decentralized actors in contributing to the framework goals is then monitored, peer-reviewed and collectively shared. Similarly, the concept of "goal-based governance" has been contrasted with rule-based governance. It stresses the importance of agreeing on ambitious but non-binding goals rather than on setting specific prescriptive rules. While the efficacy of these voluntary forms of governance has not been fully demonstrated, there is some mostly illustrative research that suggests that they can have positive consequences.

8. Reducing poverty and inequality

What can governance theories contribute to our understanding of how to reduce poverty and inequality? The first part of this chapter examines claims about the relationship between governance and poverty reduction. This discussion is related to ideas about the importance of a "Weberian" state and its ability to impartially and reliably provide public goods that both support poverty reduction efforts and that encourage economic growth. This concept of the Weberian state, which stresses the value of effective and accountable bureaucracies, is related both to claims about "good governance" and to ideas about the "developmental state." This section also returns to the consideration of decentralization, which was first examined in Chapter 5. Here, the focus is on the effects of decentralization on poverty reduction.

Following this discussion, the chapter turns to the topic of social welfare and the welfare state and investigates the relative merits of means-tested versus universalistic welfare provision for reducing poverty. This section also considers the way that social welfare can be paternalistic and punitive and briefly investigates how bureaucracy can create administrative burdens for the poor. The analysis then turns away from the state to focus on community-based strategies for addressing poverty, including discussions of collective impact, social innovation and the role of NGOs.

The final part of the chapter shifts from a focus on poverty reduction to a consideration of diversity, equity and inclusion. The analysis begins with a consideration of the concepts of institutional bias and institutional racism and then widens out the discussion to consider the concepts of equity and representative bureaucracy as they have been developed in the field of public administration. The importance of fairness and procedural justice as developed in the field of social psychology is then addressed, leading to a discussion of environmental justice, a central topic in the environmental governance literature.

GOOD GOVERNANCE AND THE WEBERIAN STATE

An important theoretical claim, often associated with the World Bank and other international organizations, is that good governance will lead to poverty reduction. Originally developed in the 1990s in the international development community, "good governance" was conceived as a strategy for guiding economic development (Rothstein, 2012). Building on the research of economic historian Douglass North (1990), among others, this work emphasized the importance of institutions, and particularly property rights and the rule of law, for creating the basis for effective economic development.

Craig and Porter (2006) describe the shift in development strategies in the late 1990s from a neoliberal structural adjustment strategy to a "poverty reduction and good governance" strategy. Behind this shift, they argue, was an emerging consensus that "good governance" was the missing ingredient for poverty reduction. They propose that this emerging consensus must be understood in historical context. With the collapse of the Soviet Union, there was renewed interest in the institutional preconditions of economic growth and liberal democracy. There was also rising concern about failed states, ethnic conflict and terrorism and a pattern of urbanization that was expanding the size of ungoverned slums and informal economies. Many states appeared both ineffective and bloated, leading to a concern with corruption and the problems of the patrimonial (clientelist) state. Thus, attention came to focus on the necessity of supporting the development of a capable and efficient state that could promote broad-based economic growth and, in turn, reduce poverty—the good governance agenda.

One important critique of this agenda was the argument that ineffective governance was not itself the primary cause of weak economic development. While acknowledging that ineffective governance was an issue, Sachs et al. (2004) diagnosed the deeper problem as a "poverty trap": low rates of savings and low foreign investment (due to weak infrastructure and human capital) were the chief culprits that led to weak economic growth. They proposed that this trap is caused by costly transportation, small markets, a low productivity agricultural sector, and inadequate adoption of technological innovations. In addition, African nations suffer from a high disease burden and the negative geopolitical legacy of colonialism. They conclude that this poverty trap can only be disrupted with large investments that address these factors, and not by reforms that focus on good governance.

More recent research, however, generally finds positive support for the relationship between good governance and poverty reduction using governance indicators developed by the World Bank (Kaufmann et al., 2008). These indices measure a wide range of governance factors that cover several distinct components of governance, including political stability and the absence of violence/terrorism, government effectiveness, regulatory quality, rule of law, voice and accountability and control of corruption. Using a composite measure for "government efficiency" constructed from this data, for example, and studying 68 low- and middle-income countries, Halleröd et al. (2013) find that more efficient governments improve four of seven indicators of childhood deprivation, including weak access to safe water, health care, lack of access to information, and malnutrition.

Other studies also find supportive—though nuanced—evidence for the relationship between good governance and poverty reduction. In a study of World Bank governance indicators, Hassan et al. (2020) find that government effectiveness, regulatory quality and voice and accountability are important for poverty reduction (they also review previous studies that find positive results of good governance). Using the World Bank governance indicators, Coccia (2021) found that government effectiveness, rule of law and regulatory quality contribute to poverty reduction. Asadullah and Savoia (2018) found that higher state administrative capacity also leads to poverty reduction. Operationalizing six "good governance" indicators, Kwon and Kim (2014) find that only the "voice and accountability" indicator has a statistically significant relationship to the reduction of poverty, leading them to conclude that "political participation of the poor in the process of policy making can lead to pro-poor policies, eventually reducing poverty" (2014, 362).

Breaking their data down further, however, Kwon and Kim (2014) find that good governance reduces poverty in middle-income countries, but not in the least developed countries (see also Jindra and Vaz, 2019). The authors argue that this finding is consistent with Sachs et al.'s (2004) argument that low-income countries are caught in poverty traps, and as a result, cannot take advantage of good governance reforms. By contrast, a province-level study in Vietnam finds support for the argument that good governance measured as a multi-dimensional concept has the most positive effects on poverty reduction in the poorest provinces (Nguyen et al., 2021).

The Limits of the Good Governance Argument

Although there appears to be support for the argument that good governance is related to poverty reduction, at least in some settings, this claim is somewhat different from claiming that a poverty reduction strategy must first prioritize achieving good governance. In her well-known article on "good enough governance," Grindle (2004) criticized the "good governance" strategy for not establishing clear priorities for governance reforms that would contribute significantly to poverty reduction. Many governance reforms, she argued, contributed only indirectly to poverty reduction and, in any case, governments often lacked motivation or capacity to actually carry out these reforms. Revisiting her argument a decade later, she also criticized the "one best way" thinking inherent in good governance prescriptions (Grindle, 2017, 17). Her analysis led her to distinguish two general approaches to governance: one focuses on the macro-institutions that permit good governance and the other targets the meso or micro levels of governing and counsels "find a problem and fix it" (Grindle, 2017, 20).

One view of governance—consistent with a macro-institutional perspective on governance—is that fostering good governance is about "getting the institutions right." From the perspective of "critical institutionalism," however, the problem with this approach is that it leads to checklists of prescriptions, which are particularly problematic when applied to natural resource management in developing country contexts (Cleaver and Whaley, 2018). Such an approach leads to superficial views of institutions that do not appreciate how they are embedded in concrete social relationships. By contrast, critical institutionalists stress the importance of paying more attention to power and to the situated negotiations and bricolage processes working with and through existing and hybrid institutions.

Finally, based on comparative case studies, Goldsmith (2007) suggests that the relationship between good governance institutions and economic development may actually be the reverse of what the good governance literature argues—that is, good governance may be an outcome of economic development rather than a precondition for it. Or, as Andrews et al. (2017, 5) put it, "success builds good institutions."

Developmental States

The reduction of poverty depends fundamentally on economic growth, a topic that goes far beyond the scope of this chapter. However, it is useful to selectively consider how governance affects economic growth. In his book, *Pathways from the Periphery*, Haggard (1990) argued that economic growth of "peripheral" nations was not the result of social-structural factors, but of choices by political elites that were conditioned by state institutions that mediate between domestic and international pressures. Such research reflected a body of scholarship that viewed the state as making key contributions to economic growth. Motivated by research on rapidly growing East Asian economies, this research on "developmental states" came to view Weberian bureaucracies as playing a key role in stimulating economic growth (Johnson, 1982).

As much of the political economy and state-building literature stress, however, states are often "predatory" or "rent-seeking," and thus may be seen as exploiting the fruits of economic development rather than helping the economy to grow. In a critique of the developmental state model, Moon and Prasad (1994) challenge an ideal-typical view of the Weberian notion of bureaucracy as glossing over the complexities of these institutions and the internal politics that limit their effectiveness. They also challenge whether the administrative state should be conceived as autonomous from society rather than as deeply entangled with it. A key question in the developmental state literature is why would an autonomous state be developmental rather than predatory?

Building on a Weberian tradition and using Zaire as an example, Peter Evans (1995, 54) argued that it was "not bureaucracy, but its absence" that made the Zairian state predatory (it may be useful here to recall Chapter 5's discussion of the difference between despotic and infrastructural power). He argues that what makes "developmental states" different from "predatory states" is the existence of a meritocratic bureaucracy that can guide economic development. While the relationship between developmental states and economic growth has never been fully specified, Evans and Rauch (1999) developed a comparative analysis of how two features of Weberian state administration impact growth. The first feature is the meritocratic recruitment of the civil service, based on education and examination (see Chapter 3 for further discussion). The second feature is the existence of a predictable career ladder. Both Weberian features are expected to enhance the competence and cohesion of the bureaucracy, leading the state to provide public goods and direction that can help guide the economy toward growth.

Examining economic growth between 1970 and 1990 in 35 countries (30 "semi-industrialized" countries and five "poorer" countries) and coding Weberian characteristics (using input from country experts), they find that these Weberian characteristics are strongly and significantly correlated with economic growth. More recent research by Besley et al. (2021) finds a particularly strong relationship between meritocratic recruitment and economic development. Related research by Arora and Chong (2018) finds a significant correlation between institutional quality and government effectiveness in delivering public services.

As discussed in Chapter 3, bureaucratic autonomy is another feature often associated with effective bureaucratic governance. Comparative research has found, for example, that higher bureaucratic autonomy is strongly associated with reductions in child mortality and TB prevalence levels over the 1990–2010 period (Cingolani et al., 2015). While arguing that autonomy is important, Peter Evans also emphasizes that bureaucracy needs to have informal networks that link bureaucrats with the private sector and with civil society. He distinguishes these informal networks from clientelist or patronage networks. It is critical, he writes, that entry into these networks is determined by competence rather than by political loyalty. He refers to this combination of a cohesive and competent bureaucracy capable of formulating its own goals and informal networks with firms and citizens as "embedded autonomy" and argues that it is a key ingredient of successful developmental states.

Moon and Prasad (1994) argue that Evans's notion of embedded autonomy is an improvement over a straightforward emphasis on bureaucratic autonomy, but it does not go far enough. They suggest that it is important to understand the policy networks that bind the state and business together, though doing so also raises some difficult questions for the developmental state perspective. Policy networks can easily be transformed into clientelist networks, they argue, and they suggest that the model developmental states of East Asia offer much evidence of this.

In an examination of whether "bureaucratic governance" or "liberal democracy" are the key institutional precursors to successful economic development, Norris (2012) argues for a "unified theory" that frames the combined importance of democracy and governance: "The unified theory assumes that development is most effective where regimes combine the qualities of democratic responsiveness and state effectiveness" (2012, 8). Her analysis provides support for her "unified" theory, but also finds that "bureaucratic state capacity" is particularly important for explaining a range of social welfare improvements (Norris, 2012, 190–191).

Decentralization and Poverty Reduction

While the argument stressing the Weberian character of the state and those emphasizing the importance of state capacity focus on the central state, some argue that state decentralization is conducive to poverty reduction (see Chapter 5 for a wider discussion of decentralization). One theoretical argument in favor of decentralization is that because "local governments have better information from the ground, they can design policies and public goods that are tailored for local needs better than the central government, resulting in welfare improvement across jurisdictions and the population in general" (Canare et al., 2020, 543). A recent study of Côte d'Ivoire, for example, found that revenue decentralization (i.e., the municipality collecting more of its own revenue) increases access to public services and reduces poverty (Sanogo, 2019). In a review of a range of country cases investigating the effects of decentralization on pro-poor policies, Crook and Sverrisson (2003) find that variations in outcomes depend on whether elites "capture" local government. Where the local mobilization of the poor is externally supported and successfully challenges elite capture, pro-poor reforms were more likely.

Decentralization may have both political and economic effects on poverty. Politically, decentralization potentially gives the poor more opportunity to demand pro-poor policies and to access social services. Economically, decentralization potentially creates more efficient government and allows for more customized targeting of social services. Reviewing the possible impacts of decentralization on poverty in 19 countries, Jütting et al. (2004) found that decentralization has mixed effects on poverty: in poorer countries that lack basic capacity, decentralization can worsen poverty; in countries with more developed capacities, decentralization can be an "excellent means of promot-

132

Rethinking theories of governance

ing improved representation of the poor and enhancing the targeting of service delivery" (2004, 5). Canare et al. (2020) also find that government effectiveness mediates the impact of decentralization on inequality. Where government effectiveness is low, decentralization is likely to increase inequality.

Some empirical research finds that fiscal decentralization has negative effects on poverty, though this depends on the context. Sepulveda and Martinez-Vazquez (2011) find that the effects of fiscal decentralization on income inequality depend on the size of the government, with negative outcomes for smaller governments and positive effects for larger governments. Based on an analysis of 54 countries between 1980 and 2009, and using measures for both political and fiscal decentralization, Lessmann (2012) finds that decentralization tends to increase regional inequalities in poorer countries, but to reduce them in wealthier countries. In a study of 33 developing countries between 1990 and 2014, Digdowiseiso et al. (2022) find that where subnational regions *independently* make their own fiscal decisions, population inequality increases, but where they make these decisions *jointly* with central governments, population inequality decreases. In a study of Ghana, Crawford (2008) argues that decentralization has had limited effects on poverty reduction and points to the limits inherent in "decentralization from above."

SOCIAL WELFARE AND THE WELFARE STATE

The development of welfare states has been one of the major mechanisms for addressing poverty and inequality. However, the social and institutional mechanisms for providing and ensuring social welfare vary significantly cross-nationally and draw on different arrangements of government, market and family (Esping-Andersen, 2002). Esping-Andersen (1990) famously identified three distinctive types of welfare state: *social democratic regimes* stress universalistic criteria and rely primarily on government to deliver social services; *liberal regimes* adopt more means-tested criteria for service delivery and rely heavily on the market for delivery; and *conservative regimes* build welfare provision around family assistance. This typology of welfare regimes remains prominent, though much scholarship has debated it and sought to extend it beyond its European focus (Rudra, 2007; Powell et al., 2020).

Providing social welfare is one important pathway to the reduction of poverty (Saleem and Donaldson, 2016). In a study of 18 Western nations between 1967 and 1997, for example, Brady (2005) found that social welfare spending, and social security transfers and public health/health spending in particular, had significant effects on poverty reduction. Analysis of more global data on social protections comes to a similar conclusion about the reduction of poverty but finds that the impact depends on how well welfare policies are targeted toward the poor (Fiszbein et al., 2014). A recent study of a sample of EU countries also finds that welfare spending reduces poverty, but that the efficiency and effectiveness of this effect varies significantly (Sawulski and Kutwa, 2022).

The design of welfare state programs is seen as a factor in the reduction of poverty and inequality. A key debate concerns how "universal" versus "targeted" (e.g., means-tested) welfare programs should be. Exploring the tradeoffs in this debate, Korpi and Palme (1998, 661) introduced what they call the paradox of redistribution: "The more we target benefits at the poor ... the less likely we are to reduce poverty and inequality." Analyzing a dataset of 18 OECD countries during the mid-1980s, along with household income data, Korpi and Palme (1998, 681) find that "by providing high-income earners with earnings-related benefits, encompassing social insurance institutions can reduce inequality and poverty more efficiently than can flat-rate or targeted benefits." In part, the paradox of redistribution reflects an underlying political dynamic: targeting is likely to undermine middle-class support for redistribution.

Utilizing a more recent and expanded dataset and refined measures, Brady and Bostic (2015) find considerable support for Korpi and Palme's "paradox of redistribution," though this support diminishes over time. They find that "transfer share" (the share of household income that is publicly provided) is a particularly important variable for reducing poverty. However, they find that the political mechanism posited by Korpi and Palme (more middle-class support for redistribution in universal welfare regimes) does not fully hold up. By defining universalism as a distinct variable (as opposed to the inverse of targeting), they also conclude that universalism and low-income targeting are not necessarily antithetical strategies.

Revisiting Korpi and Palme's analysis with new data (20 OECD countries between 2000 and 2011) and using a new indicator of universalism, Jacques and Noël (2018) also find support for Korpi and Palme's central argument: they find that "The universalism index is positively correlated with redistribution, poverty reduction and social expenditures and negatively correlated with inequality levels" (2018, 78). While there is considerable support for universalistic welfare policies as a strategy of poverty reduction, a review of research by Gugushvili and Hirsch (2014) also points to several studies that draw less positive or clear-cut conclusions.

A vast literature also exists on welfare state reforms and what consequences these reforms have for poverty and inequality (Pierson, 1996; Van Kersbergen et al., 2014). A major theme of this research over the last two decades has been the shift toward social investment strategies. These strategies prioritize active human capital development over passive transfers, both to meet the challenges of a knowledge economy and to get people into the labor market (Van Vliet and Wang, 2015). While some argue that this shift has led to a stagnation in poverty reduction in European countries (see Cantillon, 2011), Van Vliet and

134 *Rethinking theories of governance*

Wang (2015) find no support for this claim in a study of 15 European countries between 1997 and 2007.

Poverty Governance and Administrative Burdens

While the welfare state—and particularly the universalistic welfare state—is generally seen as reducing poverty and inequality, welfare has also been understood as a mechanism of social control over the poor. A body of largely U.S.-focused research on "poverty governance" analyzes the paternalistic or therapeutic elements of welfare state programs and argues that vulnerable and disadvantaged urban groups are particularly subject to state control (Soss et al., 2011; Hennigan, 2017; Collins et al., 2022). This research points to a growing range of different urban institutions—both public and private—that play an active role in processes of "coercive benevolence" (Collins et al., 2022, 4).

Poverty governance scholars often associate trends in poverty governance with neoliberalism, which emphasizes the centrality of the market and the transition from "welfare" to "workfare." Soss et al. (2011) have argued that "paternalism" and "neoliberalism" go together because a welfare-to-work agenda requires disciplining the poor. Neoliberal paternalism, they argue, is a distinctive political rationality aligned with NPM strategies (see Chapter 4). Analyzing U.S. housing voucher programs for low-income families, McCabe (2022) argues that a key characteristic of neoliberal welfare programs is that they decentralize welfare programs, which then rely on markets to discipline the poor.

Sociologists have made the argument that "poverty governance" is less directed at ameliorating poverty and more oriented toward social control (Seim, 2017). In *Punishing the Poor*, Wacquant (2009) delivers an indictment of the neoliberal state and its relationship to poverty. He argues that neoliberalism increases economic insecurity, which in turn produces public fear of crime and a turn toward more punitive policy. Essentially, the penal state replaces the welfare state. An extreme form of this dynamic is "government seizures" that Katzenstein and Waller (2015) argue are used to extract resources from the poor to finance the penal state. In an ethnographic study on the policing of homelessness in Los Angeles, Stuart (2014) finds that "marginal spaces" are policed punitively and paternalistically, with policing used to move the homeless into rehabilitative services with the goal of modifying their behavior.

More "targeted" welfare programs often use administrative rules to limit access to welfare services and benefits and public administration scholars have explored the ways that these rules impose burdens on those eligible to receive them. Herd and Moynihan (2019) develop a broad theoretical model for understanding these administrative burdens that focuses on how individual citizens experience state programs and policies. They start with the assumption that all citizen–state encounters generate some cost to citizens, which they categorize as including learning, psychological and compliance costs. These costs vary from minimal to much more significant and they are shaped by policy design, administrative capacity and expertise. Costs also fall unequally across citizens and may reinforce inequalities. Herd and Moynihan (2019) also stress that administrative burdens are a matter of politics. These burdens affect who receives government benefits and at what level and thus become a way of conducting "policymaking by other means." Third parties—including for-profit and not-for-profit institutions—may derive benefit from these administrative burdens (think of tax preparers) or they may make it their mission to assist in their reduction (think of legal aid organizations).

COMMUNITY-BASED STRATEGIES

Many strategies of poverty and inequality reduction are community-based. Indeed, community is understood to be a source of solidarity and mobilization for poverty and inequality reduction that is distinctive from the market and the state (Bowles and Gintis, 2002). Community-based strategies are also advocated by those who view poverty as resulting from cumulative and cyclical interdependencies, a view that leads to an emphasis on comprehensive programs, collaboration among a variety of different programs and groups, and community organizing to empower the poor (Bradshaw, 2007). Practitioners generally regard community participation to be a crucial component of poverty reduction strategies (Singh and Chudasama, 2020).

Research on the relationship between natural resources governance and family livelihoods also provides support for the importance of community-based strategies. For example, in an extensive review of research on how governance mediates the relationship between "ecosystem services" (a view of ecosystems as providing tangible economic benefits) and livelihoods, Nunan et al. (2021) found that inclusive, community-based governance is likely to have a positive result. Similarly, a review of forest governance finds fairly strong evidence that implementation of a community forest management strategy improves livelihoods and reduces poverty (Hajjar et al., 2021). And a six-year multi-site study of the impact of "adaptive collaborative governance" on poverty in Nepal's community forests found that adaptive collaborative governance led to increased income generation and access to micro-credit and employment opportunities for women and the poor at the hamlet level (McDougall et al., 2013).

Participatory governance is often seen as making a key contribution to community-based strategies (see Chapter 5 for a discussion of participatory governance). Participation by low-income community residents is regarded as enhancing resource access and fostering development, a strategy sometimes conceived as building social capital (Chandradasa, 2014). Schneider (1999, 522) argues that "participatory governance (PG) is an essential link in the net of causalities which have to be considered and taken into account in designing and implementing poverty reduction strategies." Participatory governance is envisioned here as a strategy of empowering the poor by establishing rights and resources that enable participation. Research suggests that poverty reduction is facilitated by pro-poor policies driven by the demands of the poor themselves (Mosley, 2012).

Urban governance scholars have observed that the fragmented, multi-scale and web-like nature of political power can undermine efforts to mobilize communities for poverty reduction (Marwell and Morrissey, 2020; Marwell et al., 2020). Moreover, participatory planning strategies may be used in a more technocratic and exclusionary fashion or may create opportunities for more privileged citizens to participate (Musso et al., 2011; Flannery et al., 2018). Some cross-national research, however, suggests that community social capital can lead to more equal incomes (Knack and Keefer, 1997).

Collaboration governance (as discussed in Chapter 5) is often seen as a strategy for bringing different community stakeholders together. Ahmed et al. (2013, 1747), for example, argue that the Bangladeshi health system has "better-than-expected performance" because it manages to harness the pluralism in the health system. Although they acknowledge that pluralism can foster weak oversight, cumbersome coordination and veto politics, they argue that systems can be improved if stakeholders can be brought into effective working partnerships. The "collective impact" framework, which has captured much attention in recent years, strongly advocates for community-based collaboration.

Collective Impact

The overriding message of collective impact theory is that social change can only be achieved by bringing different stakeholders together in a strong and joint collaborative effort that can work against the drawbacks associated with "isolated efforts." Although it is championed as a general strategy for community change, it is often used to address issues related to entrenched poverty and inequality. Kania and Kramer (2011) identify five success factors that make collective impact possible. First, relevant stakeholders must come together to build a common agenda. Second, to advance this agenda, stakeholders must develop shared measures of whether they are making progress. Third, stakeholders must develop coordinated and mutually reinforcing activities to achieve their shared agenda. Fourth, they must develop the capacity to communicate continuously about these activities and their progress in meeting goals.

Reducing poverty and inequality 137

Finally, this entire process must be supported by what they call a "backbone organization," which is capable of facilitating the first four activities.

Hanleybrown et al. (2012) further expand upon this model, describing three preconditions for success: the first is an "influential champion" who can bring the top leadership from different organizations together; the second is securing adequate financing to support and sustain the change effort; and the third is a sense of urgency that change is necessary. They then identify three phases of collective impact: initiating action, organizing for impact and sustaining impact. Initiating action requires figuring out who the players are, developing a baseline understanding of the problem and establishing a governance structure. Organizing for impact is the phase of setting a common agenda, establishing shared measures, finding ways to work together and establishing a backbone organization. Sustaining impact requires working together, but also finding ways to adapt strategies and efforts as new information becomes available.

The collective impact literature emphasizes that predetermined solutions rarely work for dealing with complex community problems (Kania and Kramer, 2013). Instead, collective change efforts need to embrace an emergent perspective, which calls for continuous monitoring of feedback and adaptation as relevant information becomes available. They suggest that an approach to evaluation known as "developmental evaluation" is appropriate in such circumstances and that stakeholders must learn collectively, as well as individually. Related research finds that communities must be prepared to change and that change efforts must be guided by a clear agenda, be flexible enough to adapt to changing circumstances and capable of mobilizing community networks and assets, and allow for the evaluation of results (Walzer et al., 2016).

Weaver (2016) suggests that the collective impact strategy can be transformational, but that meeting its conditions is difficult and requires "system leadership." Wolff (2016) provides a wider-ranging critique, arguing that the collective impact concept fails to build on prior knowledge and experience about community coalitions and coalition-building. Contrasting collective impact with an alternative set of community organizing principles, Wolff et al. (2017) argue that the collective impact strategy fails to explicitly address economic and racial injustice. They also argue that residents must be full partners in community development approaches and community change strategies need to be built from the bottom up rather than top down. Community development efforts must also build and support local leadership and they must build collaborations that can advocate for system change.

Social Innovation

Another strategy that has become prominent in recent years for addressing poverty is social innovation (Ghys, 2017). Social innovation refers to primarily private or non-profit innovation or entrepreneurship that is directed toward public or social purposes (Mulgan, 2006; Phillips et al., 2015). Most social innovation initiatives are, in fact, cross-sectoral and connect some combination of public sector, NGO and private sector actors (Howaldt et al., 2016). Quantitative research on global social innovation initiatives finds that most of them do not seek to produce "systemic change," but rather respond to particular, typically underserved, social needs (Howaldt et al., 2016). Given its entrepreneurial spirit, social innovation has been critically interpreted by some scholars as an extension of neoliberal NPM (Massey and Johnston-Miller, 2016).

The concept of social innovation is presented as a bottom-up alternative or a supplement to top-down welfare state policies and programs, one more sensitive to social relationships and local governance contexts (Oosterlynck et al., 2018). Given the shift of European welfare states toward active labor market policies, social innovation is typically seen as most aligned with "social investment" welfare strategies. Even in this case, the alignment of social innovation efforts and national welfare programs remains an open issue. However, the relationship is not necessarily antagonistic and welfare states can use social innovation to experiment—typically through the vehicle of public–civic partnerships (Oosterlynck et al., 2018). Millard et al. (2016, 158) find common agendas are the most important driver of social innovation for poverty reduction, while inadequate capacity or knowledge are the most important barriers.

Based on a review of social innovation to reduce poverty in Europe, Oosterlynck et al. (2018) have identified seven governance challenges that it encounters: (1) mainstreaming social innovations; (2) avoiding fragmentation of service delivery; (3) engaging citizens and stakeholders to participate in social innovation; (4) handling diversity in an equitable way; (5) preventing uneven access to services; (6) avoiding use of social innovation as a stalking horse to evade responsibility; and (7) working constructively in the existing legal environment. Social innovations for poverty reduction are often local and limited in scale, and attention to their "multi-scale" dimensions can improve their success and impact. Moreover, giving special attention to "empowerment," which is often implicitly or explicitly promised by social innovation projects, can increase their value.

In a study of the challenges that NGOs face in scaling-up social innovations, Westley et al. (2014) identify five different configurations of factors that characterize different paths to scaling. A "volcano" strategy scales up by channeling momentum and energy into a more centralized and systematic

Reducing poverty and inequality 139

innovation strategy. A "beanstalk" strategy remains committed to its initial vision, but "climbs up" to a more systemic level of strategy without shifting its early projects and commitments. An "umbrella" strategy starts with a system strategy and then tries to seed or stimulate its local emergence. A "LEGO" strategy scales up through a networking strategy. And a "polishing gemstones" strategy takes great effort to ensure the success and replicability of the original project. While Westley et al. (2014) argue that there is no single best way to scale up, they do suggest that scaling-up generally entails a movement toward thinking and acting on a more systemic basis.

The Role of NGOs

While social innovation research focuses specifically on the innovation process, there is also a different but related discussion about the role of non-governmental organizations (NGOs) in addressing poverty and inequality. NGOs have become central to international poverty reduction strategies (Mitlin et al., 2007). Their reputation in the world of development, however, is mixed and ranges from hero to villain. A key theoretical debate concerns whether NGOs are civil society or market-oriented actors. There is also a question of whether they are merely technocratic service providers or political advocates for the poor (Banks and Hulme, 2012). In an extensive review of the role of NGOs in development studies, Brass et al. (2018) find that research generally supports their positive effects for health and governance.

In governance studies, non-profit organizations provide a range of welfare and social services and are often referred to as the "third sector" (Enjolras et al., 2018). They play a powerful but mixed role in addressing poverty and inequality. In a study of welfare non-profits in 245 U.S. communities, for example, Berrone et al. (2016) find that an increasing number of non-profits reduces income inequality, up to a point. But this effect disappears as the field of non-profits becomes too dense, a decline they attribute to increasing non-profit competition for scarce funding resources. In a study of community planning in the Boston region, Levine (2021) argues that the professionalization of the non-profit sector has led to increasing inequality. Funding for community development is often competitive and although community-based organizations often work hard to secure funding for communities they represent, Levine (2021) argues that they are often likely to secure funding for where it is most likely to succeed rather than where it is most needed. Neighborhoods without community-based-organizations are significantly disadvantaged in the competitive world of funding.

A more positive view of the potential role of NGOs is provided by Mair and Marti (2009), who have introduced the idea of "institutional voids" to describe the weak institutions linking the poor to government and to markets. They describe NGOs as social entrepreneurs who can help to fill such voids. For example, a Bangladeshi NGO called BRAC created a variety of collaborations and participation opportunities that provided the poor with access to resources and opportunities. Panday (2018) finds that BRAC's partnership with local governments helped to mobilize the poor, and particularly women, to participate in local government. Mair et al. (2012, 822) suggest that rather than thinking of institutional voids as places where there is an absence of institutions, it is better to think of them as places where there is the "presence of plural, often contending, institutional arrangements." Their analysis of Bangladeshi villages suggests that the powerful institutions of marriage and status block women's access to market opportunity.

Building on the concept of institutional voids, van Wijk et al. (2020) develop a "process model of cascading failures" in NGO interventions based on an Ethiopian case study. A key to successful interventions, they argue, is the ability to align interventions with local needs, cultures and relationships. They observe, however, that NGOs vary in their degree of experiential knowledge and reflexivity and vary in their ability to align interventions with contexts. They argue that the failure or lack of capacity to reflect on this alignment can lead to both design and orchestration (i.e., adaptation) failures. Pradilla et al. (2022) find that a transnational NGO's deep contextual knowledge of poverty allowed it to usefully guide a range of interrelated projects addressing different dimensions of poverty.

Understanding how NGOs work in local communities is a key to understanding their success in anti-poverty activities. The Indian NGO Gram Vikas, for example, has had notable successes in facilitating Indian village sanitation by developing a number of strategies that encourage inclusiveness: first, it makes its support conditional upon a village agreeing to work across religious, social and economic differences; second, it formalizes the representation of different groups on a Village Executive Committee; third, the village must create a fund to support good sanitation if new families come to the village; and fourth, the sanitation project must be a collective effort, with individual households agreeing to contribute to the effort.

According to Mair and Seelos (2017), a key to Gram Vikas's success is that it purposefully tries to transform the structure of inequality in a village *through* governance. It does this by providing support that mobilizes existing resources and stabilizes new relational patterns while blocking elites who might coopt governance programs for their own purposes. They argue that Gram Vikas's design rules essentially coopt existing resources and power structures and redeploy them toward the goals of improved sanitation and greater village equality. Interestingly, Gram Vikas initially builds on existing social arrangements, but gradually transforms and redeploys them.

Much like the argument in favor of decentralization, NGOs are seen as more closely connected to community grassroots and thus as offering "participatory and people-centred approaches to development" (Banks and Hulme, 2012, 11). For example, studies of community forestry have found that NGOs can play a very significant role in making community participation truly effective (Fischer, 2017, 183). Gupta et al. (2020) found that NGOs were essential for educating and mobilizing communities to recognize their rights in an Indian community-based forestry program, which in turn enabled poor community members to improve their livelihoods. However, several scholars find that NGOs are driven by donor concerns and fail to understand or engage with local community perspectives (Townsend et al., 2002; Porter, 2003; Banks and Hulme, 2012; Awashreh, 2018).

DIVERSITY, EQUITY AND INCLUSION

Beyond the question of reducing poverty and economic inequality, what do theories of governance tell us about how to address issues related to the inequalities that arise from various forms of bias (race, ethnicity, gender, sexuality, etc.)? One place to begin is with discussions of diversity, an important area of public administration research since at least the early 1990s (Sabharwal et al., 2018). Moon (2018) describes two competing theories about organizational diversity. The first he calls "information/decision-making theory" which emphasizes the way that diversity has benefits because it makes additional information available that would not be in a more homogenous workforce. Essentially, diversity allows multiple perspectives to be brought to bear on an issue, encouraging productive interactions, better decisions and innovation. He refers to the second theoretical perspective as "social categorization theory," which has a less rosy view of the effects of diversity because people tend to classify themselves into various groups. These classifications can set up in-group/out-group dynamics that lead to inter-group conflict, communication problems and negative characterizations of other groups. This perspective predicts that diversity will lead to greater employee dissatisfaction as measured by greater employee turnover.

Moon argues that these outcomes are likely to be moderated by "inclusive management," which seeks to bridge across groups and create opportunities for diverse participation. Inclusive management, he hypothesizes, will help a diverse workforce realize the advantages of diversity (innovation) and reduce its negative effects (turnover). Using data on gender and racial diversity among U.S. public employees, Moon finds that the results for racial diversity are more in line with information/decision-making theory (positive for innovation), while the consequences of gender diversity are better interpreted from the vantage point of social categorization theory (positive for turnover). He also finds that inclusive management increases the positive effect on innovation and reduces the negative effect on turnover.

Other research also theorizes that active management of diversity can lead to greater job satisfaction of employees. Choi and Rainey (2014) hypothesize that organizational fairness is a key dimension of diversity management, which they hypothesize is related to procedural justice. Using data on U.S. federal employees, they find that both diversity management and perceptions of organizational fairness are positively related to job satisfaction. Somewhat surprisingly, however, they find that this relationship largely holds for non-minority personnel and not for minority personnel (though it did hold across gender differences). They theorize that this finding may reflect minority attitudes toward "identity-blind" procedures that do not reflect past histories of discrimination.

Although not focused on demographic diversity per se, Feldman and Khademian (2007) develop a theoretical framework for understanding "inclusion management." They argue that bringing together those with political, scientific-technical and experiential knowledge to share information and deliberate together is a role for public managers and important for effective policy development and implementation. Inclusion is furthered when this deliberation is used to find new ways to work together. Public managers can facilitate this action through "informational and relational work." Informational work requires public managers to operate as brokers, translators or synthesizers of knowledge. Relational work requires them to develop connections between different actors and to facilitate their collective problem-solving. In other words, their work suggests that inclusion requires active managerial effort. Ansell et al. (2020) provide support for the importance of informational and relational work in supporting inclusive collaborative governance.

Beyond the diversity of public employees, many forms of stakeholder and participatory governance raise concerns about diversity and inclusion and a considerable body of theory and research has been developed around understanding inequalities that arise in participatory and deliberative processes. One important theoretical perspective suggests that rather than designing civic forums to equalize the power of different groups, it may be preferable to allow disempowered groups to deliberate in separate "enclaves"—at least before joining a common forum (Karpowitz et al., 2009). In a study of gender inequality in deliberative settings, Karpowitz et al. (2012) add that consensus decision rules are more inclusive than majority decision rules because they create incentives for more cooperative interaction and for listening to all voices. Their research supports this argument.

Karpowitz and Mendelberg (2018) join these two streams of research by asking whether separate participation enclaves can enhance women's representation in civic forums, and how decision rules shape these outcomes. In

Reducing poverty and inequality 143

developing their analysis, they set forth a "theory of enclaves," which suggests that: (1) enclaves can empower the voices of otherwise disadvantaged actors; (2) by providing the group with mutual psychological support; (3) by prioritizing and clarifying the issues of the disadvantaged group; (4) by enhancing a sense of group and self-efficacy; and (5) by providing a basis for advocacy of the enclave's agenda. In an experimental study on gender participation, they find support for their enclave theory, but only when decision rules are consensus-based rather than majoritarian.

Institutional Bias and Institutional Racism

Another topic that intersects with governance is research on institutional bias and institutional racism. Henry (2010, 426) defines institutional bias as involving "discriminatory practices that occur at the institutional level of analysis, operating on mechanisms that go beyond individual-level prejudice and discrimination." He argues that a key theoretical step in understanding institutional bias is appreciating that it operates through mechanisms that are institutional rather than individual. He describes five different theoretical perspectives that can illuminate institutional biases, including theories of social identify, culture, economic discrimination, inter-group competition, and social networks.

Shelby (2012) has elaborated the contrast between individual-level and institutional-level racism. On the one hand, institutional racism can be viewed as resulting from decision-making by persons who hold racist views. Consequently, "[t]hough the context of action is within an institution, the target of moral appraisal is still the individual" (2012, 340). On the other hand, even where the members of an institution do not individually hold racist beliefs and where the institution's policies are race-neutral, the institution may still have negative impacts for a racially disadvantaged group. Shelby further distinguishes between "extrinsic" and "intrinsic" institutional racism. Extrinsic institutional racism occurs in the case just mentioned where an otherwise race-neutral institution produces negative outcomes. Intrinsic institutional racism, by contrast, occurs where the negative outcomes for a disadvantaged group are associated with features of the institution itself (i.e., its goals, rules, procedures, and role criteria).

Although not everyone supports the concept of institutional bias (Matthew, 2022), others argue that it is important for understanding the reproduction of racial inequalities. For example, following Shelby's distinction between "cognitive bias" and "institutional bias," Bornstein (2015) argues that the New York Police Department's "numbers-oriented management" and "zero-tolerance policing policy" are an example of institutional bias. Although this management and policy approach to crime were officially race-blind, they led to

144   *Rethinking theories of governance*

a strategy of intensive policing with important consequences for disadvantaged racial groups. This dynamic exemplifies institutional bias as distinct from cognitive bias because despite the Department's formal race neutrality, the outcome was racially inequitable. Bornstein argues that drawing a distinction between cognitive and institutional bias is critical for successful reform because the diagnosis of the problem is otherwise obscured.

There is some discussion of how to redress institutional bias and racism. Griffith et al. (2007) propose a "system change" model for addressing institutional racism, with a focus on health care. Their approach suggests that a systemic intervention is necessary for addressing historical legacies. This intervention has three legs. The first is to understand the factors producing institutional racism, which they categorize as operating at the extra-organizational, intra-organizational and individual levels. The second is anti-racist community organizing, the purpose of which is to reduce power differentials and to bring affected groups together. The third is a soft-system methodology, which they argue is a framework for analyzing and addressing complex problems.

The authors then identify several distinct steps for "dismantling racism." The first step is to create a multi-racial "change team" that leads the community toward achieving its anti-racist goals. This "change team" has many leadership responsibilities, including collecting relevant data. A second step is to engage in a series of workshops that develop a shared understanding of racism in the relevant context, with attention given to cultivating a shared vocabulary and a common appreciation of anti-racist values. A third step focuses on how relevant insights and values can be transferred to the targeted institutions. They propose a "caucusing" project that helps to support and transmit these values. A fourth step is to create opportunities for leadership development and professional growth around this agenda.

Equity

The concept of "equity" has become central to efforts to redress past biases and inequalities. Although the term is frequently used by scholars with respect to governing, there is an odd dearth of theoretical research on equity and governance, though the title of an article by Tom Perreault (2014) nicely expresses the larger issue: "What kind of governance for what kind of equity?" One important exception to the limited research on governance and equity comes from the field of public administration, where the concern about social equity is strongly indebted to philosopher John Rawls's work on justice and fairness (Wooldridge and Gooden, 2009). Still, Pitts (2011) argues that public administration has spent too much time restating the normative justification for social equity and not enough time empirically analyzing the way policies, programs and organizations affect social equity.

Frederickson (1990) argued persuasively that social equity should stand alongside efficiency and effectiveness as one of the three central pillars of public administration. He captured the value of acknowledging the centrality of equity concerns with the following phrase: "Gradually, however, public administration began to acknowledge that many public programs were implemented much more efficiently and effectively for some citizens than for others" (Frederickson, 2015, 52).

Frederickson (2015) developed what he called a compound theory of social equity, which is in essence a classification of different dimensions of equity. He first distinguishes between different types of social equity: "simple individual equalities" are cases where individuals are treated as equal; "segmented equalities" are when individuals within a group or class are treated equally but differences in treatment exist across groups; "block equalities" are cases where different groups or classes are treated equally. He next defines two different "equalities of opportunity," including "prospect equalities" and "means equalities": prospect equality refers to the probability of receiving a certain benefit or application of the law; means equality refers to the idea that those with equal endowments have equal opportunity. Frederickson (2015) also examines social equity with respect to longstanding debates about the merit of administrative discretion, arguing that administering laws without considering social equity leads to injustice.

Other public administration scholars have distinguished four aspects of social equity: *procedural fairness* includes concerns about due process, equal protection and equal rights; *access* (or *distributional equity*) refers to whether people receive the same services; *quality* refers to whether services received are of the same quality; and *outcomes* refers to whether the outcomes of receiving services are the same for all individuals or groups (Gooden, 2015, 14–15). Racial equity assessments have been developed as a methodology for analyzing government policies and programs and for developing evidence-based strategies for dealing with social equity deficits (Gooden, 2015, 2017).

Representative Bureaucracy

One potential strategy for enhancing equity and procedural justice is through what public administration scholars call "representative bureaucracy." The concept comes from a 1944 book of that title by a British public administration expert, Donald Kingsley, which critiqued the class and gender bias of the British civil service. As first introduced by Frederick Mosher (1968), this research tradition draws an important theoretical distinction between passive and active representation. *Passive representation* refers to whether the attributes or identities of individual public employees reflect, in the aggregate, those of the population they serve. *Active representation* suggests that public employees actively advocate for or serve those members of society whom they "represent."

Riccucci and Van Ryzin (2017) summarize three important implications of passive representation. First, passive representation is an indicator of and an example of social equity in the wider society. Second, government employment often has social mobility effects and thus a representative bureaucracy is one that provides equal opportunity. Third, diversity itself is understood to have a positive effect on organizational performance. However, a key point of representative bureaucracy theory, as first emphasized by Meier (1975), is that passive representation does not imply that employees will necessarily embrace or advocate for the values of the social groups whom they demographically represent. This point has led to a significant body of research on the mechanisms that lead from passive to active representation.

Defining active representation as "decision making behavior on the part of a *specific group of civil servants* which tends to affect systematically the resource allocation of a *specific group of citizens*," Hindera (1993, 419) observed that attitudes on the part of civil servants are often only loosely coupled with their behavior. In many cases, civil servants are simply not in a position to act on their personal attitudes. In a study of the U.S. Department of Agriculture's Rural Housing Loan Program, Sowa and Selden (2003) found that minority loan supervisors enjoyed the discretion to grant loans to minorities. Discretion has since been regarded as a key factor permitting passive representation to be converted into active representation.

One theoretical argument in this literature is that the transition from passive to active representation is a non-linear variable affected by certain organizational, policy and political characteristics. Meier (1993) found, for instance, that a "critical mass" of Latino administrators was necessary before Latino teachers engaged in active representation. Hindera and Young (1998) generalize the non-linear nature of the critical mass perspective by describing what they call "situational thresholds." In their study of the U.S. Equal Opportunity Employment Commission, they found that active representation was triggered when the minority investigative staff reached a plurality in the branch office (i.e., the situation threshold). Similarly, Nicholson-Crotty et al. (2017) found that black police officers became more active representatives of black citizens when black police officers reached a certain proportion of the police force.

A challenge in this literature on passive and active representation is that aggregate data at the organizational level cannot discern whether the individual-level behaviors of representative officials were the key factor producing positive benefits for those being represented (Theobald and Haider-Markel, 2009). Consequently, Bradbury and Kellough (2011, 164) note that "Only those research designs that employ measures of the individual behavior of public workers, such as those found in the criminal justice litera-

Reducing poverty and inequality 147

ture, can separate the behavior of minority or female bureaucrats from that of nonminority bureaucrats or men."

What are the mechanisms through which active representatives influence those they represent? Hindera and Young (1998) identify advocacy, attitude convergence, and communication as the three key mechanisms of direct active representation. Although these direct effects have been the primary concern of scholars, Lim (2006) notes that representative civil servants may also have indirect effects through their influence on other (non-representative) civil servants. For instance, representative civil servants may create a check or model for how non-representative civil servants behave toward a represented group, potentially creating "contagion effects" (Meier and Xu, 2022). Lim (2006) argues that these indirect effects must be accounted for in drawing conclusions about active representation.

Beyond the key distinction between passive and active representation, more recent work has also called attention to the idea of "symbolic representation" (Theobald and Haider-Markel, 2009). Whereas the idea of active representation stresses the discretionary role of government employees, symbolic representation works through the perceptions and attitudes of clients or citizens (Riccucci and Van Ryzin, 2017). Here, the issue is whether the social origins of government employees improve the trust and legitimacy that clients or citizens place in government or improve their compliance with laws or their access to services and benefits. For example, in a study of U.S. policing, Theobald and Haider-Markel (2009) find that black citizens are more likely to regard police stops as legitimate if they are stopped by a black police officer.

Symbolic representation may also produce a "demand inducement," which might occur because ethnic minorities may feel more comfortable going to a welfare office if they see their own minority group represented among office staff (Lim, 2006, 197). In an experimental study, Riccucci et al. (2016) found that women were more likely to engage in co-production related to recycling when the names used in government program announcements were female. Meier and Xu (2022) suggest that critical mass is likely to be as or more important in the case of symbolic representation than it is for active representation.

Fairness and Procedural Justice

An important discussion about fairness and procedural justice has developed in the fields of psychology and law that has important implications for governance (Mazepus and van Leeuwen, 2020). Building on social psychology, Lind and Tyler (1988) theorized that individuals distinguish between process- and outcome-based justice, a distinction that led them to focus on the importance of procedural justice. They identify two different underlying behavioral models of how individuals relate to procedural justice. The first is a self-interested model, where individuals commit to procedural justice because it helps to produce certain desired outcomes. Although research provides partial support for this model, they find that it needs to be complemented with what they call the "group value" model, which focuses on social identity. This perspective sees procedures as group norms and compliance with these norms as shaped by socialized attitudes.

In their analysis of procedural justice in policing, Sunshine and Tyler (2003) argue that public perceptions of the legitimacy of policing are related to the police's procedural fairness in applying the law. Based on this perspective, they hypothesize that individual members of the public will be more likely to comply with the law and more likely to grant the police discretion when they judge the police to be procedurally fair. They distinguish this argument from a more instrumental perspective on compliance in which individuals comply because they judge the police effective in deterring crime. Analyzing survey data on New York City residents and their attitudes toward the New York Police Department, Sunshine and Tyler find significant support for their procedural justice argument and limited support for an instrumental perspective.

Procedural justice is often understood in relationship to participation and recognition (Ruano-Chamorro et al., 2022). In an experimental study of U.S. local government, for example, Herian et al. (2012) found that having information that the public participated in policy decisions increased assessments of both procedural and outcome fairness. In a review of environmental governance research, George and Reed (2017) summarized three key dimensions of procedural justice: recognition of relevant and affected actors; participation that allows these actors to voice their concerns and views; and the cultivation of the capacity for these actors to effectively participate. However, in a review of whether 56 forest carbon projects had adopted procedural justice standards for the participation of vulnerable groups, Suiseeya and Caplow (2013) found disappointing results.

Environmental Justice

Equity and justice have been a central theme of a body of research and theory on "environmental justice" (Brulle and Pellow, 2006). Although discussions about environmental justice began in the U.S. with concerns about the racial inequities in environmental decision-making, the scope of this research has become much broader and more international (Mohai et al., 2009; Schlosberg, 2013). For example, a global literature on environmental justice with respect to indigenous peoples is now well established (Parsons et al., 2021). The concept of "climate justice" has also developed out of the environmental justice movement, raising distinct issues about intergenerational equity and historic responsibility (Schlosberg and Collins, 2014). Environmental justice also has close affinities with political ecology, a body of research that stresses the role of power in socio-ecological governance (Armitage, 2008; Bennett, 2019).

The meaning of justice in "environmental justice" has not always been clear, but generally refers to "equitable distribution of benefits, opportunities and risks" (Schlosberg, 2013; Maryudi et al., 2020, 861). Distinctions between different kinds of justice—such as distributive justice, procedural justice and recognition—are often drawn (Coolsaet, 2020; Parsons et al., 2021). Schlosberg (2013, 42) writes that "[w]hile the traditional, liberal frame of reference for the conception of justice is purely individualist, environmental justice movements address injustice at both the level of the individual and the community."

Concerns about equity have also been prominent in the wider study of environmental governance. McDermott et al. (2013), for example, explore how payments for ecosystem services might exacerbate equity issues. They identify three core dimensions of equity related to distributive, procedural and contextual justice, referring to these dimensions as "content equity" because they provide evaluative criteria for judging equity. However, they argue that "frame equity" is also important, which includes considerations of "who counts?" as a target of equity, what the equity goals are and how to design and deliver on equity commitments.

Environmental justice studies have been particularly concerned with investigating how class and race can affect exposure to environmental contaminants (Mohai et al., 2009). These studies have developed in the context of a wider civil rights movement that seeks to redress racism, inequality and injustice—hence, the "environmental justice movement." However, as a topic of research, environment justice scholars have focused on investigating whether race and class are factors in the location of environmental hazards, such as waste disposal sites.

Research on environmental justice has led to serious reflection on the underlying statistical challenges of inferring environmental inequity by race and class (Mohai et al., 2009; Banzhaf et al., 2019). In a review of studies of environmental (in)justice, Ringquist (2005, 241) finds that racial environmental inequities are ubiquitous, though their magnitudes are relatively small (he is careful to point out, however, that this does not mean that inequities are not very large in some communities). Surprisingly, he finds that low income and poverty do not prove to be significant factors in explaining environmental inequities. However, these effects are sensitive to the geographical scope of the study (U.S., regions, etc.) and to the units of community aggregation (census track, zip code, etc.).

Several causal mechanisms have been identified that can produce inequitable exposure to environmental hazards (Banzhaf et al., 2019). The first mechanism is "disproportionate siting," in which environmental hazards are located

150 *Rethinking theories of governance*

in communities of color or in low-income communities. Such siting decisions may be driven by explicit racism but also by more structural factors related to access to land, labor and transportation. The second mechanism is termed "coming to the nuisance." In this case, communities of color and low-income communities may move toward the hazard, because they are less willing or able to pay the additional costs for living further from it. The third causal mechanism is termed "Coasean bargaining" and it can be seen as an interactive blend of the first two mechanisms. Through a bargaining process between polluters and communities, different levels of pollution are negotiated. An important implication of this model is that hazardous sites might be directed toward communities with weak bargaining leverage. The fourth mechanism is "government regulation," which may shape siting and emissions decisions over which different communities may have more or less influence.

CONCLUSION

One fundamental theoretical claim that comes from the field of international development is that "good governance" will lead to reductions of poverty. Research using World Bank indicators of good governance have generally found positive support for a correlation between good governance and poverty reduction, though some research finds that this result may be less relevant for the poorest countries and some scholars challenge the implied direction of causality.

Adopting a Weberian view of the state, meritocratic, capable and autonomous bureaucracies have been identified as particularly important contributors to poverty reduction. Although the mechanisms of how Weberian states contribute to poverty reduction are not well specified, one argument is that "bureaucratic governance" reduces corruption and enhances state capacity to support anti-poverty strategies. Another related argument is that effective bureaucratic governance creates the conditions for a "developmental state," which in turn provides public goods that encourage strong economic growth.

While the Weberian model tends to stress the role of the central state, decentralization is also advocated as a strategy of poverty reduction. The positive theoretical case for decentralization is that it enables resources and services to be directed and customized in ways that aid the poor. However, empirical results for the poverty-reducing effects of decentralization are mixed, as they were for the effects of decentralization on governance effectiveness and accountability. Results seem to vary by the economic development of the country and by the institutional details of how decentralization is organized. There is some evidence suggesting that decentralization may increase interregional or interlocal inequalities, at least for poorer countries.

As expected by the welfare state literature, there is generally strong support for the argument that state provision of social services and social benefits will reduce poverty, though research suggests considerable variation in the effectiveness and efficiency of different welfare programs. Although there is no single accepted typology of welfare states, the distinction between targeted/means-tested versus universalistic welfare states and policies has been central to the debate about social welfare. While much research shows that universalistic strategies are more effective at poverty reduction, this is still an ongoing theoretical and empirical debate in the social welfare community.

While welfare state policies are generally regarded as positive for reducing poverty and inequality, there are also some negative notes. Public administration scholars have called attention to the "administrative burdens" that citizens may face in accessing welfare state services, which can either impose costs on them or reduce their access to services. While there is not much comparative research on administrative burdens, they are generally thought to be more prominent for targeted/means-tested policies. "Poverty governance" scholars also criticize the paternalistic character of the welfare state. A key argument of this literature is that neoliberalism has increased this paternalism and intensified punitive and coercive social controls over the poor.

In addition to the welfare state, governance-related research stresses the value of community-based strategies of poverty reduction. This research emphasizes the importance of mobilizing communities, empowering the poor and enhancing their capacities, and creating coordinated cross-sectoral efforts to address poverty and inequality. One relatively recent perspective on community-based change is the collective impact model, which provides an illustrative strategy for how to organize broad-based support for community change efforts. Social innovation is another recent bottom-up perspective on how to address local poverty and inequality. Scholars point out how it can be used to develop experiments in poverty and inequality reduction, though it faces challenges in scaling-up and mainstreaming these innovations. In all these models, non-governmental organizations (NGOs) often play a central role and may serve a key intermediary role in helping to overcome the "institutional voids" that inhibit the poor from accessing market opportunities. A critical note in the research on NGOs is that they tend to become focused on their own funding needs and can lose sight of the needs of the poor.

Shifting from the discussion of poverty and economic inequality to inequalities based on race, ethnicity, gender and other identity-based roles, several governance-related ideas have been advanced. One important theoretical discussion distinguishes institutional bias from individual-level cognitive bias and points out how inequitable outcomes can be produced even where individuals are not biased and where policies are officially neutral. The issue of equity also has been a central topic for the field of public administration, which has elaborated the different dimensions of this concept for use by public administrators.

One of the most important theoretical developments related to social equity is the concept of representative bureaucracy, which posits that public organizations whose employees reflect the diversity of the communities they serve will serve them better. A key theoretical distinction in this research is between passive and active representation, where the former reflects demographic representativeness, and the latter reflects the situation where representative public employees actively seek to serve the interests and needs of those for whom they are representative. A somewhat more recent discussion examines whether the effects of representative bureaucracy hold only when a certain threshold (or critical mass) of representativeness is achieved. Another recent discussion is the idea of "symbolic representation," which depends on the positive or negative perceptions of clients or citizens. Empirical research on representative bureaucracy has found positive effects in specific cases, but the overall body of research suggests that the effects of representative bureaucracy are not always straightforward.

A body of theory and empirical research in political theory and social psychology on fairness and procedural justice has important implications for governance. One of the major governance-related areas where these ideas appear is in studies of environmental justice, which stress the environmental inequities that may impact various disadvantaged communities. Research and theoretical development have focused on distinguishing different kinds of inequities and their significance and causes.

9. Managing the commons and transitioning to sustainability

Two key challenges characterize our contemporary predicament with respect to the natural environment. The first is how can we share and use common resources, like grazing lands, fisheries or groundwater, without depleting them so that they irreparably harm the biosphere or are no longer renewable? The second is how can we reform our economic and technological systems so that they are more sustainable—that is, so that they are renewable over the long term? Although both topics raise deep questions for the natural sciences and engineering, they have also produced significant governance-related research. This chapter examines some of the theoretical perspectives on governance that have developed to address commons management and transitions to sustainability, beginning with the question of how we can avoid the "Tragedy of the Commons."

In a landmark article, Garrett Hardin (1968) predicted that overexploitation of the commons was inevitable unless one of two governance arrangements was put in place—either centralized state regulation of the resource (state) or a clear assignment of private property rights (market). In perhaps the best-known response to Hardin, the landmark *Governing the Commons* (1990), Elinor Ostrom advanced a "third" solution to commons management, which she referred to as "self-organizing and self-governing" regimes. The chapter begins with a consideration of Ostrom's work and some of the related discussions that follow from it. The second half of the chapter then considers a body of theory that seeks to explain "transitions" to sustainability.

GOVERNANCE OF THE COMMONS

Ostrom did not argue that this third solution was always inherently better than the first two solutions (state or market), but she did argue that Hardin's idealized solutions had overlooked the possibility of such self-organizing and self-governing regimes. Proponents of state and market solutions had also failed to assess the diversity of existing regimes, many of which were self-organizing and self-governing. Investigating cases of common pool management from around the world, she sought to understand how some communities have successfully and sustainably managed the commons over long periods.

Drawing inspiration from collective action theory and from institutional economics, Ostrom's work has added a great deal to our understanding of "common pool resources" (CPRs), which she defined as resources that users could not be excluded from consuming *and* where this consumption subtracted from the supply available to other users (Ostrom, 2010). With her Indiana University colleagues, Ostrom also eventually developed an even broader framework to understand resource management known as the Institutional Analysis and Development (IAD) framework (Ostrom, 2011; McGinnis, 2011).

While Hardin proposed that the commons could only be sustainably managed by either "state" or "market," the basic thrust of Ostrom's work has been to suggest that we should not ignore "community" as a mechanism of commons management (Dietz et al., 2003). She and her colleagues acknowledged that community-level "self-organization" did not always work, but they also noted that state- and market-based solutions did not always work either (in many cases, no solution is ideal; see Barrett et al., 2001, 499). Based on her analysis of a range of international cases of commons management, she identified eight "design principles" that contribute to sustainable self-organizing and self-governance regimes, as summarized in Table 9.1.

Cox et al. (2010) reviewed 91 studies related to these eight design principles and found that they are mostly well supported empirically (though Cox et al. tweak them a bit). However, they also identified three types of criticism of the principles: the first is that the eight design principles are incomplete and need to take account of additional social, resource, and external factors; the second is that the principles may be relevant to local cases, but are not necessarily relevant to commons management on a larger scale; the third critique is that a "principle-based" logic is itself problematic because it glosses over the uniqueness of local communities.

With respect to the first criticism—the incompleteness of the theory—this is a typical challenge for many social science theories, which also face the reciprocal challenge of too many variables. As scholars investigate new cases and deepen their exploration, the number of relevant factors or variables typically multiplies. Agrawal (2001) combines Ostrom's eight principles with findings from other researchers and develops an even more elaborated list of 36 (or more) "critical enabling conditions" for the sustainability of the commons. This expansion of variables presents not only a methodological challenge for researchers, but also a practical challenge for users who might wish to use the factors to assess strategies of commons governance. The point here is that Ostrom's eight design principles are certainly incomplete, but a "complete" theory presents challenges of its own and is probably a chimerical goal.

Managing the commons and transitioning to sustainability 155

Table 9.1   Ostrom's eight design principles for long-enduring commons management

1. *Clearly defined boundaries*: the boundaries of the resource must be clearly defined and the individuals or households with rights to use the resource must be identified.

2. *Congruence between appropriation and provision rules and local conditions*: rules defining how the resource can be appropriated must be aligned with local conditions and with rules about the provision of labor, material, and/or money.

3. *Collective-choice arrangements*: most of the individuals affected by these operational rules can participate in modifying them.

4. *Monitoring*: those who actively monitor resource use must be accountable to the users of the resource.

5. *Graduated sanctions*: users who violate the rules of resource use are punished by graduated sanctions that reflect the seriousness of their offense and these sanctions are imposed by the users themselves or by those accountable to them.

6. *Conflict-resolution mechanisms*: users and those accountable to them must have easy access to local, low-cost conflict mediation.

7. *Minimal recognition of rights to organize*: government authorities recognize the rights of users to design and implement their own institutions to regulate resource use.

8. *Nested enterprises*: relevant institutions are organized at different levels and scales in a nested fashion—that is, in ways that take each other into account (see the discussion of polycentricity below).

Source: Ostrom (1990, 90).

With respect to the second criticism, Stern (2011) investigates the difference between commons management at a small scale (e.g., a fishery in one bay) versus at a large scale (e.g., an ocean) and discusses how the eight design principles are affected. As scale increases significantly, Ostrom's first principle—delineate clear boundaries—becomes impossible, and her second principle—devising principles congruent with local conditions—becomes more or less unworkable. The remainder of the design principles remain relevant but confront specific challenges related to scale. For example, allowing most users to participate in decision-making is unrealistic, but the principle can be reformulated as "Ensure meaningful participation of the range of interested and affected parties in developing rules" (Stern, 2011, 221). He suggests similar revisions to each of the design principles to make them relevant for larger-scale commons.

A significant challenge for community-based governance also occurs when a resource is mobile and not easily localized, because this limits the ability to clearly bound the resource and its users. However, a study of a highly mobile resource, tuna, concludes that Ostrom's design principles remain relevant at a large scale (Epstein et al., 2014). In a review of Ostrom's critique of Hardin,

156   *Rethinking theories of governance*

however, Araral (2014) argues that while her critique is valid for small-scale commons, Hardin's analysis has validity for the global commons.

With respect to the third criticism, Young (2002) has discussed some of the challenges of Ostrom's design principles. He refers to both the scope conditions of the design principles (do the principles apply to the global commons as well as to the small-scale commons that Ostrom studied?) and the underlying heterogeneity of cases and whether they fit the implied scope conditions (is a small-scale fishery similar enough to a small-scale forest to warrant application of the same principles?). He points to the heterogeneity of environmental problems to suggest the difficulty (though not the irrelevance) of design principles, proposing a different approach that he calls "institutional diagnosis" (Young, 2002, 176). Cox et al. (2010) suggest that "diagnostic" and "design" principles can be seen as complementary rather than as alternatives.

Scaling and Polycentricity

Young (2002) has developed an institutional theory approach to environmental problems that identifies three related concepts: fit, interplay and scale. "Fit" refers to the idea that an institution that works well in one place or for one issue, may not work well for others. Fit becomes particularly problematic, he writes, when the environmental or human aspects of given situations become heterogeneous, increasing the possibility of "misfits" between institutions and environmental problems. "Interplay" refers to the idea that institutions deployed to address a particular environmental issue will interact with other institutions. He observes that this interplay may be vertical (between institutions operating at different governing levels) or horizontal (between institutions operating on the same governing level) and it may be driven by interdependencies that arise between institutions or that result from the design or management of institutions. "Scale" refers to the spatial or temporal level at which a particular environmental issue manifests itself and the corresponding scale of institutions that correspond to it (local to global). Fit, interplay and scale, Young argues, all need to be considered in designing institutions to address environmental problems.

This framework makes sense in general but can be difficult to apply in practice. Vatn and Vedeld (2012) point out that institutions do not simply "fit" a particular environmental context, but also to some extent create that context. "Fit" also focuses attention on the alignment between an institution and an environmental context, but the functioning of institutions also depends on the motivation and behavior of actors (they suggest that this is an ambiguous point in Young's perspective). They also suggest that it is often difficult to distinguish "fit" and "interplay," since it is interplay with other institutions that often determines fit. Finally, they observe that Young primarily links the issue of scale to the issue of whether knowledge scales up or down. They argue that this is a limited view of scale and that other important factors are also relevant to scale.

The multi-scale nature of environmental problems is often addressed by the concept of polycentricity, an idea associated with the work of Victor and Elinor Ostrom (Aligica and Tarko, 2012; Ostrom, 2010; McGinnis and Ostrom, 2012). Their analysis of polycentricity began with a challenge to the orthodoxy that the institutional fragmentation of metropolitan regions was inefficient. They argued that the scale of efficient production varies considerably and that some services are better produced on a small scale. Based on this logic, organizing service provision in a variegated fashion at multiple scales (a polycentric system) can outperform a more uniform and consolidated system of service provision (a monocentric system). Although polycentric systems have a fragmented authority structure, their decentered nature is intended to facilitate self-organization and respond to heterogeneity.

Carlisle and Gruby (2019) observe that a polycentric resource governance system is organized around multiple decision centers operating at different scales. They note some of the potential drawbacks of polycentric systems (e.g., high transaction costs) while also pointing out that polycentric systems are often purported to be more adaptive to environmental change, exhibit a better fit with the scale of resource use, and reduce risk by increasing institutional redundancy. Building on Victor Ostrom's work, they argue that a functional polycentric system has two key features: (1) multiple, overlapping decision centers with some degree of autonomy; (2) that engage with one another via cooperation, competition, conflict and conflict resolution. In a review of research on polycentric governance, Thiel (2017, 66) concludes that "polycentric governance is mostly used as a concept to frame and sensitize research."

Several "enabling conditions" are expected to support the adaptability of polycentricity to resource governance. Adaptability is facilitated by (1) institutional diversity encouraged by the multiplicity and relative autonomy of decision-making centers; (2) generally applicable rules that create incentives for productive action; (3) mechanisms that support learning between decision centers; (4) the ability to hold individual decision centers accountable for their actions; and (5) the existence of mechanisms for conflict resolution (Carlisle and Gruby, 2019). The institutional fit of a polycentric system will be facilitated by (1) organizing decision centers at multiple levels and across different political jurisdictions; and (2) aligning the scale of the decision-making jurisdiction with specific resource governance problems. Reduction of risk follows from many of these same properties, but in general is derived from the fact that that decision centers have overlapping jurisdictional concerns and the failure of one jurisdiction can be partly compensated for by the continued service of another.

Co-management

Although Elinor Ostrom's emphasis on community self-organization and her critique of centralized state regulation generally favor a decentralized view of resource management, Andersson and Ostrom (2008) and Nagendra and Ostrom (2012) have argued that polycentric systems are better thought of as "nested" rather than centralized or decentralized. While decentralized systems are important for fitting institutional arrangements to local contexts, they observed that it is also important that higher-level authorities provide support for decentralized units. They argue that polycentric systems better capture the multi-scalar and multi-level nature of natural resource governance than do either strictly centralized or decentralized regimes.

One way to think about resource governance that avoids a strict separation between centralization and decentralization is through the idea of co-management. Co-management is generally understood to be the joint management of natural resources by the state and by local communities and is often framed as a "partnership" between a resource management agency and local community actors (public and private). Co-management is also perceived as a response to the "failure" of top-down governance to deal with the overexploitation of the commons (particularly in the fisheries sector), as well as a cause and consequence of decentralization (Sen and Nielsen, 1996; Jentoft et al., 1998; Pomeroy and Berkes, 1997). In a review of decentralized natural resource management, however, Larson and Soto (2008, 218) argue that "Comanagement arrangements may increase the participation of local entities but are often designed to strengthen state control."

The forms that such partnerships take vary from limited, informal cooperation and negotiation to more extensive and formal cooperation (for a useful typology, see Sen and Nielsen, 1996). A key point is that the precise relationship between state and community is multi-dimensional and pluralistic, such that "in many real-life cases, we can expect to find rich webs of relations and agreements linking different parts of the public sector to a similarly heterogeneous set of private actors, all within the same area or in the same resource system" (Carlsson and Berkes, 2005, 69). How the community is defined and represented thus becomes a critical issue for the functioning of co-management regimes (Jentoft et al., 1998).

Co-management is understood to be a collaborative and iterative approach to solving resource management problems and power-sharing between state and community is best understood as the *result* of this interaction (Plummer and Fitzgibbon, 2004; Carlsson and Berkes, 2005). Carlsson and Berkes (2005) set out a six-step process for engaging in co-management: (1) define the relevant socio-ecological system; (2) identify problems and tasks to address; (3) establish who should participate, and in what fashion; (4) probe the linkages

Managing the commons and transitioning to sustainability 159

between people, problems, tasks and socio-ecological system; (5) determine what capacity is needed to address problems; and (6) identify solutions.

Co-management has been widely implemented and scholars have identified conditions that support or constrain it (Noble, 2000). Jentoft (2005) argues that empowerment is an important aspect of co-management, one that requires capacity-building and community-building. "People are empowered," he writes, "when they act in concert to form organizations, and when they acquire rights and responsibilities in fisheries management" (2005, 4). Property rights are also likely to strongly influence how co-management is designed and operated (Jentoft et al., 1998). Successful co-management depends on supportive central government policies and programs *and* on effective decentralization of management (Pomeroy and Berkes, 1997).

In a study of co-management regimes in Asia, Pomeroy et al. (2001) found that government and other external agents (e.g., NGOs) must be supportive of co-management. At the community level, management boundaries and membership must be well defined and affected actors must be included in the management process. Local leadership from within the community is critical and local politicians must be supportive and provide adequate funding. Community empowerment and capacity-building are also important and collective community organization can contribute significantly. Effective co-management processes will build a sense of commitment, common ownership and trust, and mutual respect. They will also be open and transparent in order to garner a sense of accountability. Straightforward objectives, clear and fair monitoring and enforcement, and individual incentives that support compliance are also important factors contributing to co-management success.

A discussion of the success and failure of co-management raises some general issues. Does a governance strategy like co-management "fail" because having been put in practice it does not produce the anticipated benefits or does it "fail" because the strategy is not successfully implemented in the first place? In an extensive investigation of the application of co-management to marine protected areas in Central America, for example, Bown et al. (2013) found that co-management did not live up to its promise. But they note that this failure arose from not giving local fishers a seat at the table. In a review of co-management in 22 different fisheries cases, Sen and Nielsen (1996) observe that co-management has generally been a form of "crisis management" where "[g]overnments, observing the failure of their own management regime take the decision to bring users into the management process" (1996, 417). It is clear from these and other studies that co-management is not an easy task (Nadasdy, 2003; Natcher et al., 2005).

Berkes (2009) stresses that successful co-management requires a "knowledge partnership" and he suggests the importance of "bridging organizations" that act as the interface between local knowledge and scientific knowledge.

Knowledge production and integration, however, are often a flashpoint in resource management (Nadasdy, 2003). Based on a worldwide survey of over 13,000 fisheries experts, Mora et al. (2009, 6) found that "policymaking transparency" was the most important factor contributing to sustainable fisheries. In sustainable fisheries, transparency implies that scientific advice is central to the policy process and that pressures from corruption or interest groups are limited. This focus on the importance of knowledge leads us to a discussion of strategies for adaptive management and adaptive governance.

Adaptive Management and Governance

The idea of "adaptive management" began as a strategy to deal more constructively with the uncertainty related to natural resource management (Holling, 1978; Walters, 1986). It is worth pointing out that this governance theory is rooted in the tradition of modeling natural resource systems (like fisheries), but it led to a fundamental reconsideration of how resource managers should approach uncertainty. Adaptive management counsels managers to engage in active experimentation (as opposed to trial-and-error or mere updating) to learn from the feedback from management interventions and resource policies.

The strategy of adaptive management has been popular with resource management agencies. However, scholars have pointed to the challenges of putting adaptive management into practice. A key challenge is whether stakeholders are actually willing to learn from experiments (Lee, 1999). Analyzing three case studies in Canada and the U.S. where adaptive management was applied, McLain and Lee (1996) found that system modeling remained politically contested and iterative hypothesis testing was difficult to implement. Although adaptive management increased information flow and deliberation about management objectives, it did not provide sufficient opportunities for stakeholders to develop shared understandings about goals. The authors concluded that "the adaptive management literature pays little attention to the question of what types of institutional structures and processes are required for the approach to work on a large-scale basis" (1996, 446).

Allen et al. (2011) identify five key implementation challenges that resource management agencies face in putting adaptive management into practice: (1) lack of operational clarity; (2) lack of success stories to imitate; (3) pressures to be reactive rather than proactive; (4) inadequate acknowledgment of shifting objectives; and (5) lack of attention to the social sources of disruption. They suggest that adaptive management is most appropriate where uncertainty and "controllability" are high (for a discussion of what controllability means in the context of adaptive management, see Gregory et al., 2006).

The concept of "adaptive governance" broadens out the discussion of adaptive management to talk about how the governance of natural resources can adapt to a broader set of challenges. Dietz et al. argued that:

> Devising effective governance systems is akin to a coevolutionary race. A set of rules crafted to fit one set of socioecological conditions can erode as social, economic, and technological developments increase the potential for human damage to ecosystems and even to the biosphere itself. Furthermore, humans devise ways of evading governance rules. Thus, successful commons governance requires that rules evolve. (2003, 1907–1908)

They argue that to manage the commons, institutions must be prepared to adapt to changing social, environmental and technological conditions. Moreover, they have to be able to adapt to changing knowledge and information about the commons. As Gunderson and Light (2006, 325) nicely put it: "adaptive governance is aimed at integrating science, policy and decision making in systems that assume and manage for change, rather than against change." In other words, the focus is not so much on how to adapt the management regime to new information about prior resource management interventions, but how governance regimes must adapt to social, technological and environmental change. Scholars, however, see adaptive management and adaptive governance as mutually supportive (Chaffin et al., 2014).

Adaptive governance theory is built, in part, on a critique of existing scientific, bureaucratic and engineering approaches to ecosystem management that impose prescriptive rules and constraints poorly suited to the dynamic nature of ecosystems, and which have been described as creating a "rigidity trap" (Brunner et al., 2005; Gunderson and Light, 2006, 330). In a general review, Folke et al. (2005) concluded that the key elements of adaptive governance include: (1) building and mobilizing the knowledge base for adapting to environmental change; (2) engaging in continuous monitoring and testing to evaluate (and reevaluate) management practices; (3) creating institutions that allow flexible adaptation and facilitate cooperation among stakeholders and across levels; and (4) building capacity to deal with surprise and uncertainty.

Rijke et al. (2012) point to three practical challenges of implementing adaptive governance—ambiguous purposes, unclear context, and uncertain outcomes. They argue that "supporting tools are still required to shift adaptive governance from rhetoric to practice" (2012, 76), and they suggest a "fit for purpose" framework to operationalize it. The first step in the framework requires stakeholders to develop common objectives for adaptive governance. The second step requires stakeholders to map the context in which adaptive governance will develop in order to identify the ecological, social, political etc. conditions that will affect governance in that context. The third step requires a strategy for evaluating the outcomes of adaptive governance.

162   *Rethinking theories of governance*

"Adaptive co-management" links experimental/experiential (adaptive) and collaborative (co-management) approaches together. Armitage et al. (2009) argue that learning is the common denominator that unites them. Co-management becomes adaptive co-management if learning accumulates over time (Berkes, 2009). Since "learning" is itself complex and multi-dimensional, the adaptive co-management literature has taken pains to elaborate what it means in this context (Armitage et al., 2008). Learning is likely to be more successful if it is supported and if it is an intentional strategy. Moreover, it requires the building of trust, the acknowledgment of diversity, and the development of shared objectives (Armitage et al., 2009).

Networks

Scholars have also linked adaptive and multi-level governance. Armitage (2008) links the following features to adaptive multi-level governance: the centrality of participation, collaboration and deliberation; the multi-layered nature of effective governance efforts; an emphasis on accountability for avoiding inequities; the importance of interactive dynamics and networks between actors and levels; the facilitating or catalyzing role of leadership; and the pluralism of knowledge and the importance of learning and trust. He concludes that managing the commons "necessitates flexible and distributed institutional forms" (2008, 25). Giest and Howlett (2014) argue that a precondition for commons governance is a network leader who can help to build trust and social capital.

Building on five case studies of adaptive governance from around the world, Olsson et al. (2006) explore conditions for the transformability of natural resource governance regimes and find that leadership is an important factor in preparing regimes for change. Transformation often occurs during "windows of opportunity" where awareness of problems with the resource are increasing. However, a crisis does not guarantee transformation to a more sustainable system. A key innovation of this paper is their observation that sustainability solutions often develop through the formation of "shadow networks" that generate the knowledge and solutions to guide natural regimes through change. These shadow networks tend to exist outside of formal institutional arrangements, and they require leadership to function well, but these networks can also provide leadership for adaptive change (see also Gunderson and Light, 2006).

Social network research on adaptive governance finds that brokerage can help to facilitate cross-scale governance (Ernstson et al., 2010). In a study of how the San Francisco Bay CALFED program created a number of institutions to address specific watershed issues, Lejano and Ingram (2009) argue that the key to the success of these institutions was that they promoted new patterns

Managing the commons and transitioning to sustainability 163

of cross-boundary interaction. Examining co-management from a network perspective, Carlsson and Sandström (2008) suggest that heterogeneous, but centrally coordinated and densely connected networks are likely to provide the most favorable conditions for co-management. Comparing three estuarine systems, Berardo and Lubell (2016) found that bridging ties were more important than expected in two of the estuaries.

International Environmental Regimes

As developed in Chapter 7, international cooperation is challenging and this is also certainly true for international cooperation on environmental protection. In a review of international environmental regimes, Young (1999a, 249) observes that international regimes do make a difference, but they are far from perfect and "there is considerable variation in the extent to which specific institutions shape collective outcomes at the international level." He argues that they can be effective when "they can redirect the interplay of political forces within the domestic policymaking arenas of key members" (1999a, 276).

Building on prior studies and several quantitative techniques to analyze available datasets on international environmental regimes, Breitmeier et al. (2011) find that when problems are poorly understood or the politics around the problem are heated ("malignant"), regimes will tend to perform less well. When these two factors interact negatively, they can sound the death knell for international regimes. Regimes that invest in knowledge production about the problem, however, can improve regime effectiveness, and a high level of collaboration enhances regime effectiveness. "Deep and dense rules" and a power distribution in favor of regime advocates can both enhance effectiveness (although this latter factor is less robust across analyses).

Using a qualitative comparative analysis (QCA), Breitmeier et al. (2011) find that one combination of factors stands out in terms of producing high effectiveness—a combination of strong knowledge base, either majority voting or high institutional capacity, and a power distribution favoring regime advocates. They point out that if they had to identify one factor that makes a particularly important contribution, they would emphasize the importance of a strong knowledge base. It appears to be a common factor in regime effectiveness in nearly all the combinations of factors they explore. Reciprocally, weak rules appear to be a common factor characterizing most combinations of factors producing weak regimes. They also draw the conclusion that power operates in a complex and differentiated way across different regimes depending on combinations of levels of knowledge, the degree of political contestation, and voting rules.

SUSTAINABILITY TRANSITIONS AND TRANSITION MANAGEMENT

In addition to research on governing the commons, there is an extensive body of research on the factors that contribute to transitions to sustainability. While this research focuses on the technological conditions that can produce sustainability, governance factors also play an important role. Such systems are both "social" and "technological," and hence regimes are understood to be "socio-technical" (Markard et al., 2012).The sustainability transitions literature calls attention to how the "locked-in" or "path-dependent" nature of unsustainable socio-technical regimes, can block incremental change toward sustainability.

Transition management is conceived as a form of change management that aims to usher socio-technological regimes toward a more sustainable future. This change process is understood to be a dynamic "coevolutionary" and "multi-level" process as opposed to a linear change process guided by a blueprint. As a result, the focus is on the interaction of top-down support and bottom-up innovation and the "multiplicity of steering activities by different actors, different mechanisms and different instruments" (Kemp et al., 2007, 83). Transition management is thus conceived as a "directed incrementalism" that stands somewhere between planning and incrementalism. Another way to describe this approach is to say that it focuses on "system innovation" (Smith et al., 2005).

A transition management approach is intended to provide a framework for guiding transitions policy, and research in this domain has sought to analyze the conditions under which significant shifts in unsustainable socio-economic regimes can be brought about (Kemp et al., 2007; Köhler et al., 2019). Köhler et al. (2019) summarize key characteristics of sustainability transitions: they have many different elements that "coevolve"; they involve many different actors with different perspectives and interests, leading to disagreement and conflict over desirable strategies; unsustainable regimes are often deeply entrenched; change is thus a long-term process; and although there are multiple possibilities for change, the success of any given strategy is uncertain; and finally, government must intervene to provide direction to the transition.

Several different theoretical frameworks for understanding sustainability transitions have been developed (Markard et al., 2012; Köhler et al., 2019). A multi-level perspective examines the interplay between niche, regime, and socio-economic landscape in producing transitions (Rip and Kemp, 1998). A technological innovation approach focuses on the conditions necessary for effective innovation (Hekkert et al., 2007). A strategic niche management approach focuses on the importance of nurturing innovations in protected

Managing the commons and transitioning to sustainability 165

"niches" so that they can develop and diffuse (Geels and Raven, 2006). A common aspect of all these frameworks is that innovation must be encouraged, protected and channeled in ways that will produce transitions from unsustainable to sustainable technology (Markard et al., 2020).

Building on complexity theory and experiences in managing sustainability projects in Belgium and the Netherlands, Loorbach (2010) outlines four steps in transition management: (1) a core group of forerunners structure the problem and develop a long-term strategy; (2) an expanded transition network, built around self-formed coalitions, develops a more specific transition agenda to guide the transition process; (3) transition "experiments" are conducted; and (4) these experiments are monitored and evaluated and the strategy and transition agenda are updated to reflect lessons learned. As these four steps suggest, transition management is conceived as an adaptive, experimental, and learning-based approach to achieving sustainability.

A further contribution is to call attention to how sustainability innovations are likely to occur through multilevel processes in which "niches" (micro level), "regimes" (meso level) and "societal landscapes" (macro level) interact (Rijke et al., 2013). In particular, there is a focus on how incumbent regime-level systems can create barriers to the diffusion or scaling-up of "niche" innovations and a concern with the development of "widely shared, specific, realistic, and achievable" innovations (Seyfang and Haxeltine, 2012, 390). Markard et al. (2020) identify five distinctive transition challenges: (1) components are innovated but they fail to change the surrounding socio-technical system; (2) adjacent socio-technical systems negatively constrain a focal innovation; (3) incumbent and competing socio-technical regimes are not successfully phased out; (4) unsustainable consumer practices are not successfully transformed; and (5) appropriate governance strategies and structures to support transitions are not available or provided.

Socio-technical regime transitions often begin in "early niche markets" (Raven, 2007). The literature distinguishes a "niche accumulation" strategy, where the goal is to protect outsider innovations until they can build up the steam to challenge mainstream regimes, from a "niche hybridization" strategy, where innovation occurs within mainstream regimes, but seeks to redirect them in more sustainable directions. Both strategies have strengths and weaknesses. Niche accumulation strategies are valuable where radical innovation from incumbent regimes is critical, but this strategy can easily lead to innovations that remain marginalized. Niche accumulation has the opposite profile: it is strong in mainstreaming innovations, but weaker on creating a clearly differentiated technological profile. Infrastructural systems are particularly hard to transition to sustainability because they are large, interdependent systems with long lifespans that require extensive investment (Frantzeskaki and Loorbach, 2010).

Several authors specifically investigate the governance dimensions of sustainability transitions. Building on an evolutionary perspective, Smith et al. (2005) conceptualize "selection pressures" in sustainability transitions. A key question is whether these selection pressures, which include governance factors, push system-level evolution in a particular direction—something the authors label "articulation." Thus, governance may vary in terms of how clearly and strongly it articulates pressure to change. A second issue has to do with the adaptive capacity of socio-technical regimes and whether they have the necessary resources and knowledge to adapt over time. Smith et al. (2005) argue that more "adaptive" regimes will have survival advantages over time.

Smith et al. (2005) link this focus on articulation and adaptive capacity directly to governance, which is understood to be a process of organizing and negotiating these selection pressures. At the system level, the governance of transitions may be more or less intentionally coordinated and the locus of the capacities for change may be more internal or external to the regime. This framing leads them to typologize different types of transition governance:

Purposive transition (high coordination, external resources): the case where focused programs are developed to bring a particular vision of sustainable regimes to fruition.

Endogenous renewal (high coordination, internal resources): change is steered by and adaptation capacity comes from within the incumbent regimes, thus leading to incremental change toward sustainability. If this is seen as moving in a positive direction, then the role of governance is to provide support to these incremental change processes.

Emergent transformation (low coordination, external resources): these transitions occur as the result of distributed innovation supported from outside the regime, but with the difficulty of knowing which innovations will catch on or take off. Governance strategy in this context might include identifying favorable innovations and then helping to coordinate and support them.

Reorientation of trajectories (low coordination, internal resources). In this case, transitions toward sustainability may come about through internal reorganizations in response to external shocks. Because the trajectory is unpredictable, governance must operate on the "back end" of the transition process—for example through regulation.

Thus, depending on the character of change and change management, governance may look quite different.

The transitions literature has begun to explore the importance of "policy mixes" on sustainability transitions (Kern et al., 2019), conceptualizing them as a series of positive or negative feedbacks on socio-economic innovation

(Edmondson et al., 2019). Kemp et al. (2005) write that governance for sustainability requires policy integration, process tools, and mixes of policy instruments that provide incentives and, information and programs for system innovation. The transitions literature recognizes that sustainability transitions are highly political and draws, to various degrees, on policy process models to explore the political dynamics of transitions (Avelino et al., 2016).

Grassroots Innovation

One conceptualization of sustainability transitions emphasizes the role of citizens, communities, social movements, and NGOs in driving niche innovation (Seyfang and Smith, 2007). These civil society-centered innovations are distinguished from the market- and state-centric innovation stressed by much of the transitions literature (Seyfang and Haxeltine, 2012). The groups that support these "grassroots innovations," are diverse in form, funding, degree of professionalization and ideology, but collectively they represent a potent force for driving sustainability innovation.

Seyfang and Smith (2007) distinguish between the "intrinsic benefits" and the "diffusion benefits" of grassroots innovation. Grassroots innovators can provide direct benefits for their communities, often in ways that align well with local contexts and needs ("intrinsic benefits"). Grassroots innovators can also provide the basis for innovations that depart from the mainstream and can test these ideas and demonstrate their potential, thus becoming models for others ("diffusion benefits"). Smith and Seyfang (2013) note that apart from the actual innovation that grassroots communities may produce, they also collectively generate and store knowledge and information about sustainability and innovation, though this knowledge and information is often informally held by networks of activists and not always generally available.

Despite this potential, research finds that grassroots innovators also face significant challenges: they often have limited access to funding and lack critical skills or manpower and their non-mainstream or counter-cultural agendas may create barriers to the diffusion or replication of their innovation (Seyfang and Smith, 2007; Fressoli et al., 2014). Feola and Nunes (2014) examine the success and failure of grassroots innovations for climate change, analyzing a network of local initiatives known as the "Transition Movement." They find that these local initiatives are interdependent with global networking efforts, though their early development is still very situated in local contexts. Training by the wider network is particularly important. They also find that an "incubation period" of roughly four years seems to be an important success factor for local initiatives and that these initiatives often undergo a cyclical development process that moves between coherence and fragmentation. Place attachment may be an important success factor, with less successful initiatives often having weaker attachment to place.

In a study of the U.K.'s "transition towns" movement, Seyfang and Haxeltine (2012) find that the movement was extremely successful in replicating itself in many locales and describe how intra-niche networking and learning are key strategies of the movement. And in a similar study of grassroots innovation in the U.K., Martiskainen (2017) finds that community leadership is important for helping local initiatives to connect to funding and to relevant skills and capacity. With a focus on Latin America, Smith et al. (2014) describe three paradoxes that grassroots movements are likely to encounter. The first is that they must create generally applicable innovations while fitting them into local contexts. The second is that they must fit in locally, while also disrupting existing structures and dynamics. The third is that they must create systemic or structural change on a project-by-project basis.

Leverage Points

Donella Meadows (1999) proposed that "leverage points"—a concept drawn from systems analysis—is useful for understanding and affecting sustainability transitions. A leverage point, according to Meadows, is a place you can strategically intervene in a system. She starts by examining aspects of systems that make them weak leverage points. She argues that "systems parameters," while critical for system performance, are, counterintuitively, not places where one can get great leverage on a system. Nor do "system buffers" or "system infrastructure" generally make promising leverage points. She argues that negative and positive feedback loops offer greater opportunity for leverage and using information to create new feedback loops can be a particularly useful systems intervention. Changing the system's rules is another key leverage point (which usually entails changing who controls the rules), particularly if it facilitates the ability of the system to self-organize in response to changing conditions. Introducing new system goals or changing the overall system paradigm have even more power to produce system transformation.

Fischer and Riechers (2019) argue that a value of the leverage point perspective is that it combines "causal" (explanatory) and "teleological" (goal-directed) thinking. They also suggest that it is valuable to think about the interaction of leverage points, such that they might provide synergistic pathways to change. Building on Meadows's concept of leverage points, Abson et al. (2017) argue that the problem with sustainability science is that it has not identified strong "leverage points" to affect change. They identify three broad leverage points—restructuring institutions, connecting people to nature, and reconceiving how knowledge is produced. Leventon et al. (2021) argue that incorporating diverse values into governance is a leverage point for addressing

Managing the commons and transitioning to sustainability 169

biodiversity. Williams et al. (2020) propose an integrated modeling approach in conjunction with a "capital analysis" to identify leverage points in local governance. Leverage points might go together with the idea of a diagnostic approach (e.g., Bartkowski and Bartke, 2018).

The metaphor of leverage points also implies the idea of levers. Chan et al. (2020) draw on a multinational expert deliberation to identify leverage points and levers for achieving system transformation for sustainability. They identify five key levers for system transformation, including incentives and capacity-building, cross-boundary coordination, adaptive governance and resilience, a precautionary approach to risk and enforcement and implementation of environmental laws. Linnér and Wibeck (2021) argue, however, that the concept of lever is only appropriate for simple, linear systems. Instead, they identify common "drivers" of system transformations. Technological innovation is a prominent driver of system change, but needs to be considered together with other behavioral, political and economic factors. Political economy is another key driver in the sense that transformations have to address existing power imbalances, differences in capacity, and the legitimacy of change. A third driver includes "new narratives" that can motivate action for change. Finally, transformative learning is necessary to challenge the cultural assumptions around which current systems are built.

Reflexive Governance

Theories of environmental governance often talk about the idea of reflexive governance, which grew, in part, out of Ulrich Beck's (1986) description of "risk society" and Beck et al.'s (1994) elaboration of the idea of "reflexive modernization." The idea of "reflexivity" also draws on neo-evolutionary theories of law that describe "reflexive law" as oriented toward controlling and guiding self-regulation (Teubner, 1982). Feindt and Weiland (2018, 665) argue that "a governance mode can be called reflexive if it includes the perspectives, values and norms of a variety of actors, which in turn has consequences for the interventions of the governance system." They observe that interest in the concept of reflexive governance grew out of a disappointment with first-generation environmental policies and strategies.

Stirling (2006) argues that reflexivity goes beyond reflectiveness, which refers to a mirror-like situation that implies serious consideration of the full range of issues and externalities involved in a governance situation. By contrast, reflexivity refers to a more recursive relationship in which there is an ongoing review of the very perspectives, issues and institutions that are intended to address the situation of concern. He argues that criticism of technology, as well as strategies of acting on these criticisms (including aspects of

170   *Rethinking theories of governance*

the precautionary principle) are often reflective rather than reflexive. Greater reflexivity calls for widening deliberation about technological futures.

Reflexive governance calls for an examination of the assumptions that guide governance and calls into question our basic strategies of rational problem-solving. While these strategies are powerful for achieving techno-logical and social control, the high degree of analytical specialization they entail increasingly produces unintended consequences that arise from the nar-rowness of their control objectives and the interdependence they produce. In part, reflexive governance is the response to these unintended consequences, such that they themselves become the object of governance. As a result, "second-order governance" is required to steer and complement modernist strategies of problem-solving with a more learning-oriented approach (Voß and Kemp, 2006).

Voß and Kemp (2006) argue that sustainability problems are complex and characterized by heterogeneous elements that call for integrated knowledge, uncertain dynamics and systems that demand adaptive and experimental learning, and path-dependent effects that must be avoided. Thus, the reflexive governance of sustainability depends on the production of transdisciplinary knowledge, on the ability of governance institutions to adapt their strategies as conditions change, and on the ability to anticipate long-term impacts via methods of scenario planning. Sustainability strategies must be developed interactively and with the possibility of revising goals as circumstances and knowledge changes.

A common theme of the reflexive governance literature is that successful sustainability transitions must bring multiple types of knowledge together. In a case study of the city of Bristol in the U.K., Ersoy and Hall (2020) argue that the Bristol Green Capital Project was an exemplar of reflexive governance, bringing together a wide range of urban stakeholders with their different perspectives and knowledge to develop strategies for making the city more sustainable. By contrast, Leonard and Lidskog (2021) argue that the city of South Durban in South Africa lacked the governance capacity and the practices of participation and deliberation to engage in reflexive governance. In addi-tion, distributed and asymmetric power may frustrate reflexive governance. In a case study of reflexive governance about the relationship between agriculture and pesticides in the Netherlands, for example, Hendriks and Grin (2007) explore how actors who stand to lose through greater attention to an issue will take steps to undermine reflexivity. Such efforts are partly counterbalanced by efforts to expand the range of actors involved in the discussion and by efforts to accommodate power differences.

Voß and Bornemann (2011, 14) point to concepts of adaptive management and transition management as specific "designs" for reflexive governance and argue that they have paid limited attention to politics. The result is unrealistic designs that "build on an idealized image of cognitive learning that assumes unbiased observers of systemic changes, open-minded consideration of developmental options, and unequivocal interpretations of results from experimentation" (2011, 14). They argue that safeguards must be built into these processes to safeguard them from politicization and capture and they identify three generic strategies that might be called on to address this challenge: (1) to exclude politics from these processes with procedures that enhance rationality; (2) to surface political conflicts and then engage in "frame reflection" to move forward; and (3) to engage in a democratic process of "mutual partisan adjustment."

CONCLUSION

This chapter investigates two broad issues with respect to environmental governance: how do theories of governance help us understand common resource management and how do they contribute to our understanding of how to promote transitions to sustainability? Starting with ideas about managing the commons, we began with Elinor Ostrom's response to the debate started by Garrett Hardin about the Tragedy of the Commons. In response to Hardin's argument that the commons would inevitably be overexploited in the absence of either centralized regulation or clear specification of private property rights, Ostrom suggested a third way—community-based self-governance of the commons—that she demonstrated was a viable alternative through a range of international case studies.

Ostrom's research ultimately led her to formulate eight design principles for community-based commons management, which are presented in Table 9.1. These principles have attracted much theoretical and empirical attention and research provides considerable warrants for their value, at least on a relatively small-scale basis. Research has also found many other variables that may be important in successfully managing common pool resources and the principles have been challenged with respect to whether they hold at larger scales (e.g., oceans). Some research suggests that Ostrom's design principles do scale, with appropriate modifications, but this remains a somewhat open question.

Ostrom and colleagues did, however, have a particular concept of scaling, which she referred to as "nesting" or "polycentricity." Arguing against either decentralization or centralization, Ostrom and colleagues have argued that relatively self-governing institutions operating at different scales and loosely cooperating as a system (polycentricity) can provide an effective means of regulating the commons at multiple scales. Although the concept of polycentricity has received less serious theoretical and empirical attention than the concept of community-based self-governance, scholars have begun to identify the conditions under which it works or does not work.

Another important theoretical concept in research on environmental governance is co-management. Like Ostrom's research on the commons, it emphasizes local community participation in governance, but also stresses that local communities do this in conjunction with the state—hence the idea of *co*-management. Theoretical perspectives on co-management start with a view of communities as being socially and ecologically complex and as requiring the development of horizontal collaboration within the community and vertical collaboration with the state. While co-management is often seen as valuable and necessary, it is also understood to be quite challenging. A common theme is that state and politician support is important for increasing the likelihood of success.

Another strategy stresses the adaptive nature of governance in the face of uncertainty about ecosystems. Adaptive management began as an expert-oriented approach to refining resource management regimes through experimentation. While adaptive management has been widely used by resource management agencies, some critics have suggested that it is often improperly applied, and they identify the types of conditions under which it is more likely to be successfully implemented. The concept of "adaptive governance" broadens out the idea of adaptive management, envisioning it as a strategy implemented through the collaboration of many stakeholders and responding to a wider set of social and ecological changes. Most importantly, it builds directly on ideas of community self-government and co-management, including Ostrom's eight principles.

Theories of environmental governance also stress the importance of networks for mobilizing and leading environmental protection efforts both within and across communities and across levels and scales of governance. One important idea is that the change efforts that lead communities toward greater sustainability are often guided by informal "shadow networks." Using social network analysis to analyze community-based and polycentric governance, environmental governance scholars have begun to identify the characteristics of networks that support mobilization and cooperation.

While the Ostrom tradition of commons management emphasizes local efforts, an important body of environmental governance research focuses on the international level. Many of the issues discussed in Chapter 7 on the challenges of global cooperation and coordination are relevant to understanding environmental governance at this level. Global environmental regimes face many challenges, but it is theorized that they will be more effective when they invest in and develop a solid and deep knowledge base. Well-articulated rules and a balance of power that favors regime advocates will also contribute toward regime effectiveness.

The second broad governance issue dealt with in this chapter is the idea of a sustainability transition. An extensive body of theory and research characterizes sustainability transitions as coevolutionary processes where incumbent institutions and technologies are challenged by innovations and experiments developing in "niches." While there are a variety of different theoretical specifications of a sustainability transition, most of them emphasize that it is a multi-level process, that unsustainable technologies and institutions are path-dependent and resistant to change, and that positive change must be tackled from a systems point of view. A key theoretical concern is how to protect, nurture and scale niche innovations. Opportunities and demands for governance are understood from within this coevolutionary dynamic and they depend on the pattern of change observed. While empirical research on sustainability transitions has explored many different domains, this research is generally more illustrative than conclusive.

One somewhat heterodox view of sustainability transitions comes from research on "grassroots innovation." This body of research suggests that much of the sustainability transitions literature is still too "top-down" in its view of how change occurs and stresses that some patterns of innovation are more bottom-up in nature, and to some extent take the form of social movements. While grassroots innovators are often highly motivated and committed to change, they also face significant constraints related to funding, resources and capacity. Another perspective on change is the concept of "leverage points." Like the sustainability transitions literature, the idea of leverage points is drawn from a systems theory perspective. Scholars have begun to discuss how leverage points can be identified, though this research remains at a high level of generality.

A final conception of change relevant to environmental governance is the concept of "reflexive governance," which arises out of the work of Beck et al. (1994). The basic idea is that as modernization produces more negative impacts, politics becomes more critically focused on evaluating the potentially negative consequences of these developments. As a result, politics becomes more "reflexive," which means that learning and knowledge integration become central to governance efforts. While useful at a very general level as an orientation to the issues of environmental governance, research on reflexive governance operates at a relatively abstract level and has only generated a limited empirical base.

10. Rethinking theories of governance

This book has asked whether governance theories are useful for confronting the challenges of contemporary governing. At the outset, it was acknowledged that truly answering this question depends on asking "useful for whom?" and that probing this deeply was beyond the scope of the book. More modestly, the book set out a generic standard for thinking about the usefulness of theory. In doing so, it was motivated by criticisms of the idea of "evidence-based policymaking." While this book has no quarrel with the idea of "evidence" or the value that it can serve in policymaking, it is much more cautious about the prescriptive implications of "evidence-based policy." Such an approach tends to become reductive and to support the idea of "blueprint" strategies that ignore contextual conditions.

In a way, this prescriptive approach to theory and evidence also undersells what theory is good at doing, which is helping us to orient ourselves to the world and assisting us in interpreting it. As a result, the book began by setting out three general criteria for thinking about the usefulness of theory. The first is whether the theory is *warranted*. A theory is more warranted when the strength of evidence supporting the theory's descriptions, interpretation, explanation or expectations is strong. This criterion leads to an approach to evidence that is in many respects indistinguishable from an "evidence-based" approach. Even where there is a wealth of evidence and considerable consensus about it, however, warranted theory is understood as providing the basis for further inquiry rather than a prescription for what to do. As summarized in Table 1.1, theories that provide the basis for subsequent inquiry shift attention from "what to do" to "what to ask." They encourage dialogue between the theory and the situation and aid in its diagnosis. Thus, in addition to being warranted, useful theory is also *dialogical* and *diagnostic*.

GOVERNANCE THEORIES: WARRANTED, DIALOGICAL AND DIAGNOSTIC?

Governance research on public problems, as analyzed in Chapter 2, has created useful analytical frameworks for understanding the challenging nature of public problems. The concepts of wicked, ill-structured, messy, or complex problems and the idea of problems as traps provide significant insights into why such problems can be so hard to solve. Their strength is their usefulness for diagnosing the nature of public problems and they can help policymakers, administrators and citizens identify attributes and dynamics that are often surprising or frustrating in hindsight.

These problem-oriented theories are somewhat weaker on diagnostic insights into how to manage challenging problems, though they point to important types of solutions. They are also somewhat less helpful for dialoguing with a problem as it unfolds dynamically, though they offer useful advice on how to structure ill-structured problems, how to use small wins to dynamically address difficult problems, and how to approach problems in adaptive and innovative ways. The warranted nature of these frameworks is perhaps their weakest characteristic. Although significant case study research is available, it is typically more illustrative than evaluative of their claims.

The next three chapters investigate the factors and conditions that contribute to the effectiveness and accountability of public organizations and governance processes. Chapter 3 examines broad political factors and conditions that shape the effectiveness and accountability of public organizations. It finds general empirical support for the theoretical claim favoring a separation between politics and administration and the establishment of a meritocratic civil service. Politicization of the bureaucracy generally weakens its effectiveness by undermining professionalism and accountability and by fostering the conditions for clientelism and corruption. Where states have not achieved these Weberian conditions, diagnosis and dialogue are less well developed, though "islands of excellence" research makes some important contributions.

Consistent with the Weberian argument, different theoretical perspectives generally agree that bureaucratic effectiveness and accountability are enhanced when public organizations have a significant degree of autonomy. However, this autonomy is necessarily relative and democratic political control over the bureaucracy is essential for achieving accountability. Principal–agent theories have done a great deal to analyze the different conditions, processes and mechanisms for achieving this control, with considerable analysis of scope conditions (e.g., multiple principals). Beyond principal–agent theories, a burgeoning body of research on accountability has discerned many distinctive types of accountability and identified some of the challenges of applying accountability in practice. While the evidence base for accountability research remains limited (with the exception of the psychological research tradition), it does provide useful diagnostic insights.

Chapter 4 shifts attention to the administrative and managerial conditions for effective and accountable public organizations, distinguishing between two broad theoretical approaches that call attention to the importance of different institutional mechanisms. New Public Management stresses the importance of "managing by results" and suggests that the key to achieving results is agency design ("agencification" and "incentive design"), use of markets and quasi-markets ("contracting out") and effective performance measurement and management ("accountability for results"). NPM has provided a powerful model of diagnosis, which may have been part of the reason it was so wildly popular, and it has identified many important factors that can help agency managers to dialogue with their situation. However, the warrants for its claims have been at best mixed, though they have been stronger for some of its elements (e.g., performance management).

The other theoretical approach to public organization effectiveness and accountability was dubbed an "institutional" approach and it also provides an umbrella to draw together another set of related theoretical ideas. It stresses the importance of motivating and coordinating public employees around a strong sense of organizational mission, of building agency professionalism, of leading through models of transformative leadership, and of cultivating public service motivation. It is not as cohesive in its overall diagnosis of agency performance as NPM, but the warrants for some of its elements (e.g., mission orientation, professionalism, transformative leadership and public service motivation) are more generally positive.

While public organizations often play a central role in governance, the governance literature generally expands the focus beyond a single agency and beyond government. Chapter 5 begins by investigating claims about the state itself. There is a general sense that state capacity is a critical variable for effective governance and there is some empirical evidence to warrant this claim. Scholars have also usefully distinguished different kinds of capacity. However, the diagnostic and dialogical character of these perspectives is not particularly fine-grained. There is a relatively elaborate body of research on the value of centralization and decentralization. While governance has often been associated with decentralized conditions, the warrants for decentralization improving the effectiveness and accountability of governance are not particularly strong, though these findings have encouraged research to identify the conditions and factors that contribute to better outcomes (e.g., local state capacity).

Network and collaborative governance lie at the heart of governance research. Theories have identified different modes of network and collaborative governance and specified some of the key drivers and barriers of success. Network management, sufficient resources and long-term commitment are three well-established factors for producing effective network governance and leadership, trust, and effective process management are regarded as essential factors in successful collaboration. Accountability has been a particular source of concern in research on decentered governance, but scholars have done much to explore the potential for state meta-governance to steer, support and hold networks democratically accountable. Empirical support for these arguments is still thin, but the literature has identified how meta-governance works in practice.

Governance theories have analyzed a range of ways that various modes of governance contribute to or detract from the quality and legitimacy of democracy. Various modes of citizen participation have been studied in some depth by governance scholars, who have focused on identifying both the potential and the limits of these modes of governance (Chapters 5 and 6). This research generally finds that effective citizen participation is difficult to achieve but can be productive and successful if a strong partnership is established between the state and civil society. Generally, research suggests that that the state must play an active role in supporting effective participation, but that successful participation can cultivate a sense of citizenship and support for government.

Cross-national research finds that effective governance supports citizen satisfaction with democracy and suppresses societal conflict. As discussed in Chapter 6, the governance literature per se has not been particularly attentive to the question of how governance can contribute to and mediate conflict, but collaborative governance clearly has an important conflict-mediation role. Widening our perspective, however, political science has made important contributions to thinking about how to forestall or mitigate violent conflict. Research has extensively explored the role of power-sharing arrangements and federalism to mitigate high-intensity conflicts, particularly inter-ethnic conflict. Research generally supports claims that power-sharing and federalism are positive conflict management strategies, though there remains tension over whether they also help to institutionalize these conflicts.

Global governance, a distinctive subfield of governance research, is discussed in Chapter 7. Discussions about governance have been particularly intense at the global level because weak collective leadership by states often leads to what has been called a "governance gap." Governance scholars have identified the challenges faced by international organizations and regimes in governing at the global level and discussed the increasing fragmentation of global governance. They have identified and analyzed the important role of various kinds of networks (epistemic, regulatory, public policy, public–private partnerships and advocacy) in filling this gap. Overall, it is doubtful that these networks could effectively fill the governance gap, though they do probably contribute to improved global cooperation and coordination.

While the structure of the global order significantly limits effective global governance, scholars have contributed significant insights into how global cooperation and coordination can be enhanced under these constrained circumstances. A notable contribution is research on "orchestration," which identifies the ways that international organizations can facilitate cooperation among states. So far, research in this domain has primarily identified how orchestration works in practice and has identified some of the opportunities and constraints in using it.

Global governance scholars have also focused their attention on the various forms of private and hybrid transnational regulation that have emerged at the international level. While they remain divided on how optimistic or pessimistic to be about these forms of regulation, they have done much to help us understand how they work in practice. Global governance scholars have also identified and probed two forms of governance—global experimentalist governance and governance by goals—that operate in the context of weak international authority. They demonstrate that these forms have potential to increase global cooperation and coordination, but they operate in the face of significant challenges.

Chapter 8 asks whether governance theories have contributed to our understanding of how to reduce poverty and inequality. Comparative research has provided supportive evidence that "good governance" reduces poverty and that the Weberian state (effective bureaucratic governance) contributes to economic growth. Research on the expected impacts of decentralization on poverty and inequality, however, show quite mixed results, reinforcing the findings of Chapter 5. By contrast, comparative research generally supports the claim that welfare states reduce poverty and inequality, as one might expect. Scholars generally agree that how benefits are provided matters and there is considerable support for the idea that more universalistic welfare programs do a better job than targeted benefits. Still, the details of how the design of welfare programs impact poverty reduction remain a topic of lively debate. While state-centric views of poverty reduction have been prominent, more bottom-up theories have also been developed. These theories focus on the role of community-building and the empowerment of the poor and give significant attention to the important but variable role of NGOs.

Chapter 8 also examines some of the ways that discussions of governance intersect with issues of diversity, equity and inclusion. One important development is the growing interest in the concept of institutional bias or institutional racism, which has carved out a distinctive but still mostly illustrative perspective on how governance institutions might contribute to inequitable outcomes. The issue of equity itself has been important in public administration research, which has identified the general tenets of equity for public administrators. Although an empirical body of research on equity has only been established to a limited degree, the public administration literature has made quite significant strides in theorizing and researching "representative bureaucracy." This research has done much to identify the mechanisms that lead from passive, active or symbolic representation of certain groups to the increased legitimacy and responsiveness of public organizations vis-à-vis these groups. Research on environmental justice has made similar contributions in the field of environmental governance, particularly with respect to identifying different aspects of justice.

Research on environmental governance is vast and Chapter 9 focuses attention on what governance theories have contributed toward understanding the management of common pool resources and transitions to sustainability. The chapter begins with a consideration of Elinor Ostrom's landmark contributions to addressing the "tragedy of the commons." In contrast with prior perspectives, her work suggests that community self-governance is a viable approach when certain conditions are met and she identified eight design principles for effective commons governance. A significant body of research provides support for her analysis, though many factors beyond these eight have been found to be relevant and the applicability of the principles is limited for larger-scale commons. Her research has also contributed to the development of the concept of the "co-management" of environmental resources by local communities and the state. Research on co-management suggests that it faces many challenges but can be effective when there is strong state support for local management.

An extremely large body of literature has now developed around analyzing transitions to sustainability, with a focus on the development of new and more sustainable technologies. The sustainable transitions literature has generally adopted an evolutionary view of transitions, which focuses on how sustainable innovations that develop in niches can eventually scale up to challenge and replace incumbent technological regimes. Case studies of these evolutionary processes have identified important insights into how niche innovations can be protected and diffused. While much of the sustainability transitions literature has seen transitions through the lens of state policymaking, some scholars have stressed the importance of grassroots innovation and have identified some of the specific challenges of bottom-up innovation.

Governance theories (broadly interpreted) cover an amazing range of important topics and concerns. Judging their usefulness in terms of whether they are warranted, diagnostic and dialogical is itself a difficult (and even painful!) task, but an important one. A first point to make, as stressed by a number of governance theorists, is that there are no governance panaceas—alas, no magic formulas or recipes that, if followed, will cure our collective ills (Ostrom, 2007; Young, 2021). Over and over, the research reviewed in this book suggests that governance is perplexing, tedious, and politicized and all the "solutions" are to be taken with a grain of salt. Indeed, this is part of the point of why relying on evidence-based prescription is a hazardous strategy.

The fact that governance is hard and theory does not tell us precisely what to do does not be mean that we should throw up our hands in resignation. Governance theories have examined many of the challenges that confront us and provided many insights about the challenges themselves, the strategies we have available to respond to them, and the pitfalls that we may face when we try to implement them. It is hardly a definitive body of knowledge, but it is still extremely useful. One observation is that these theories do a pretty good job helping us to develop an initial diagnosis of the challenges of governance and the prospects for overcoming them. Although governance theorists do not always think of their theories in terms of diagnosis, doing so might help governance theorizing to be more helpful in practice.

In terms of empirical support for the claims of governance, we see a very wide range of outcomes. In some cases, we see supportive and generally consensual evidence for some claims (e.g., for the value of the separation of politics and administration) and in other cases much more mixed and inconclusive evidence and divided scholarly opinion (e.g., with respect to value of decentralization or the effectiveness of NPM). In some cases, we see relatively extensive data collection for evaluating specific theoretical claims (e.g., studies of the effects of World Bank "good governance" indicators) and in other cases we see a more illustrative use of case studies to demonstrate an argument or to suss out key explanatory mechanisms (e.g., collective impact studies). A general observation is that judging whether a governance theory is warranted is quite a different task from evaluating whether they provide good diagnostic insights or help practitioners to dialogue with their specific context.

The theories reviewed have had the least to say about the dialogical nature of governance theories. In a mundane sense, all the theories reviewed are dialogical in the sense that they invite us to engage in a dialogue between the theory and specific issues. A theory of poverty governance requires us to ask whether a particular governance strategy is punitive or paternalistic. A theory of transnational private regulation bids us to examine whether third-party certification can be effective. A theory of international orchestration invites us to consider whether and how this might work in a specific domain of global governance. In this sense, governance theories stimulate further inquiry and shape our imagination. In another sense, governance theories have been weaker on this dialogical criterion than on the warranted or diagnostic criteria. Governance is often as much about process as it is about structure. Yet there seems to be a general weakness in many governance theories in terms of imagining the dynamic nature of governance challenges, which call for those addressing them to continue to query and respond to changing conditions. Governance theory clearly understands this in abstract terms and stresses the adaptive or interactive nature of governance, but our theories are less geared toward an ongoing conversation with a dynamic world.

STATE–SOCIETY SYNERGY

Having summarized the book "bird-by-bird," as they say, it is worthwhile to now "think across" the different topics considered, as Alistair Roberts advises (2020). One of the key cross-cutting themes that emerges in the book is a recurring tension between a Weberian state perspective and a more bottom-up perspective on the role of citizens and stakeholders. On the one hand, there is quite a bit of empirical support in favor of Weberian states. An impartial, meritocratic and professional public administration that enjoys a measure of bureaucratic autonomy and effective political oversight can increase government effectiveness and accountability.

Effective and accountable state institutions, in turn, are important for other valued outcomes. They contribute to the legitimacy of the state and citizen satisfaction with democracy. They increase economic growth and reduce societal conflict and poverty. State capacity matters for effective governance and decentralization is only effective when it can ensure that local governments have adequate capacity and do not increase corruption.

These findings support a state-centric perspective on effective and accountable governance. Yet there is also quite a bit of support for a more "bottom-up" or "society-centric" perspective. Development scholars have called attention to the failures of top-down blueprint strategies and argued that development needs to work more closely and adaptively with local communities. Social capital embedded in communities has been found to have a positive influence on effective governance and public participation and bottom-up social accountability also generally have positive effects, though these benefits can be difficult to realize in practice. Scholars of violence suggest that power-sharing arrangements and decentralization may ameliorate ethnic conflict and that informal social mechanisms are often critical for conflict management. Research on poverty stresses the value of community-building for addressing issues of poverty and inequality and theories of commons management stress the value of community self-governance.

While it is tempting to pose state-centric and society-centric as alternative or conflicting accounts of governance, this book points more toward the value of thinking in terms of what Peter Evans (1996, 1997) dubbed a "state–society synergy," which emphasizes the possibility of positive interactions between state and society. This perspective runs across the chapters and is implicit in many governance ideas. Concepts of collaborative governance, co-production, co-creation and co-management, polycentricity and various forms of "new governance" stress possibilities of positive-sum interactions between the state and citizens, communities and stakeholders.

Standing back from the broad range of theory reviewed here, the possibilities of understanding governance through the lens of state–society synergy remain underexplored. There are several reasons why. Perhaps the single most important reason is "neoliberalism." The classic claim that we are transitioning from "government to governance" is often viewed in terms of the criticism that neoliberalism is undermining the public sphere (Brown, 2015), hollowing out, de-territorializing and depoliticizing the state (Milward and Provan, 2000; Craig and Porter, 2006; Flinders and Buller, 2006) and transforming the welfare state into a punitive workfare state (Jessop, 2002a; Wacquant, 2009). The most encompassing critique is a Foucault-inspired argument that governance represents a neoliberal "governmentality" where the state extends its rule over subjects by governing at a distance (Rose et al., 2006; Bevir, 2011).

The concern that governance is a neoliberal stalking horse is not, however, the only reason that the possibilities of "state–society synergy" remain underexplored. A second reason is that governance tends to blur the boundary between public and private that underpins much of our understanding of liberal representative democracy. As Peters and Pierre (2016, 4) note, many descriptions of governance counter the "traditional notion in liberal democratic theory about a clear empirical and normative distinction between state and society and between governors and governed." Any erosion of these distinctions creates a fundamental anxiety about the accountability of various governance mechanisms, as discussed in Chapters 3–5. New forms of governance are particularly threatening to populists who stress majoritarian control over the state (Stoker, 2019).

Thus, governance can be critiqued as both advancing neoliberalism and eroding the state or as challenging liberalism and eroding representative democracy. As a result, the critical focus has been on the negative relationship between governance, on the one hand, and the democratic state, on the other. These criticisms are valuable, but they tend to lump all discussions of governance into a single bucket. But there is great variety in the governance literature. Triantafillou (2020), for example, argues that New Public Governance, which is understood as a corrective to New Public Management, is also a form of liberalism, but it differs from both classical liberalism and neoliberalism. It is fundamentally concerned, he suggests, about the legitimacy problems created by societal complexity and particularly about the ability of citizens to engage in democratic self-governance. He infers that New Public Governance has a "positive conception of freedom enabling citizens and communities to participate in political and administrative processes, and a freedom equipping them with the powers necessary to solve the problems affecting them" (2020, 1233).

One way to "rethink" governance is to accept neoliberal and liberal critiques of governance as possible outcomes, but then to ask when, where and how governance contributes to and expresses a strong state–society synergy. It is useful to consider this synergy as flowing in two directions: how can the state contribute to strengthening the societal capacity to engage effectively and accountably in governance, and reciprocally, how can societal mobilization strengthen the capacity of the state to engage effectively and accountably in governance? Posed from this perspective there is not one, but many possible theoretical ideas developed in the governance literature that already speak to these questions.

A common but implicit thread in Chapter 2 is that as problems become more challenging, the state as *external governor* of those problems becomes less efficacious. In a sense, the more challenging problems are, the more the state must govern from *inside* the problem and coevolve with it. Moreover, challenging problems are dynamic and contextual and do not respond well to blueprint solutions. Thus, they require "adaptive governance" or "small win" strategies where the state must engage incrementally and innovatively in collaboration with societal actors. None of this should imply that states can offload their responsibilities onto society (the governmentality critique) or escape accountability for their legal responsibilities (the liberal critique).

Closer engagement with society is, of course, viewed as problematic from the perspective of the Weberian model. The closed and apolitical character of bureaucracy is precisely what endows it with professionalism and reduces its tendency toward corruption, though it may also lead it to embrace blueprint-type approaches to problem-solving and to "see like a state" (Scott, 2020). Peter Evans's analysis of development states in terms of their "embedded autonomy" is one important attempt to reconcile the Weberian model with greater state–society synergy. However, the institutional model of public organizations outlined in Chapter 4 may offer a somewhat different perspective. While it overlaps with the Weberian model in several respects, it differs in ways that may make it more adaptive to constructive interaction with society. Notably, this model stresses a strong mission orientation and a concern for public reputation (see Ansell, 2011, for additional discussion).

The point here is not to say that we already have a well-oiled theory of how the state can be both autonomous and impartial and work in and through society. But there are some ideas touched on in this book that offer avenues for further refinement of a state–society synergy meta-theory. Gerring et al.'s (2005) concept of "centripetal" institutions, for instance, provides one approach for thinking about how to combine top-down and bottom-up forces (Chapter 5). Research on network, collaborative and participatory governance also offers a range of insights on the opportunities and limits of state–society synergy—and they are often at least implicitly understood from this vantage point by governance theorists. To take one explicit discussion, research on "empowered participatory governance" has emphasized the importance of

184   *Rethinking theories of governance*

"accountable autonomy" and explored the conditions under which it can be achieved (Chapter 6).

Another example of where an analysis of state–society synergy can be potentially observed from a network governance perspective is in the discussion of meta-governance, where the state acts as a meta-governor of self-governing networks (Chapter 5). The concept of orchestration (Chapter 7) also provides possible insights, though it is generally seen as a strategy adopted because international organizations have limited direct authority. Nevertheless, both ideas could be further probed from the perspective of state–society synergy.

Another place to look for state–society synergy is in discussions of welfare and equity (Chapter 8). Although not explored in this book, the provision of social benefits and public goods impacts the trust and legitimacy that citizens place in the state, which in turn produces favorable conditions for effective and accountable governance. The social psychological research on fairness also offers significant insights about the possibilities for state–society synergy. While the findings about representative bureaucracy are not straightforward, this research tradition also suggests lines of inquiry into state–society synergy.

A state–society synergy perspective must investigate not only how the state works constructively with society, but also how societies can mobilize to elicit and demand the best from their states. One of the places we see this is in discussions of social capital, which can contribute to effective and accountable governance (Chapter 6). A state–society synergy perspective would, however, always try to see both sides of the state–society relation. Thus, it might stress—as some governance theorists do—that the state can help cultivate social capital and build capacity for societal mobilization.

All this may sound insufficiently political, and a narrowly instrumental perspective on governance can often miss the political context in which governance takes place. Houtzager (2009) calls for a "polity" approach that connects state and society by looking at how pro-reform coalitions coalesce around the state. One way to do this is to further investigate the relationship between states, NGOs, and communities. The discussion in Chapter 8 shows that NGOs sometimes serve as effective intermediaries between state and society, although they can sometimes serve as agents of donors or states and lose sight of the communities they ostensibly serve.

In advancing the idea of state–society synergy, it is important to acknowledge some of its more ominous prospects. For example, in *The Art of Political Control in China*, Daniel Mattingly (2019) describes the way that the Chinese state works through society to achieve control over society. It does this, he finds, by cultivating non-state groups, by coopting communal elites and by building local networks of grassroots informants. His research shows "how a strong society can in fact complement a strong state" (Mattingly, 2019,

183). This instrumentalization of society is not what is envisioned here, but Mattingly's work serves as a cautionary note.

This brief sketch of a state–society synergy perspective is not meant to demonstrate that it either currently exists or that it is unproblematic. The important point is that a state–society synergy perspective provides a meta-theoretical framework for rethinking—or at least, refining—our thinking about governance. It suggests, in broad brushstrokes, a general benchmark against which governance developments can be probed and analyzed. This benchmark can be used to analyze how current modes of governance contribute to or fall short of state–society synergy.

HOW WE THEORIZE

The analysis in this book prompts several observations about governance theories *as* theories and suggests some strategies for improving theorizing in the future. The first observation is about the general terrain of governance theories. Collier and Mahon (1993) have drawn a distinction between classical and radial concepts, where the former have a distinct and clearly distinguishable set of defining features while the latter have a more variable and less well-bounded set. Extending this idea from concepts to theories, we would have to conclude that, on the whole, governance theories are more radial than classical in nature. They are more like a network of overlapping ideas than clearly demarcated domains of rival hypotheses.

Judged against Thomas Kuhn's conception of a scientific paradigm, these complexly overlapping ideas clearly look like the preparadigmatic stage that Kuhn called "proto-science." While such a judgement would be negative with respect to the development of an evidence base, it is less so with respect to the dialogical and diagnostic character of theories. A radial view of theories treats a theory as less of a prescriptive and deductive application of theory-to-case, and more as a toolbox of possible theories and concepts that may be used in combination to understand a particular situation. Access to a toolbox of governance ideas may be in practice more useful for dialoging and diagnosing specific situations than a single preeminent paradigm. As Weick (2007, 16) argues, we need a "headful of theories" to detect the richness of the world and, as Braithwaite (1996) suggests, we often need to scan through theories to find one that is useful for a particular context.

To say that radial theories have some potential advantages when it comes to dialogue and diagnosis, however, is not to say that this inevitably produces useful theory. A second very general observation is that many governance theories are highly descriptive as opposed to explanatory in nature. Descriptive theory is not per se a problem because description is fundamental to good theorizing (Gerring, 2012). Moreover, the discernment provided by good descriptive theory is essential for dialoging with and diagnosing specific cases. Governance theories often begin with a classification or typology that distinguishes different types, kinds, qualities or dimensions of governance and these distinctions can provide useful insights.

Too often, however, descriptive theory does not specify why the description matters. Various classifications are proposed, but they often remain "high-level" descriptions that are often of limited usefulness to theory users. Simple typologies often do not take us far into diagnosing cases and typically provide a static analysis. Phase, stage, or pathway models are better at capturing dynamics, but often at the cost of oversimplification or the imposition of linear thinking. While there is no simple recipe for improving description, keeping in mind how it can be used for dialogue and diagnosis may make it more powerful.

A third general observation is that our theories do have the tendency, as Mark Bevir and Rod Rhodes (2016) have argued, toward "reification"—that is, to abstract away from the meanings and agency that animates governance in practice. There are many Platonic ideal forms in the study of governance, and they can be useful for theorizing. But they can also be seriously misleading "on the ground" if they lose sight of the lived experiences of those who inhabit them (Hallett and Ventresca, 2006; Cleaver and De Koning, 2015). Systems perspectives, which have been particularly influential in governance theories, are particularly prone to reification.

This tendency toward institutional reification is related to a wider challenge for governance theories, and perhaps for all theories: the challenge of reconciling theoretical generality with contextual specificity. Consider the research on wicked problems. Scholars have made some progress toward identifying general approaches to addressing wicked problems, but the strategies they identify still feel frustratingly generic. This is not meant to be a criticism of specific theoretical work because this is a common dilemma: how can generic theory suggest meaningful strategies that apply to highly context-specific situations?

There is no easy resolution of this dilemma. Cox (2008, 6) discusses this challenge in the context of understanding common pool resource management and Ostrom's eight principles:

> the basic lesson is that concepts based on the aggregation of highly varied units are less meaningful and produce less meaningful theory when used. More important information describing low-level diversity is lost. This is the risk that Ostrom (1990) took when she constructed her design principles: the risk that they might lose meaning and be less applicable to particular CPR settings where someone might attempt to apply them.

This generality–specificity dilemma is softened somewhat when we think of theory in dialogical and diagnostic terms because theory tells us what to ask, not what to do. By querying the local context, users of theory may quickly discover that the questions are irrelevant or misleading. In this spirit, Pahl-Wostl et al. (2012, 25) call for a "generic but contextual diagnostic approach."

The tensions between generality and specificity are old ones. Ragin and Zaret (1983) note that our founding social scientists wrestled with just such issues and came up with different solutions. Weber sought to reconcile generality and specificity with his concept of "ideal types" (like "bureaucracy") and developed a "genetic" approach that sought to make "modest generalizations about historical diversity" (Ragin and Zaret, 1983, 741). Durkheim, by contrast, sought to identify "social species" that are "transhistorical generalizations, not concrete knowledge about specific cases," which led him toward a variable-oriented comparative method (Ragin and Zaret, 1983, 740). An implication of Ragin and Zaret's analysis for governance theories is that the variable-oriented approach tends to seek an overall theoretical account that subsumes diversity within the general account, whereas the genetic method tends to focus on explaining the diversity of types rather than arriving to a general account.

One possible way to think about the generality–specificity tension is in terms of "zooming in" and "zooming out." As we zoom in to any social situation, our observations become more fine-grained and what matters often changes. For example, Hulme (2004) argues that "thinking small" can be an important complement to "thinking big." Exploring the life histories of a single Bangladeshi household, Hulme shows that factors that are not really considered in "thinking big" become visible when investigating life histories. Most importantly, this focus on a single household reveals the household's own agency as a critical resource in addressing poverty. However, zooming out can also reveal patterns that might not be visible from such an intimate family portrait. They may identify structural forces or conditions that impinge on many families or communities, producing similar kinds of opportunities and constraints.

Another possible way that the generality–specific challenge might be managed is through better specification of generic or causal mechanisms. Rather than seeking to articulate general theories that apply across contexts, theories might be thought of as identifying a range of generic mechanisms that might be found in specific contexts. McAdam et al. (2001) put forward such a strategy in their ambitious effort to reformulate social movement theory. An instructive critical lesson is that this approach can lead to a growing "laundry list" of mechanisms. From the perspective of a search for a general theory that covers many cases, this is not helpful. However, viewed from a dialogical and diagnostic perspective, each case may be viewed as a unique combination of generic or causal mechanisms that must be identified through further inquiry.

Various other approaches have been proposed for bridging the distance between general theory and specific cases, including contingency theory (Ansell and Gash, 2008), middle-range theory (Cartwright, 2020), phronesis (Flyvbjerg et al., 2012) and configurational theory (Rihoux and Ragin, 2008). The configurational or set-theoretic approach is particularly promising, though it has mostly been adopted to date as a methodological rather than a theory-building tool. However, Raab et al. (2015) develop a configurational theory of network effectiveness that might serve as a useful model (see also, Smith, 2020 and Cristofoli and Markovic, 2016). This approach suggests that different "configurations" of conditions may come together in an "equifinal" way to produce a particular outcome, an approach that is more sensitive to contextual effects than to "net effects" (roughly speaking, the mean effects across contexts).

THE FUTURE OF GOVERNANCE THEORIES

This final section reflects on some broader themes about the nature of governance theories. Some of the tensions around governance theory arise from the different purposes that social scientists bring to understanding governance. Perhaps the dominant theoretical approach in the governance literature is *instrumental*. Instrumental theorists ask: how can governance be improved? How can we solve challenging problems, reduce poverty, or improve our protection of the environment? When does governance work well and when does it work poorly? As these questions suggest, this book is largely structured in an instrumental way. Instrumental theorists tend to seek solutions to governance problems and they are interested in how to design governing arrangements in ways that improve our capacity to govern. They tend to take power for granted or place it in the background. Although transforming power relations may be implicit in the ideas they develop (think, for example, of research on social accountability or sustainability transitions), they rarely frontload the discussion of power. They do not zero in on social movements, unionization or political protest as ways to amass the power needed to bring about governance change.

A very different kind of purpose is brought to the table by *critical* theorists. Their goal is not to improve governance or find better solutions to public problems or to design institutions that are more effective and accountable. Instead, the central agenda of critical theory is to critique the prevailing or proposed relations of society, including governance, for the purpose of liberating individuals and groups from the shackles of societal control. Critical theorists might ask: "whom does this governance arrangement serve?" They are highly attentive to the inequities created by governing institutions, and they foreground issues of power and dominance. They are keen observers of the insidious aspects of governance—such as how efforts to depoliticize or rationalize governance may in fact be another form of power or subordination. Critical theorists are deeply interested in the meaning of things and tend to adopt an interpretive approach to governance that is skeptical of the goals of positivist social science.

A third major purpose of governance theorists is *explanation*. The major goal of an explanatory theorist is to develop authoritative explanations of how the world is in order to improve our collective understanding of how it works. While this goal may overlap with either the goals of instrumental or critical theorists, explanatory theorists are cautious about moving into the realm of either design or ethical judgement. The central standard for explanatory theorists is to uphold the quality of explanations, and design and critique tend to threaten this quality through speculation or ideology. The theoretical questions they ask are often expressed as empirical hypotheses that can be judged and falsified through the collection of data with hypotheses such as "public service motivation will increase public employee satisfaction and reduce turnover" or "federalism will reduce ethnic violence."

While these different theoretical agendas—instrumental, critical, and explanatory—are not necessarily mutually exclusive and may be combined in various ways, they are often in tension or simply ignore or talk past one another. Consider the relationship between instrumental and critical theories of network governance. Instrumental theories, for example, tend to see network governance as a solution to a problem of complexity or divided power. They see network governance as emerging in situations where other strategies of governance have failed, and they are interested in investigating the conditions that make networks more or less successful in achieving particular societal goals. Critical theorists might approach network governance quite differently. They might see the public–private nature of networks as reflecting a larger political project of neoliberalism or the erosion of publicness.

This is a scenario in which instrumental and critical theorists talk past one another. From an instrumental perspective, the broader critical theory analysis does not really perceive or address the everyday challenges of governing and the need to respond to them. Its global critique, however valid, is mostly irrelevant from the perspective of getting services delivered under straightened conditions or coordinating groups with different interests and perspectives. Critical theorists are critical without offering up anything constructive for dealing with such governance challenges. From a critical perspective, instrumental theories may be well intentioned but by helping the trains run on time they may be aiding and abetting the enemy. They miss the bigger picture and the bigger fight, and by placing power in the background, they are politically naïve.

190   *Rethinking theories of governance*

The main point here is that instrumental and critical theorists mostly talk past each other, and this is a loss for both. Instrumental theorists need to build more reflexive criticism of governance practices into their analysis and critical theorists need to find ways to target their criticism in more constructive ways (people cannot be liberated simply by freeing them from dominant institutions). Instrumental theorists need to scale up their analysis to reflect on how they intersect with wider political currents and projects and critical theorists need to scale down their analysis so they can speak to concrete governance challenges. These adjustments are not easy for either side to make, but they could improve governance theories. A good example of how this might work is Turnbull's (2006) critique of the "problem-solving" perspective. He argues that an "instrumental approach" that prioritizes "discovering discrete solutions to a finite problem" (2006, 6) often fails to understand the meaning of problems and that analysis should begin by considering what makes a problem a problem (*problematicity*). Here, he manages to be both critical and constructive.

Instrumental and critical theorists also talk past explanatory theorists to varying degrees. Instrumental and explanatory theorists are perhaps naturally closer in spirit because many concerns about how well governance works can be framed as explanatory projects. However, the more that instrumental theorists probe possible futures or deviant cases, they tend to depart from the comfort zone of explanatory theorists. In addition, instrumental theory tends to foreground consequentialist reasoning (how can we improve governance?) that explanatory theories are more inclined to leave in the background. From an explanatory view, instrumental theorists are too willing to depart from standards of explanatory excellence to speculate on the design of governance institutions. From an instrumental point of view, explanatory theorists produce too many high-quality analyses that do not matter much.

The tension between explanatory and critical theories tends to be sharper. The standard of excellence for explanatory theorists is the ability to demonstrate causation, a difficult endeavor. Critical theorists, by contrast, tend to eschew causal explanation altogether. While explanatory theorists are interested in how people think, they tend to adopt a relatively schematic perspective on meaning that is tractable for causal analysis. Unconcerned about causal explanation, critical theorists tend to adopt a richer view of meaning, stressing its ambiguities and paradoxes, and they often rely on this richness to interpret the meaning of situations.

There is no simple resolution to these differences, because they are grounded in principled commitments and express different standards, values and purposes. But thinking of governance theories in terms of whether they are warranted, dialogical and diagnostic can go some distance toward drawing them together. A warranted theory is one that has marshaled evidence to support its claims to the satisfaction of those who would wish to use the theory. Warranted theories typically build on causal explanation and rely on the standards of excellence that explanatory theorists advocate. However, this book has argued that warranted theory is only the beginning of inquiry and useful theory goes further and helps us dialogue with and diagnose specific governance situations. Critical and instrumental theories are particularly useful for these purposes. Critical analysis can help those who would use governance theories to reflect critically on the ethical and political problems that all efforts at governance encounter, while instrumental analysis can help identify possible success and failure factors in a given governance situation. Bringing instrumental, critical and explanatory approaches into a constructive dialogue can enhance the value of future theories of governance.

References

Abbott, K. W., & Bernstein, S. (2015). The high-level political forum on sustainable development: Orchestration by default and design. *Global Policy, 6*(3), 222–233.

Abbott, K. W., & Snidal, D. (2009). Strengthening international regulation through transmittal new governance: Overcoming the orchestration deficit. *Vanderbilt Journal of Transnational Law, 42*, 501–578.

Abbott, K. W., & Snidal, D. (2010). International regulation without international government: Improving IO performance through orchestration. *Review of International Organizations, 5*(3), 315–344.

Abbott, K. W., Genschel, P., Snidal, D., & Zangl, B. (Eds.) (2015). *International Organizations as Orchestrators*. Cambridge: Cambridge University Press.

Abend, G. (2008). The meaning of "theory". *Sociological Theory, 26*(2), 173–199.

Aberbach, J., Putnam, R. D., & Rockman, B. (1981). *Bureaucrats and Politicians in Western Democracies*. Cambridge, MA: Harvard University Press.

Abson, D. J., Fischer, J., Leventon, J., Newig, J., Schomerus, T., Vilsmaier, U., & Lang, D. J. (2017). Leverage points for sustainability transformation. *Ambio, 46*, 30–39. https://doi.org/10.1007/s13280-016-0800-y.

Adler, P. S., & Kwon, S. W. (2002). Social capital: Prospects for a new concept. *Academy of Management Review, 27*(1), 17–40.

Agranoff, R. (1986). *Intergovernmental Management: Human Services Problem-solving in Six Metropolitan Areas*. Albany: SUNY Press.

Agranoff, R., & McGuire, M. (2001). Big questions in public network management research. *Journal of Public Administration Research and Theory, 11*(3), 295–326.

Agrawal, A. (2001). Common property institutions and sustainable governance of resources. *World Development, 29*(10), 1649–1672.

Ahmed, S. M., Evans, T. G., Standing, H., & Mahmud, S. (2013). Harnessing pluralism for better health in Bangladesh. *The Lancet, 382*(9906), 1746–1755.

Aleksovska, M., Schillemans, T., & Grimmelikhuijsen, S. (2019). Lessons from five decades of experimental and behavioral research on accountability: A systematic literature review. *Journal of Behavioral Public Administration, 2*(2). https://doi.org/10.30636/jbpa.22.66.

Alford, J. (2014). The multiple facets of co-production: Building on the work of Elinor Ostrom. *Public Management Review, 16*(3), 299–316.

Alford, J., & Head, B. W. (2017). Wicked and less wicked problems: A typology and a contingency framework. *Policy and Society, 36*(3), 397–413.

Aligica, P. D., & Tarko, V. (2012). Polycentricity: From Polanyi to Ostrom, and beyond. *Governance, 25*(2), 237–262.

Allen, C. R., Fontaine, J. J., Pope, K. L., & Garmestani, A. S. (2011). Adaptive management for a turbulent future. *Journal of Environmental Management, 92*(5), 1339–1345.

Alonso, J. M., Clifton, J., & Díaz-Fuentes, D. (2015). Did new public management matter? An empirical analysis of the outsourcing and decentralization effects on public sector size. *Public Management Review, 17*(5), 643–660.

Alter, K. J., & Raustiala, K. (2018). The rise of international regime complexity. *Annual Review of Law and Social Science, 14*, 329–349.

Altunbaş, Y., & Thornton, J. (2012). Fiscal decentralization and governance. *Public Finance Review, 40*(1), 66–85.

Amirkhanyan, A. A., Kim, H. J., & Lambright, K. T. (2007). Putting the pieces together: A comprehensive framework for understanding the decision to contract out and contractor performance. *International Journal of Public Administration, 30*(6–7), 699–725.

An, J., & Yoo, I. T. (2019). Internet governance regimes by epistemic community: Formation and diffusion in Asia. *Global Governance: A Review of Multilateralism and International Organizations, 25*(1), 123–148.

Andersen, L. B., Boesen, A., & Pedersen, L. H. (2016). Performance in public organizations: Clarifying the conceptual space. *Public Administration Review, 76*(6), 852–862.

Andersson, K. P., & Ostrom, E. (2008). Analyzing decentralized resource regimes from a polycentric perspective. *Policy Sciences, 41*, 71–93.

Andeweg, R. B. (2000). Consociational democracy. *Annual Review of Political Science, 3*(1), 509–536.

Andonova, L. B. (2017). *Governance Entrepreneurs: International Organizations and the Rise of Global Public–Private Partnerships*. Cambridge: Cambridge University Press.

Andrews, M. (2008). The good governance agenda: Beyond indicators without theory. *Oxford Development Studies, 36*(4), 379–407.

Andrews, M., Pritchett, L., & Woolcock, M. (2013). Escaping capability traps through problem driven iterative adaptation (PDIA). *World Development, 51*, 234–244.

Andrews, M., Pritchett, L., & Woolcock, M. (2017). *Building State Capability: Evidence, Analysis, Action*. Oxford: Oxford University Press.

Ansell, C. (2011). *Pragmatist Democracy: Evolutionary Learning as Public Philosophy*. New York: Oxford University Press.

Ansell, C., & Gash, A. (2008). Collaborative governance in theory and practice. *Journal of Public Administration Research and Theory, 18*(4), 543–571.

Ansell, C., & Gash, A. (2012). Stewards, mediators, and catalysts: Toward a model of collaborative leadership. *Innovation Journal, 17*(1), 1–21.

Ansell, C., & Geyer, R. (2017). "Pragmatic complexity": A new foundation for moving beyond "evidence-based policy making"? *Policy Studies, 38*(2), 149–167.

Ansell, C., & Torfing, J. (Eds.) (2016). *Handbook on Theories of Governance*. Cheltenham, UK and Northampton, MA, USA: Edward Elgar Publishing.

Ansell, C., & Torfing, J. (2021a). Co-creation: The new kid on the block in public governance. *Policy & Politics, 49*(2), 211–230.

Ansell, C., & Torfing, J. (2021b). *Public Governance as Co-creation: A Strategy for Revitalizing the Public Sector and Rejuvenating Democracy*. Cambridge: Cambridge University Press.

Ansell, C. K., Comfort, L., Keller, A., LaPorte, T., & Schulman, P. (2021). The loss of capacity in public organizations: A public administration challenge. *Perspectives on Public Management and Governance, 4*(1), 24–29.

Ansell, C., Doberstein, C., Henderson, H., Siddiki, S., & 't Hart, P. (2020). Understanding inclusion in collaborative governance: A mixed methods approach. *Policy and Society, 39*(4), 570–591.

Ansell, C., Sørensen, E., & Torfing, J. (2021). When governance theory meets democratic theory: The potential contribution of cocreation to democratic governance. *Perspectives on Public Management and Governance*, *4*(4), 346–362.

Araral, E. (2014). Ostrom, Hardin and the commons: A critical appreciation and a revisionist view. *Environmental Science & Policy*, *36*, 11–23.

Armitage, D. (2008). Governance and the commons in a multi-level world. *International Journal of the Commons*, *2*(1), 7–32.

Armitage, D., Marschke, M., & Plummer, R. (2008). Adaptive co-management and the paradox of learning. *Global Environmental Change*, *18*(1), 86–98.

Armitage, D. R., Plummer, R., Berkes, F., Arthur, R. I., Charles, A. T., Davidson-Hunt, I. J., Johnson, D. S., Marschke, M., McConney, P., Pinkerton, E. W., & Wollenberg, E. K. (2009). Adaptive co-management for social–ecological complexity. *Frontiers in Ecology and the Environment*, *7*(2), 95–102.

Arnstein, S. R. (1969). A ladder of citizen participation. *Journal of the American Institute of Planners*, *35*(4), 216–224.

Arora, P., & Chong, A. (2018). Government effectiveness in the provision of public goods: The role of institutional quality. *Journal of Applied Economics*, *21*(1), 175–196.

Asadullah, M. N., & Savoia, A. (2018). Poverty reduction during 1990–2013: Did millennium development goals adoption and state capacity matter? *World Development*, *105*, 70–82.

Åström, J., Jonsson, M. E., & Karlsson, M. (2017). Democratic innovations: Reinforcing or changing perceptions of trust? *International Journal of Public Administration*, *40*(7), 575–587.

Avelino, F., Grin, J., Pel, B., & Jhagroe, S. (2016). The politics of sustainability transitions. *Journal of Environmental Policy & Planning*, *18*(5), 557–567.

Awashreh, R. (2018). Palestinian NGOs: External governance, stakeholders, and accountability. *Journal of Governance and Public Policy*, *5*(2), 165–210.

Bache, I., Bartle, I., & Flinders, M. (2016). Multi-level governance. In C. Ansell & J. Torfing (Eds.) *Handbook on Theories of Governance*. Cheltenham, UK and Northampton, MA, USA: Edward Elgar Publishing, pp. 486–498.

Bäckstrand, K., Khan, J., Kronsell, A., & Lovbrand, E. (2010). Environmental politics after the deliberative turn. In *Environmental Politics and Deliberative Democracy*. Cheltenham, UK and Northampton, MA, USA: Edward Elgar Publishing, pp. 217–234.

Baekgaard, M., & Serritzlew, S. (2016). Interpreting performance information: Motivated reasoning or unbiased comprehension. *Public Administration Review*, *76*(1), 73–82.

Bali, A. S., Capano, G., & Ramesh, M. (2019). Anticipating and designing for policy effectiveness. *Policy and Society*, *38*(1), 1–13.

Banks, N., & Hulme, D. (2012). The role of NGOs and civil society in development and poverty reduction. Brooks World Poverty Institute Working Paper, 171.

Banzhaf, S., Ma, L., & Timmins, C. (2019). Environmental justice: The economics of race, place, and pollution. *Journal of Economic Perspectives*, *33*(1), 185–208.

Bardhan, P. (2002). Decentralization of governance and development. *Journal of Economic Perspectives*, *16*(4), 185–205.

Barnett, M., & Finnemore, M. (2012). *Rules for the World: International Organizations in Global Politics*. Ithaca: Cornell University Press.

Barrett, C. B., & Carter, M. R. (2013). The economics of poverty traps and persistent poverty: Empirical and policy implications. *Journal of Development Studies, 49*(7), 976–990.

Barrett, C. B., & Swallow, B. M. (2006). Fractal poverty traps. *World Development, 34*(1), 1–15.

Barrett, C. B., Brandon, K., Gibson, C., & Gjertsen, H. (2001). Conserving tropical biodiversity amid weak institutions. *BioScience, 51*(6), 497–502.

Bartkowski, B., & Bartke, S. (2018). Leverage points for governing agricultural soils: A review of empirical studies of European farmers' decision-making. *Sustainability, 10*(9), 3179.

Bartley, T. (2018). Transnational corporations and global governance. *Annual Review of Sociology, 44*, 145–165.

Bartley, T. (2022). Power and the practice of transnational private regulation. *New Political Economy, 27*(2), 188–202.

Bartley, T., Andersson, K., Jagger, P., & Laerhoven, F. V. (2008). The contribution of institutional theories to explaining decentralization of natural resource governance. *Society and Natural Resources, 21*(2), 160–174.

Bass, B. M. (1990). From transactional to transformational leadership: Learning to share the vision. *Organizational Dynamics, 18*(3), 19–31.

Bass, B. M., & Avolio, B. J. (1993). Transformational leadership and organizational culture. *Public Administration Quarterly, 17*(1), 112–121.

Bauer, M. W., & Becker, S. (2020). Democratic backsliding, populism, and public administration. *Perspectives on Public Management and Governance, 3*(1), 19–31.

Beck, U. (1986). *Risk Society: Towards a New Modernity*. London: Sage Publications.

Beck, U., Giddens, A., & Lash, S. (1994). *Reflexive Modernization: Politics, Tradition and Aesthetics in the Modern Social Order*. Palo Alto: Stanford University Press.

Behn, R. D. (2001). *Rethinking Democratic Accountability*. Washington, DC: Brookings Institution Press.

Behn, R. D. (2003). Why measure performance? Different purposes require different measures. *Public Administration Review, 63*(5), 586–606.

Behn, R. (2009). *Leadership Counts: Lessons for Public Managers from the Massachusetts Welfare, Training, and Employment Program*. Cambridge, MA: Harvard University Press

Benner, T., Reinicke, W. H., & Witte, J. M. (2004). Multisectoral networks in global governance: Towards a pluralistic system of accountability. *Government and Opposition, 39*(2), 191–210.

Bennett, J., Sjölander-Lindqvist, A., Sandström, C., & Larsson, S. (2022). Addressing the Swedish large carnivore controversy: Identifying roadblocks in collaborative governance to reduce conflict. *Frontiers in Conservation Science, 3*. article id 952242.

Bennett, N. J. (2019). In political seas: Engaging with political ecology in the ocean and coastal environment. *Coastal Management, 47*(1), 67–87.

Berardo, R., & Lubell, M. (2016). Understanding what shapes a polycentric governance system. *Public Administration Review, 76*(5), 738–751.

Berdej, S. M., & Armitage, D. R. (2016). Bridging organizations drive effective governance outcomes for conservation of Indonesia's marine systems. *PloS One, 11*(1), e0147142.

Berkes, F. (2009). Evolution of co-management: Role of knowledge generation, bridging organizations and social learning. *Journal of Environmental Management, 90*(5), 1692–1702.

Berkman, E. T., & Wilson, S. M. (2021). So useful as a good theory? The practicality crisis in (social) psychological theory. *Perspectives on Psychological Science, 16*(4), 864–874.

Bernauer, J., Bühlmann, M., Vatter, A., & Germann, M. (2016). Taking the multidimensionality of democracy seriously: Institutional patterns and the quality of democracy. *European Political Science Review, 8*(3), 473–494.

Berrone, P., Gelabert, L., Massa-Saluzzo, F., & Rousseau, H. E. (2016). Understanding community dynamics in the study of grand challenges: How nonprofits, institutional actors, and the community fabric interact to influence income inequality. *Academy of Management Journal, 59*(6), 1940–1964.

Bersch, K., Praça, S., & Taylor, M. M. (2017). State capacity, bureaucratic politicization, and corruption in the Brazilian state. *Governance, 30*(1), 105–124.

Berwick, E., & Christia, F. (2018). State capacity redux: Integrating classical and experimental contributions to an enduring debate. *Annual Review of Political Science, 21*, 71–91.

Besada, H., Agarwal, M., & McMillan Polonenko, L. (Eds.) (2017). *Did the Millennium Development Goals Work? Meeting Future Challenges with Past Lessons*. Bristol: Policy Press.

Besley, T. J., Burgess, R., Khan, A., & Xu, G. (2021). Bureaucracy and development. NBER Working Paper 29163.

Betsill, M. M., & Bulkeley, H. (2006). Cities and the multilevel governance of global climate change. *Global Governance, 12*, 141–159.

Betts, A. (2013). Regime complexity and international organizations: UNHCR as a challenged institution. *Global Governance: A Review of Multilateralism and International Organizations, 19*(1), 69–81.

Bevir, M. (2010). *Democratic Governance*. Princeton: Princeton University Press.

Bevir, M. (2011). Governance and governmentality after neoliberalism. *Policy & Politics, 39*(4), 457–471.

Bevir, M. (2013). *A Theory of Governance*. Berkeley: Global, Area, International Archives.

Bevir, M., & Krupicka, B. (2011). On two types of governance theory: A response to B. Guy Peters. *Critical Policy Studies, 5*(4), 450–453.

Bevir, M., & Rhodes, R. A. W. (2016). *Rethinking Governance: Ruling, Rationality, Resistance*. London: Routledge.

Bianchi, C., Bovaird, T., & Loeffler, E. (2017). Applying a dynamic performance management framework to wicked issues: How coproduction helps to transform young people's services in Surrey County Council, UK. *International Journal of Public Administration, 40*(10), 833–846.

Biermann, F., & Pattberg, P. (2008). Global environmental governance: Taking stock, moving forward. *Annual Review of Environment and Resources, 33*(1), 277–294.

Biermann, F., Kanie, N., & Kim, R. E. (2017). Global governance by goal-setting: The novel approach of the UN Sustainable Development Goals. *Current Opinion in Environmental Sustainability, 26*, 26–31.

Biermann, F., Man-san Chan, A. M., & Pattberg, P. (2007). Multi-stakeholder partnerships for sustainable development: Does the promise hold? In P. Glasbergen, F. Biermann, & A. P. Mol (Eds.) *Partnerships, Governance and Sustainable Development: Reflections on Theory and Practice*. Cheltenham, UK and Northampton, MA, USA: Edward Elgar Publishing, pp. 239–260.

Bingham, L. B., Nabatchi, T., & O'Leary, R. (2005). The new governance: Practices and processes for stakeholder and citizen participation in the work of government. *Public Administration Review*, *65*(5), 547–558.

Boege, V., Brown, M. A., & Clements, K. P. (2009). Hybrid political orders, not fragile states. *Peace Review*, *21*(1), 13–21.

Bogaards, M., Helms, L., & Lijphart, A. (2019). The importance of consociationalism for twenty-first century politics and political science. *Swiss Political Science Review*, *25*(4), 341–356.

Boin, A. (2001). *Crafting Public Institutions: Leadership in Two Prison Systems*. Boulder: Lynne Rienner Publishers.

Boin, A., & Christensen, T. (2008). The development of public institutions: Reconsidering the role of leadership. *Administration & Society*, *40*(3), 271–297.

Boix, C., & Posner, D. N. (1998). Social capital: Explaining its origins and effects on government performance. *British Journal of Political Science*, *28*(4), 686–693.

Bornstein, A. (2015). Institutional racism, numbers management, and zero-tolerance policing in New York City. *North American Dialogue*, *18*(2), 51–62.

Borrás, S., & Conzelmann, T. (2007). Democracy, legitimacy and soft modes of governance in the EU: The empirical turn. *European Integration*, *29*(5), 531–548.

Börzel, T. A., & Risse, T. (2010). Governance without a state: Can it work? *Regulation & Governance*, *4*(2), 113–134.

Bours, S. A., Wanzenböck, I., & Frenken, K. (2021). Small wins for grand challenges: A bottom-up governance approach to regional innovation policy. *European Planning Studies*, *30*(11), 2245–2272.

Bovaird, T., & Loeffler, E. (2012). From engagement to co-production: The contribution of users and communities to outcomes and public value. *Voluntas: International Journal of Voluntary and Nonprofit Organizations*, *23*(4), 1119–1138.

Bovaird, T., Flemig, S., Loeffler, E., & Osborne, S. P. (2019). How far have we come with co-production—and what's next? *Public Money & Management*, *39*(4), 229–232.

Bovens, M. (2007). Analysing and assessing accountability: A conceptual framework. *European Law Journal*, *13*(4), 447–468.

Bowles, S., & Gintis, H. (2002). Social capital and community governance. *Economic Journal*, *112*(483), F419–F436.

Bown, N., Gray, T. S., & Stead, S. M. (2013). *Contested Forms of Governance in Marine Protected Areas: A Study of Co-Management and Adaptive Co-Management*. London: Routledge.

Boyne, G. A. (2014). Performance management: Does it work? In R. M. Waltker, G. A. Boyne, & G. A. Brewer (Eds.) *Public Management and Performance: Research Directions*. Cambridge: Cambridge University Press, pp. 207–226.

Boyne, G. A., & Walker, R. M. (2010). Strategic management and public service performance: The way ahead. *Public Administration Review*, *70*, s185–s192.

Bradbury, M., & Kellough, J. E. (2011). Representative bureaucracy: Assessing the evidence on active representation. *American Review of Public Administration*, *41*(2), 157–167.

Bradshaw, T. K. (2007). Theories of poverty and anti-poverty programs in community development. *Community Development*, *38*(1), 7–25.

Brady, D. (2005). The welfare state and relative poverty in rich western democracies, 1967–1997. *Social Forces*, *83*(4), 1329–1364.

Brady, D., & Bostic, A. (2015). Paradoxes of social policy: Welfare transfers, relative poverty, and redistribution preferences. *American Sociological Review*, *80*(2), 268–298.

Braithwaite, J. (1996). Beyond positivism: Learning from contextual integrated strategies. *Journal of Research in Crime and Delinquency*, *30*(4), 383–399.

Braithwaite, V. (1998). Communal and exchange trust norms: Their value base and relevance to institutional trust. In V. Braithwaite & M. Levi (Eds.) *Trust and Governance*. New York: Russell Sage Foundation, pp. 46–74.

Braithwaite, V., & Levi, M. (Eds.). (1998). *Trust and Governance*. New York: Russell Sage Foundation.

Brandsen, T., & Honingh, M. (2016). Distinguishing different types of coproduction: A conceptual analysis based on the classical definitions. *Public Administration Review*, *76*(3), 427–435.

Brandsen, T., Trommel, W., & Verschuere, B. (2017). The state and the reconstruction of civil society. *International Review of Administrative Sciences*, *83*(4), 676–693.

Brass, J. N., Longhofer, W., Robinson, R. S., & Schnable, A. (2018). NGOs and international development: A review of thirty-five years of scholarship. *World Development*, *112*, 136–149.

Brehm, J. O., & Gates, S. (1999). *Working, Shirking, and Sabotage: Bureaucratic Response to a Democratic Public*. Ann Arbor: University of Michigan Press.

Breitmeier, H., Underdal, A., & Young, O. R. (2011). The effectiveness of international environmental regimes: Comparing and contrasting findings from quantitative research. *International Studies Review*, *13*(4), 579–605.

Brewer, G. A., & Selden, S. C. (2000). Why elephants gallop: Assessing and predicting organizational performance in federal agencies. *Journal of Public Administration Research and Theory*, *10*(4), 685–712.

Brewer, G. A., Choi, Y., & Walker, R. M. (2007). Accountability, corruption and government effectiveness in Asia: An exploration of World Bank governance indicators. *International Public Management Review*, *8*(2), 204–225.

Briggs, X. D. S. (2008). *Democracy as Problem Solving: Civic Capacity in Communities Across the Globe*. Cambridge, MA: MIT Press.

Brinkerhoff, D. W. (2011). State fragility and governance: Conflict mitigation and subnational perspectives. *Development Policy Review*, *29*(2), 131–153.

Brinkerhoff, D. W., & Wetterberg, A. (2016). Gauging the effects of social accountability on services, governance, and citizen empowerment. *Public Administration Review*, *76*(2), 274–286.

Brown, T. L., Potoski, M., & Van Slyke, D. M. (2006). Managing public service contracts: Aligning values, institutions, and markets. *Public Administration Review*, *66*(3), 323–331.

Brown, W. (2015). *Undoing the Demos: Neoliberalism's Stealth Revolution*. Cambridge, MA: MIT Press.

Brulle, R. J., & Pellow, D. N. (2006). Environmental justice. *Annual Review of Public Health*, *27*, 103–124.

Brunner, R. D., Steelman, T. A., Coe-Juell, L., Cromley, C. M., Edwards, C. M., & Tucker, D. W. (2005). *Adaptive Governance: Integrating Science, Policy, and Decision Making*. New York: Columbia University Press.

Bryson, J. M. (2018). *Strategic Planning for Public and Nonprofit Organizations: A Guide to Strengthening and Sustaining Organizational Achievement*. New York: John Wiley & Sons.

Burns, J. M. (1978). *Leadership*. New York: Harper and Row.

Buse, K., & Harmer, A. M. (2007). Seven habits of highly effective global public–private health partnerships: Practice and potential. *Social Science & Medicine, 64*(2), 259–271.

Buse, K., & Tanaka, S. (2011). Global public–private health partnerships: Lessons learned from ten years of experience and evaluation. *International Dental Journal, 61*, 2–10.

Buse, K., & Walt, G. (2000a). Global public–private partnerships: Part I—a new development in health? *Bulletin of the World Health Organization, 78*, 549–561.

Buse, K., & Walt, G. (2000b). Global public–private partnerships: Part II—what are the health issues for global governance? *Bulletin of the World Health Organization, 78*, 699–709.

Caillier, J. G. (2016). Do transformational leaders affect turnover intentions and extra-role behaviors through mission valence? *American Review of Public Administration, 46*(2), 226–242.

Cairney, P. (2018). Three habits of successful policy entrepreneurs. *Policy & Politics, 46*(2), 199–215.

Cairney, P. (2022). The myth of "evidence-based policymaking" in a decentred state. *Public Policy and Administration, 37*(1), 46–66.

Cairney, P., & Geyer, R. (2017). A critical discussion of complexity theory: How does complexity thinking improve our understanding of politics and policymaking? *Complexity, Governance and Networks, 3*(2), 1–11.

Campbell, S. P. (2018). *Global Governance and Local Peace: Accountability and Performance in International Peacebuilding.* Cambridge: Cambridge University Press.

Canare, T., Francisco, J. P., & Caliso, R. A. C. (2020). Decentralization and income inequality in a panel and cross-section of countries. *Journal of International Development, 32*(4), 543–579.

Cantillon, B. (2011). The paradox of the social investment state: Growth, employment and poverty in the Lisbon era. *Journal of European Social Policy, 21*(5), 432–449.

Capano, G., & Woo, J. J. (2017). Resilience and robustness in policy design: A critical appraisal. *Policy Sciences, 50*(3), 399–426.

Capano, G., & Woo, J. J. (2018). Designing policy robustness: Outputs and processes. *Policy and Society, 37*(4), 422–440.

Capano, G., Howlett, M., Jarvis, D. S., Ramesh, M., & Goyal, N. (2020). Mobilizing policy (in) capacity to fight COVID-19: Understanding variations in state responses. *Policy and Society, 39*(3), 285–308.

Carlisle, K., & Gruby, R. L. (2019). Polycentric systems of governance: A theoretical model for the commons. *Policy Studies Journal, 47*(4), 927–952.

Carlsson, L., & Berkes, F. (2005). Co-management: Concepts and methodological implications. *Journal of Environmental Management, 75*(1), 65–76.

Carlsson, L., & Sandström, A. (2008). Network governance of the commons. *International Journal of the Commons, 2*(1), 33–54.

Carpenter, D. (2001). The forging of bureaucratic autonomy. In *The Forging of Bureaucratic Autonomy.* Princeton, NJ: Princeton University Press.

Cartwright, N. (2020). Middle-range theory. *Theoria: An International Journal for Theory, History and Foundations of Science, 35*(3), 269–323.

Cashore, B. (2002). Legitimacy and the privatization of environmental governance: How non-state market-driven (NSMD) governance systems gain rule-making authority. *Governance: An International Journal of Policy, Administration, and Institutions, 15*(4), 503–529.

Cashore, B., Knudsen, J. S., Moon, J., & van der Ven, H. (2021). Private authority and public policy interactions in global context: Governance spheres for problem solving. *Regulation & Governance, 15*(4), 1166–1182.

Cento Bull, A., & Jones, B. (2006). Governance and social capital in urban regeneration: A comparison between Bristol and Naples. *Urban Studies, 43*(4), 767–786.

Cepiku, D., Giordano, F., Mastrodascio, M., & Wang, W. (2021). What drives network effectiveness? A configurational approach. *Public Management Review, 23*(10), 1479–1503.

Chaffin, B. C., Gosnell, H., & Cosens, B. A. (2014). A decade of adaptive governance scholarship: Synthesis and future directions. *Ecology and Society, 19*(3), 56.

Chan, K. M., Boyd, D. R., Gould, R. K., Jetzkowitz, J., Liu, J., Muraca, B., ... & Brondízio, E. S. (2020). Levers and leverage points for pathways to sustainability. *People and Nature, 2*(3), 693–717.

Chandradasa, A. M. (2014). Effectiveness and impact of community governance approach to alleviate poverty: A case study of Care International Hambantota Sri Lanka. *Journal of Asian Scientific Research, 4*(7), 392–407.

Chang, E. C., & Kerr, N. N. (2017). An insider–outsider theory of popular tolerance for corrupt politicians. *Governance, 30*(1), 67–84.

Chhotray, V., & Stoker, G. (2009). Governance: From theory to practice. In *Governance Theory and Practice*. London: Palgrave Macmillan, pp. 214–247.

Chisholm, D. (1995). Problem solving and institutional design. *Journal of Public Administration Research and Theory, 5*(4), 451–492.

Choi, S., & Rainey, H. G. (2014). Organizational fairness and diversity management in public organizations: Does fairness matter in managing diversity? *Review of Public Personnel Administration, 34*(4), 307–331.

Christensen, R. K., Paarlberg, L., & Perry, J. L. (2017). Public service motivation research: Lessons for practice. *Public Administration Review, 77*(4), 529–542.

Christensen, T., & Lægreid, P. (2007). Regulatory agencies—The challenges of balancing agency autonomy and political control. *Governance, 20*(3), 499–520.

Christensen, T., & Lægreid, P. (2011). Democracy and administrative policy: Contrasting elements of New Public Management (NPM) and post-NPM. *European Political Science Review, 3*(1), 125–146.

Cingolani, L., & Fazekas, M. (2020). The role of agencification in achieving value-for-money in public spending. *Governance, 33*(3), 545–563.

Cingolani, L., Thomsson, K., & De Crombrugghe, D. (2015). Minding Weber more than ever? The impacts of state capacity and bureaucratic autonomy on development goals. *World Development, 72*, 191–207.

Clarke, N., Jennings, W., Moss, J., & Stoker, G. (2018). *The Good Politician: Folk Theories, Political Interaction, and the Rise of Anti-politics*. Cambridge: Cambridge University Press.

Cleaver, F., & De Koning, J. (2015). Furthering critical institutionalism. *International Journal of the Commons, 9*(1), 1–18.

Cleaver, F., & Whaley, L. (2018). Understanding process, power, and meaning in adaptive governance. *Ecology and Society, 23*(2), 49.

Coccia, M. (2021). How a good governance of institutions can reduce poverty and inequality in society? In N. Faghih & A. H. Samadi (Eds.) *Legal-Economic Institutions, Entrepreneurship, and Management, Perspectives on the Dynamics of Institutional Change from Emerging Markets*. Cham: Springer Nature pp. 65–94

Cohen, F. S. (1997). Proportional versus majoritarian ethnic conflict management in democracies. *Comparative Political Studies, 30*(5), 607–630.

Colander, D., & Kupers, R. (2014). *Complexity and the Art of Public Policy*. Princeton, NJ: Princeton University Press.

Collier, D., & Mahon, J. E. (1993). Conceptual "stretching" revisited: Adapting categories in comparative analysis. *American Political Science Review, 87*(4), 845–855.

Collins, D., Beckett, K., & Brydolf-Horwitz, M. (2022). Pandemic poverty governance: Neoliberalism under crisis. *City & Community*, 15356841221140078.

Conklin, J. (2005). *Dialogue Mapping: Building Shared Understanding of Wicked Problems*. New York: John Wiley & Sons, Inc.

Coolsaet, B. (Ed.) (2020). *Environmental Justice: Key Issues*. London: Routledge.

Cornelissen, J., Höllerer, M. A., & Seidl, D. (2021). What theory is and can be: Forms of theorizing in organizational scholarship. *Organization Theory, 2*(3), 26317877211020328.

Cortright, D., Seyle, C., & Wall, K. (2017). *Governance for Peace: How Inclusive, Participatory and Accountable Institutions Promote Peace and Prosperity*. Cambridge: Cambridge University Press.

Cox, M. (2008). Balancing accuracy and meaning in common-pool resource theory. *Ecology and Society, 13*(2), 44.

Cox, M., Arnold, G., & Tomás, S. V. (2010). A review of design principles for community-based natural resource management. *Ecology and Society, 15*(4), 38.

Craig, D. A., & Porter, D. (2006). *Development beyond Neoliberalism? Governance, Poverty Reduction and Political Economy*. London: Routledge.

Crawford, G. (2008). Decentralization and the limits to poverty reduction: Findings from Ghana. *Oxford Development Studies, 36*(2), 235–258.

Crick, B. (1962). *In Defence of Politics*. London: Weidenfeld & Nicolson.

Cristofoli, D., & Markovic, J. (2016). How to make public networks really work: A qualitative comparative analysis. *Public Administration, 94*(1), 89–110.

Crook, R., & Sverrisson, A. S. (2003). Does decentralization contribute to poverty reduction. In P. P. Houtzager & M. P. Moore (Eds.) *Changing Paths: International Development and the New Politics of Inclusion*. Ann Arbor: University of Michigan Press, pp. 233–259.

Crosby, B. C., & Bryson, J. M. (2005). *Leadership for the Common Good: Tackling Public Problems in a Shared-Power World*. New York: John Wiley & Sons.

Crosby, B. C., & Bryson, J. M. (2010). Integrative leadership and the creation and maintenance of cross-sector collaborations. *Leadership Quarterly, 21*(2), 211–230.

Crosby, B. C., & Bryson, J. M. (2018). Why leadership of public leadership research matters: And what to do about it. *Public Management Review, 20*(9), 1265–1286.

Crosby, B. C., 't Hart, P., & Torfing, J. (2017). Public value creation through collaborative innovation. *Public Management Review, 19*(5), 655–669.

Cross, M. D. (2013). Rethinking epistemic communities twenty years later. *Review of International Studies, 39*(1), 137–160.

Crowley, K., & Head, B. W. (2017). The enduring challenge of "wicked problems": Revisiting Rittel and Webber. *Policy Sciences, 50*(4), 539–547.

Cucciniello, M., Porumbescu, G. A., & Grimmelikhuijsen, S. (2017). 25 years of transparency research: Evidence and future directions. *Public Administration Review, 77*(1), 32–44.

Curato, N., & Böker, M. (2016). Linking mini-publics to the deliberative system: A research agenda. *Policy Sciences, 49*(2), 173–190.

Da Cruz, N. F., Rode, P., & McQuarrie, M. (2019). New urban governance: A review of current themes and future priorities. *Journal of Urban Affairs, 41*(1), 1–19.

Dahlberg, S., & Holmberg, S. (2014). Democracy and bureaucracy: How their quality matters for popular satisfaction. *West European Politics, 37*(3), 515–537.

Dahlström, C., & Lapuente, V. (2017). *Organizing Leviathan: Politicians, Bureaucrats, and the Making of Good Government.* Cambridge: Cambridge University Press.

Dahlström, C., Lapuente, V., & Teorell, J. (2012). The merit of meritocratization: Politics, bureaucracy, and the institutional deterrents of corruption. *Political Research Quarterly, 65*(3), 656–668.

Dan, S., & Pollitt, C. (2015). NPM Can Work: An optimistic review of the impact of New Public Management reforms in central and eastern Europe. *Public Management Review, 17*(9), 1305–1332.

Daviter, F. (2017). Coping, taming or solving: Alternative approaches to the governance of wicked problems. *Policy Studies, 38*(6), 571–588.

De Búrca, G. (2017). Human rights experimentalism. *American Journal of International Law, 111*(2), 277–316.

De Búrca, G., Keohane, R. O., & Sabel, C. (2014). Global experimentalist governance. *British Journal of Political Science, 44*(3), 477–486.

Dellmuth, L. M., & Tallberg, J. (2017). Advocacy strategies in global governance: Inside versus outside lobbying. *Political Studies, 65*(3), 705–723.

Denhardt, J. V., & Campbell, K. B. (2006). The role of democratic values in transformational leadership. *Administration & Society, 38*(5), 556–572.

Destler, K. N. (2016). Creating a performance culture: Incentives, climate, and organizational change. *American Review of Public Administration, 46*(2), 201–225.

De Vries, H., Bekkers, V., & Tummers, L. (2016). Innovation in the public sector: A systematic review and future research agenda. *Public Administration, 94*(1), 146–166.

Dewey, J. (1941). Propositions, warranted assertibility, and truth. *Journal of Philosophy, 38*(7), 169–186.

Dietz, T., Ostrom, E., & Stern, P. C. (2003). The struggle to govern the commons. *Science, 302*(5652), 1907–1912.

Digdowiseiso, K., Murshed, S. M., & Bergh, S. I. (2022). How effective is fiscal decentralization for inequality reduction in developing countries? *Sustainability, 14*(1), 505.

DiMaggio, P. J. (1995). Comments on "What theory is not". *Administrative Science Quarterly, 40*(3), 391–397.

Dincecco, M. (2015). The rise of effective states in Europe. *Journal of Economic History, 75*(3), 901–918.

Dincecco, M., & Katz, G. (2016). State capacity and long-run economic performance. *Economic Journal, 126*(590), 189–218.

Dingwerth, K., & Pattberg, P. (2006). Global governance as a perspective on world politics. *Global Governance, 12*, 185–203.

Dingwerth, K., & Pattberg, P. (2009). World politics and organizational fields: The case of transnational sustainability governance. *European Journal of International Relations, 15*(4), 707–743.

Dingwerth, K., Witt, A., Lehmann, I., Reichel, E., & Weise, T. (2019). *International Organizations under Pressure: Legitimating Global Governance in Challenging Times.* Oxford: Oxford University Press.

Di Nucci, M. R., Isidoro Losada, A. M., & Themann, D. (2021). Confidence gap or timid trust building? The role of trust in the evolution of the nuclear waste governance in Germany. *Journal of Risk Research, 25*(5), 594–612.

Djelic, M. L., & Sahlin-Andersson, K. (Eds.). (2006). *Transnational Governance: Institutional Dynamics of Regulation*. Cambridge: Cambridge University Press.

Doberstein, C. (2016). Designing collaborative governance decision-making in search of a "collaborative advantage". *Public Management Review, 18*(6), 819–841.

Doberstein, C., & Millar, H. (2014). Balancing a house of cards: Throughput legitimacy in Canadian governance networks. *Canadian Journal of Political Science/Revue Canadienne de Science Politique, 47*(2), 259–280.

Doh, S. (2014). Social capital, economic development, and the quality of government: How interaction between social capital and economic development affects the quality of government. *Public Administration, 92*(1), 104–124.

Doorenspleet, R., & Pellikaan, H. (2013). Which type of democracy performs best? *Acta Politica, 48*(3), 237–267.

Douglas, M., & Wildavsky, A. (1983). *Risk and Culture: An Essay on the Selection of Technological and Environmental Dangers*. Oakland, CA: University of California Press.

Dowding, K. (1995). Model or metaphor? A critical review of the policy network approach. *Political Studies, 43*(1), 136–158.

Dryzek, J. S. with S. Niemeyer (2010). *Foundations and Frontiers of Deliberative Governance*. Oxford: Oxford University Press.

Dubnick, M. (2005). Accountability and the promise of performance: In search of the mechanisms. *Public Performance & Management Review, 28*(3), 376–417.

Dubnick, M. J., & Frederickson, H. G. (Eds.) (2014). *Accountable Governance: Problems and Promises*. London: Routledge.

Duckett, D., Feliciano, D., Martin-Ortega, J., & Munoz-Rojas, J. (2016). Tackling wicked environmental problems: The discourse and its influence on praxis in Scotland. *Landscape and Urban Planning, 154*, 44–56.

Duit, A., & Galaz, V. (2008). Governance and complexity—emerging issues for governance theory. *Governance, 21*(3), 311–335.

Dunleavy, P., & Hood, C. (1994). From old public administration to new public management. *Public Money & Management, 14*(3), 9–16.

Dunleavy, P., Margetts, H., Bastow, S., & Tinkler, J. (2006). New public management is dead—long live digital-era governance. *Journal of Public Administration Research and Theory, 16*(3), 467–494.

Dunlop, C. A., & Radaelli, C. M. (2018). Does policy learning meet the standards of an analytical framework of the policy process? *Policy Studies Journal, 46*, S48–S68.

Dunn, W. N. (1988). Methods of the second type: Coping with the wilderness of conventional policy analysis. *Review of Policy Research, 7*(4), 720–737.

Dunn, W. N. (1997). Probing the boundaries of ignorance in policy analysis. *American Behavioral Scientist, 40*(3), 277–298.

Durose, C., Justice, J., & Skelcher, C. (2015). Governing at arm's length: Eroding or enhancing democracy? *Policy & Politics, 43*(1), 137–153.

Eberlein, B. (2019). Who fills the global governance gap? Rethinking the roles of business and government in global governance. *Organization Studies, 40*(8), 1125–1145.

Edelenbos, J., & van Meerkerk, I. (2015). Connective capacity in water governance practices: The meaning of trust and boundary spanning for integrated performance. *Current Opinion in Environmental Sustainability, 12*, 25–29.

Edelenbos, J., van Meerkerk, I., & Schenk, T. (2018). The evolution of community self-organization in interaction with government institutions: Cross-case insights from three countries. *American Review of Public Administration, 48*(1), 52–66.

Edmondson, D. L., Kern, F., & Rogge, K. S. (2019). The co-evolution of policy mixes and socio-technical systems: Towards a conceptual framework of policy mix feedback in sustainability transitions. *Research Policy, 48*(10), 103555.

Elbanna, S., Andrews, R., & Pollanen, R. (2016). Strategic planning and implementation success in public service organizations: Evidence from Canada. *Public Management Review, 18*(7), 1017–1042.

Emerson, K., & Nabatchi, T. (2015). *Collaborative Governance Regimes*. Washington, DC: Georgetown University Press.

Emerson, K., Nabatchi, T., & Balogh, S. (2012). An integrative framework for collaborative governance. *Journal of Public Administration Research and Theory, 22*(1), 1–29.

Enjolras, B., Salamon, L. M., Sivesind, K. H., & Zimmer, A. (2018). *The Third Sector as a Renewable Resource for Europe: Concepts, Impacts, Challenges and Opportunities*. Cham: Springer Nature.

Ennser-Jedenastik, L. (2016). The politicization of regulatory agencies: Between partisan influence and formal independence. *Journal of Public Administration Research and Theory, 26*(3), 507–518.

Epstein, G., Nenadovic, M., & Boustany, A. (2014). Into the deep blue sea: Commons theory and international governance of Atlantic Bluefin Tuna. *International Journal of the Commons, 8*(2), 277–303.

Ernstson, H., Barthel, S., Andersson, E., & Borgström, S. T. (2010). Scale-crossing brokers and network governance of urban ecosystem services: The case of Stockholm. *Ecology and Society, 15*(4)

Ersoy, A., & Hall, S. (2020). The Bristol Green Capital Partnership: An exemplar of reflexive governance for sustainable urban development. *Town Planning Review, 91*(4), 397–413.

Esping-Andersen, G. (1990). *The Three Worlds of Welfare Capitalism*. Princeton: Princeton University Press.

Esping-Andersen, G. (2002). Toward the good society, once again? In G. Esping-Andersen, D. Gallie, A. Hemerijck, & J. Myles (Eds.) *Why We Need a New Welfare State*. Oxford: Oxford University Press, pp. 1–25.

Evans, P. B. (1995). *Embedded Autonomy: States and Industrial Transformation*. Princeton: Princeton University Press.

Evans, P. (1996). Government action, social capital and development: Reviewing the evidence on synergy. *World Development, 24*(6), 1119–1132.

Evans, P. (1997). *State–Society Synergy: Government and Social Capital in Development*. University of California, Berkeley, Research Series, no. 94.

Evans, P., & Rauch, J. E. (1999). Bureaucracy and growth: A cross-national analysis of the effects of "Weberian" state structures on economic growth. *American Sociological Review, 64*(5), 748–765.

Evans, P. P., Rueschemeyer, D., & Skocpol, T. (Eds.) (1985). *Bringing the State Back In*. Cambridge: Cambridge University Press.

Faguet, J. P. (2012). *Decentralization and Popular Democracy: Governance from Below in Bolivia*. Ann Arbor, MI: University of Michigan Press.

Faguet, J. P. (2014). Decentralization and governance. *World Development, 53*, 2–13.

Fan, C. S., Lin, C., & Treisman, D. (2009). Political decentralization and corruption: Evidence from around the world. *Journal of Public Economics, 93*(1–2), 14–34.

Farrell, D., & Curato, N. (2021). *Deliberative Mini-Publics: Core Design Features*. Bristol: Bristol University Press.

Favero, N., Meier, K. J., & O'Toole Jr, L. J. (2016). Goals, trust, participation, and feedback: Linking internal management with performance outcomes. *Journal of Public Administration Research and Theory, 26*(2), 327–343.

Favoreu, C., Carassus, D., & Maurel, C. (2016). Strategic management in the public sector: A rational, political or collaborative approach? *Revue Internationale des Sciences Administratives, 82*(3), 465–482.

Fawcett, P., Flinders, M. V., Hay, C., & Wood, M. (Eds.) (2017). *Anti-Politics, Depoliticization, and Governance.* Oxford: Oxford University Press.

Feindt, P. H., & Weiland, S. (2018). Reflexive governance: Exploring the concept and assessing its critical potential for sustainable development. Introduction to the special issue. *Journal of Environmental Policy & Planning, 20*(6), 661–674.

Feldman, M. S., & Khademian, A. M. (2007). The role of the public manager in inclusion: Creating communities of participation. *Governance, 20*(2), 305–324.

Feola, G., & Nunes, R. (2014). Success and failure of grassroots innovations for addressing climate change: The case of the Transition Movement. *Global Environmental Change, 24*, 232–250.

Ferguson, J. (1994). *The Anti-Politics Machine: "Development," Depoliticization, and Bureaucratic Power in Lesotho.* Minneapolis: University of Minnesota Press.

Ferlie, E., Fitzgerald, L., McGivern, G., Dopson, S., & Bennett, C. (2011). Public policy networks and "wicked problems": A nascent solution? *Public Administration, 89*(2), 307–324.

Fischer, F. (2017). *Climate Crisis and the Democratic Prospect: Participatory Governance in Sustainable Communities.* Oxford: Oxford University Press.

Fischer, J., & Riechers, M. (2019). A leverage points perspective on sustainability. *People and Nature, 1*(1), 115–120.

Fisher, J., Stutzman, H., Vedoveto, M., Delgado, D., Rivero, R., Quertehuari Dariquebe, W., Contrerase, L. S., Soutob, T., Harden, A., & Rhee, S. (2020). Collaborative governance and conflict management: Lessons learned and good practices from a case study in the Amazon Basin. *Society & Natural Resources, 33*(4), 538–553.

Fiszbein, A., Kanbur, R., & Yemtsov, R. (2014). Social protection and poverty reduction: Global patterns and some targets. *World Development, 61*, 167–177.

Flannery, W., Healy, N., & Luna, M. (2018). Exclusion and non-participation in Marine Spatial Planning. *Marine Policy, 88*, 32–40.

Fledderus, J., & Honingh, M. (2016). Why people co-produce within activation services: The necessity of motivation and trust :An investigation of selection biases in a municipal activation programme in the Netherlands. *International Review of Administrative Sciences, 82*(1), 69–87.

Fledderus, J., Brandsen, T., & Honingh, M. (2014). Restoring trust through the co-production of public services: A theoretical elaboration. *Public Management Review, 16*(3), 424–443.

Flinders, M., & Buller, J. (2006). Depoliticisation: Principles, tactics and tools. *British Politics, 1*(3), 293–318.

Flinders, M., & Wood, M. (2014). Depoliticisation, governance and the state. *Policy & Politics, 42*(2), 135–149.

Flyvbjerg, B., Landman, T., & Schram, S. (Eds.) (2012). *Real Social Science: Applied Phronesis.* Cambridge: Cambridge University Press.

Folke, C., Hahn, T., Olsson, P., & Norberg, J. (2005). Adaptive governance of social-ecological systems. *Annual Review of Environmental Resources, 30*, 441–473.

Fowler, P. J., Wright, K., Marcal, K. E., Ballard, E., & Hovmand, P. S. (2019). Capability traps impeding homeless services: A community-based system dynamics evaluation. *Journal of Social Service Research*, *45*(3), 348–359.

Fox, J. A. (2015). Social accountability: What does the evidence really say? *World Development*, 72, 346–361.

Frantzeskaki, N., & Loorbach, D. (2010). Towards governing infrasystem transitions: Reinforcing lock-in or facilitating change? *Technological Forecasting and Social Change*, *77*(8), 1292–1301.

Frederickson, H. G. (1990). Public administration and social equity. *Public Administration Review*, *50*, 228–237.

Frederickson, H. G. (2005). Whatever happened to public administration? Governance, governance everywhere. In E. Ferlie, L. E. Lynn Jr., & C. Pollitt (Eds.) *The Oxford Handbook of Public Management*. Oxford: Oxford University Press, pp. 282–304.

Frederickson, H. G. (2015). *Social Equity and Public Administration: Origins, Developments, and Applications: Origins, Developments, and Applications*. London: Routledge.

Freeman, J. (1997). Collaborative governance in the administrative state. *UCLA Law Review*, *45*, 1.

Fressoli, M., Arond, E., Abrol, D., Smith, A., Ely, A., & Dias, R. (2014). When grassroots innovation movements encounter mainstream institutions: Implications for models of inclusive innovation. *Innovation and Development*, *4*(2), 277–292.

Fukuyama, F. (2001). Social capital, civil society and development. *Third World Quarterly*, *22*(1), 7–20.

Fukuyama, F. (2013). What is governance? *Governance*, *26*(3), 347–368.

Fung, A. (2001). Accountable autonomy: Toward empowered deliberation in Chicago schools and policing. *Politics & Society*, *29*(1), 73–103.

Fung, A. (2006). Varieties of participation in complex governance. *Public Administration Review*, *66*, 66–75.

Fung, A. (2015). Putting the public back into governance: The challenges of citizen participation and its future. *Public Administration Review*, *75*(4), 513–522.

Fung, A., & Wright, E. O. (2003). *Deepening Democracy: Institutional Innovations in Empowered Participatory Governance*. London: Verso.

Fung, A., Graham, M., & Weil, D. (2007). *Full Disclosure: The Perils and Promise of Transparency*. Cambridge: Cambridge University Press.

Gailmard, S. (2009). Multiple principals and oversight of bureaucratic policy-making. *Journal of Theoretical Politics*, *21*(2), 161–186.

Gailmard, S. (2012). Accountability and principal–agent models. In M. Bovens, R. E. Goodin, & T. Schillemans (Eds.) *The Oxford Handbook Public Accountability*. Oxford: Oxford University Press, pp. 90–105.

Gailmard, S., & Patty, J. W. (2007). Slackers and zealots: Civil service, policy discretion, and bureaucratic expertise. *American Journal of Political Science*, *51*(4), 873–889.

Gaventa, J., & Barrett, G. (2012). Mapping the outcomes of citizen engagement. *World Development*, *40*(12), 2399–2410.

Geddes, B. (1994). *Politician's Dilemma*. Berkeley: University of California Press.

Geels, F., & Raven, R. (2006). Non-linearity and expectations in niche-development trajectories: Ups and downs in Dutch biogas development (1973–2003). *Technology Analysis and Strategic Management*, *18*(3–4), 375–392.

George, A. L. (1994). The two cultures of academia and policy-making: Bridging the gap. *Political Psychology*, *15*(1), 143–172.

George, B. (2021). Successful strategic plan implementation in public organizations: Connecting people, process, and plan (3Ps). *Public Administration Review, 81*(4), 793–798.

George, B., Walker, R. M., & Monster, J. (2019). Does strategic planning improve organizational performance? A meta-analysis. *Public Administration Review, 79*(6), 810–819.

George, C., & Reed, M. G. (2017). Revealing inadvertent elitism in stakeholder models of environmental governance: Assessing procedural justice in sustainability organizations. *Journal of Environmental Planning and Management, 60*(1), 158–177.

Gerring, J. (2012). Mere description. *British Journal of Political Science, 42*(4), 721–746.

Gerring, J., Thacker, S. C., & Moreno, C. (2005). Centripetal democratic governance: A theory and global inquiry. *American Political Science Review, 99*(4), 567–581.

Gerrish, E. (2016). The impact of performance management on performance in public organizations: A meta-analysis. *Public Administration Review, 76*(1), 48–66.

Getha-Taylor, H., Grayer, M. J., Kempf, R. J., & O'Leary, R. (2019). Collaborating in the absence of trust? What collaborative governance theory and practice can learn from the literatures of conflict resolution, psychology, and law. *American Review of Public Administration, 49*(1), 51–64.

Geyer, R., & Rihani, S. (2012). *Complexity and Public Policy: A New Approach to 21st Century Politics, Policy and Society*. Abingdon, UK: Routledge.

Ghys, T. (2017). Analysing social innovation through the lens of poverty reduction: Five key factors. *European Public & Social Innovation Review, 2*(2), 1–14.

Giessen, L., Burns, S., Sahide, M. A. K., & Wibowo, A. (2016). From governance to government: The strengthened role of state bureaucracies in forest and agricultural certification. *Policy and Society, 35*(1), 71–89.

Giest, S., & Howlett, M. (2014). Understanding the pre-conditions of commons governance: The role of network management. *Environmental Science & Policy, 36*, 37–47.

Gilley, B. (2006). The determinants of state legitimacy: Results for 72 countries. *International Political Science Review, 27*(1), 47–71.

Gjaltema, J., Biesbroek, R., & Termeer, K. (2020). From government to governance… to meta-governance: A systematic literature review. *Public Management Review, 22*(12), 1760–1780.

Goldfinger, J., & Ferguson, M. R. (2009). Social capital and governmental performance in large American cities. *State and Local Government Review, 41*(1), 25–36.

Goldsmith, A. A. (2007). Is governance reform a catalyst for development? *Governance, 20*(2), 165–186.

Goldstein, G., & Ansell, C. (2018). Experimentalist governance in global public health: The case of UNAIDs. *Arizona Journal of International & Comparative Law, 35*, 219–255.

Gooden, S. T. (2015). *Race and Social Equity: A Nervous Area of Government*. London: Routledge.

Gooden, S. T. (2017). Social equity and evidence: Insights from local government. *Public Administration Review, 77*(6), 822–828.

Goodin, R. E., & Dryzek, J. S. (2006). Deliberative impacts: The macro-political uptake of mini-publics. *Politics & Society, 34*(2), 219–244.

Goodsell, C. T. (2010). *Mission Mystique: Belief Systems in Public Agencies*. Thousand Oaks: Sage.

Goodsell, C. T. (2014). *The New Case for Bureaucracy*. Washington, DC: CQ Press.

Grabs, J., Auld, G., & Cashore, B. (2021). Private regulation, public policy, and the perils of adverse ontological selection. *Regulation & Governance, 15*(4), 1183–1208.

Grafton, R. Q. (2005). Social capital and fisheries governance. *Ocean & Coastal Management, 48*(9–10), 753–766.

Graham, E. R. (2014). International organizations as collective agents: Fragmentation and the limits of principal control at the World Health Organization. *European Journal of International Relations, 20*(2), 366–390.

Gray, B. (1989). *Finding Common Ground for Multiparty Problems.* San Francisco: Jossey-Bass.

Greenhalgh, T., & Russell, J. (2009). Evidence-based policymaking: A critique. *Perspectives in Biology and Medicine, 52*(2), 304–318.

Gregory, R., Ohlson, D., & Arvai, J. (2006). Deconstructing adaptive management: Criteria for applications to environmental management. *Ecological Applications, 16,* 2411e2425.

Griffith, D. M., Mason, M., Yonas, M., Eng, E., Jeffries, V., Plihcik, S., & Parks, B. (2007). Dismantling institutional racism: Theory and action. *American Journal of Community Psychology, 39*(3), 381–392.

Grindle, M. S. (2004). Good enough governance: Poverty reduction and reform in developing countries. *Governance, 17*(4), 525–548.

Grindle, M. S. (2017). Good governance, RIP: A critique and an alternative. *Governance, 30*(1), 17–22.

Grindle, M. S., & Hilderbrand, M. E. (1995). Building sustainable capacity in the public sector: What can be done? *Public Administration and Development, 15*(5), 441–463.

Groenleer, M. L. (2014). Agency autonomy actually: Managerial strategies, legitimacy, and the early development of the European Union's agencies for drug and food safety regulation. *International Public Management Journal, 17*(2), 255–292.

Gruendel, A. (2022). The technopolitics of wicked problems: Reconstructing democracy in an age of complexity. *Critical Review, 34*(2), 202–243.

Guevara, J., Garvin, M. J., & Ghaffarzadegan, N. (2017). Capability trap of the US highway system: Policy and management implications. *Journal of Management in Engineering, 33*(4), 04017004.

Gugushvili, D., & Hirsch, D. (2014). Means-tested and universal approaches to poverty: International evidence and how the UK compares. Centre for Research in Social Policy. Working paper, 640.

Gulbrandsen, L. H. (2010). *Transnational Environmental Governance: The Emergence and Effects of the Certification of Forest and Fisheries.* Cheltenham, UK and Northampton, MA, USA: Edward Elgar Publishing.

Gunderson, L., & Light, S. S. (2006). Adaptive management and adaptive governance in the Everglades ecosystem. *Policy Sciences, 39*(4), 323–334.

Gupta, D., Lele, S., & Sahu, G. (2020). Promoting a responsive state: The role of NGOs in decentralized forest governance in India. *Forest Policy and Economics, 111,* 102066.

Gustafson, P., & Hertting, N. (2017). Understanding participatory governance: An analysis of participants' motives for participation. *American Review of Public Administration, 47*(5), 538–549.

Gustavson, M., & Sundström, A. (2018). Organizing the audit society: Does good auditing generate less public sector corruption? *Administration & Society, 50*(10), 1508–1532.

Haas, P. M. (1992). Introduction: Epistemic communities and international policy coordination. *International Organization, 46*(1), 1–35.

References

Haas, P. M. (2017). Addressing the global governance deficit. In *International Environmental Governance*. London: Routledge, pp. 499–513.

Haas, P. (2021). Epistemic communities. In L. Rajamani & J. Peel (Eds.) *The Oxford Handbook of International Environmental Law*. Oxford: Oxford University Press, pp. 699–715.

Haggard, S. (1990). *Pathways from the Periphery: The Politics of Growth in the Newly Industrializing Countries*. Ithaca: Cornell University Press.

Haggard, S., & Simmons, B. A. (1987). Theories of international regimes. *International Organization, 41*(3), 491–517.

Hajjar, R., Newton, P., Ihalainen, M., Agrawal, A., Alix-Garcia, J., Castle, S. E., ... & Timko, J. A. (2021). Levers for alleviating poverty in forests. *Forest Policy and Economics, 132*, 102589.

Hale, T., Held, D., & Young, K. (2013). *Gridlock: Why Global Cooperation is Failing When We Need it Most*. Cambridge: Polity.

Halleröd, B., Rothstein, B., Daoud, A., & Nandy, S. (2013). Bad governance and poor children: A comparative analysis of government efficiency and severe child deprivation in 68 low-and middle-income countries. *World Development, 48*, 19–31.

Hallett, T., & Ventresca, M. J. (2006). Inhabited institutions: Social interactions and organizational forms in Gouldner's Patterns of Industrial Bureaucracy. *Theory and Society, 35*, 213–236.

Halliday, T. C. (2018). Plausible folk theories: Throwing veils of plausibility over zones of ignorance in global governance. *British Journal of Sociology, 69*(4), 936–961.

Hammerschmid, G., Van de Walle, S., Andrews, R., & Mostafa, A. M. S. (2019). New public management reforms in Europe and their effects: Findings from a 20-country top executive survey. *Revue Internationale des Sciences Administratives, 85*(3), 411–431.

Han, Y., & Hong, S. (2019). The impact of accountability on organizational performance in the US federal government: The moderating role of autonomy. *Review of Public Personnel Administration, 39*(1), 3–23.

Hanleybrown, F., Kania, J., & Kramer, M. (2012). Channeling change: Making collective impact work. *Stanford Social Innovation Review*, website.

Hardin, G. (1968). The tragedy of the commons. *Science, 162*(3859), 1243–1248

Hardin, R. (1998). Trust in government. In V. Braithwaite & M. Levi (Eds.). *Trust and Governance*. New York: Russell Sage Foundation, pp. 9–27.

Hargrove, E. C., & Glidewell, J. C. (Eds.) (1990). *Impossible Jobs in Public Management*. Lawrence: University Press of Kansas.

Harlow, C., & Rawlings, R. (2007). Promoting accountability in multilevel governance: A network approach. *European Law Journal, 13*(4), 542–562.

Hartley, K., & Howlett, M. (2021). Policy assemblages and policy resilience: Lessons for non-design from evolutionary governance theory. *Annual Review of Policy Design, 9*(1), 1–20.

Hassan, M. S., Bukhari, S., & Arshed, N. (2020). Competitiveness, governance and globalization: What matters for poverty alleviation? *Environment, Development and Sustainability, 22*(4), 3491–3518.

Head, B. W. (2008). Wicked problems in public policy. *Public Policy, 3*(2), 101–118.

Head, B. W. (2016). Toward more "evidence-informed" policy making? *Public Administration Review, 76*(3), 472–484.

Head, B. W. (2022). *Wicked Problems in Public Policy: Understanding and Responding to Complex Challenges*. Cham: Springer Nature.

Head, B. W., & Alford, J. (2015). Wicked problems: Implications for public policy and management. *Administration & Society*, *47*(6), 711–739.

Head, B. W., & Xiang, W. N. (2016). Why is an APT approach to wicked problems important? *Landscape and Urban Planning*, *154*, 4–7.

Healey, P. (2003). Collaborative planning in perspective. *Planning Theory*, *2*(2), 101–123.

Heclo, H. (2011). *On Thinking Institutionally*. Oxford: Oxford University Press.

Hegre, H., & Nygård, H. M. (2015). Governance and conflict relapse. *Journal of Conflict Resolution*, *59*(6), 984–1016.

Hekkert, M. P., Suurs, R. A., Negro, S. O., Kuhlmann, S., & Smits, R. E. (2007). Functions of innovation systems: A new approach for analysing technological change. *Technological Forecasting and Social Change*, *74*(4), 413–432.

Hendriks, C. M., & Dzur, A. W. (2021). Citizens' governance spaces: Democratic action through disruptive collective problem-solving. *Political Studies*, *70*(3), 680–700.

Hendriks, C. M., & Grin, J. (2007). Contextualizing reflexive governance: The politics of Dutch transitions to sustainability. *Journal of Environmental Policy & Planning*, *9*(3–4), 333–350.

Hennigan, B. (2017). House broken: Homelessness, housing first, and neoliberal poverty governance. *Urban Geography*, *38*(9), 1418–1440.

Henry, P. J. (2010). Institutional bias. In J. F. Dovidio, J. P. Glick, & M. Hewstone (Eds.) *The SAGE Handbook of Prejudice, Stereotyping and Discrimination*. Thousand Oaks: Sage, pp. 426–440.

Herd, P., & Moynihan, D. P. (2019). *Administrative Burden: Policymaking by Other Means*. New York: Russell Sage Foundation.

Herian, M. N., Hamm, J. A., Tomkins, A. J., & Pytlik Zillig, L. M. (2012). Public participation, procedural fairness, and evaluations of local governance: The moderating role of uncertainty. *Journal of Public Administration Research and Theory*, *22*(4), 815–840.

Héritier, A., & Lehmkuhl, D. (2008). The shadow of hierarchy and new modes of governance. *Journal of Public Policy*, *28*(1), 1–17.

Hickel, J. (2016). The true extent of global poverty and hunger: Questioning the good news narrative of the Millennium Development Goals. *Third World Quarterly*, *37*(5), 749–767.

Hickey, S., & King, S. (2016). Understanding social accountability: Politics, power and building new social contracts. *Journal of Development Studies*, *52*(8), 1225–1240.

Higgins, E. T. (2004). Making a theory useful: Lessons handed down. *Personality and Social Psychology Review*, *8*(2), 138–145.

Hindera, J. J. (1993). Representative bureaucracy: Further evidence of active representation in the EEOC district offices. *Journal of Public Administration Research and Theory*, *3*(4), 415–429.

Hindera, J. J., & Young, C. D. (1998). Representative bureaucracy: The theoretical implications of statistical interaction. *Political Research Quarterly*, *51*(3), 655–671.

Hisschemöller, M., & Hoppe, R. (1995). Coping with intractable controversies: The case for problem structuring in policy design and analysis. *Knowledge and Policy*, *8*(4), 40–60.

Hodge, G. A., & Greve, C. (2017). On public–private partnership performance: A contemporary review. *Public Works Management & Policy*, *22*(1), 55–78.

Hofstad, H., Sørensen, E., Torfing, J., & Vedeld, T. (2022). Designing and leading collaborative urban climate governance: Comparative experiences of co-creation from Copenhagen and Oslo. *Environmental Policy and Governance, 32*(3), 203–216.

Holling, C. S. (Ed.) (1978). *Adaptive Environmental Assessment and Management.* Chichester, UK: Wiley,

Holmberg, S., Rothstein, B., & Nasiritousi, N. (2009). Quality of government: What you get. *Annual Review of Political Science, 12*, 135–161.

Homsy, G. C., Liu, Z., & Warner, M. E. (2019). Multilevel governance: Framing the integration of top-down and bottom-up policymaking. *International Journal of Public Administration, 42*(7), 572–582.

Hood, C. (1991). A public management for all seasons? *Public Administration, 69*(1), 3–19.

Hood, C., & Dixon, R. (2015). What we have to show for 30 years of new public management: Higher costs, more complaints. *Governance, 28*(3), 265–267.

Hood, C., & Lodge, M. (2006). *The Politics of Public Service Bargains: Reward, Competency, Loyalty and Blame.* Oxford: Oxford University Press.

Hooghe, L. and Marks, G. (2003). Unraveling the central state, but how? Types of multi-level governance. *American Political Science Review, 97*(2), 233–243.

Hoornbeek, J. A., & Peters, B. G. (2017). Understanding policy problems: A refinement of past work. *Policy and Society, 36*(3), 365–384.

Hoppe, R. (2011). *The Governance of Problems: Puzzling, Powering, Participation.* Bristol: Policy Press.

Hoppe, R. (2018). Heuristics for practitioners of policy design: Rules-of-thumb for structuring unstructured problems. *Public Policy and Administration, 33*(4), 384–408.

Houtzager, P. (2009). Introduction: From polycentrism to the polity, In P. P. Houtzager & M. P. Moore (Eds.) *Changing Paths: International Development and the New Politics of Inclusion.* Ann Arbor: University of Michigan Press, pp. 1–31.

Howaldt, J., Schröder, A., Kaletka, C., Rehfeld, D., & Terstriep, J. (2016). *Mapping the World of Social Innovation: Key Results of a Comparative Analysis of 1.005 Social Innovation Initiatives at a Glance.* https://www.iat.eu/aktuell/veroeff/2016/howaldt01.pdf.

Howlett, M. (2009). Governance modes, policy regimes and operational plans: A multi-level nested model of policy instrument choice and policy design. *Policy Sciences, 42*(1), 73–89.

Howlett, M., Mukherjee, I., & Woo, J. J. (2015). From tools to toolkits in policy design studies: The new design orientation towards policy formulation research. *Policy & Politics, 43*(2), 291–311.

Huang, W. L., & Feeney, M. K. (2016). Citizen participation in local government decision making: The role of manager motivation. *Review of Public Personnel Administration, 36*(2), 188–209.

Huber, J. D., & Shipan, C. R. (2002). *Deliberate Discretion? The Institutional Foundations of Bureaucratic Autonomy.* Cambridge: Cambridge University Press.

Hui, I., & Smith, G. (2022). Private citizens, stakeholder groups, or governments? Perceived legitimacy and participation in water collaborative governance. *Policy Studies Journal, 50*(1), 241–265.

Hulme, D. (2004). Thinking "small" and the understanding of poverty: Maymana and Mofizul's story. *Journal of Human Development, 5*(2), 161–176.

Hupe, P., & Hill, M. (2007). Street-level bureaucracy and public accountability. *Public Administration, 85*(2), 279–299.

Hurd, I. (2019). Legitimacy and contestation in global governance: Revisiting the folk theory of international institutions. *Review of International Organizations*, *14*(4), 717–729.

Hustedt, T., & Salomonsen, H. H. (2014). Ensuring political responsiveness: Politicization mechanisms in ministerial bureaucracies. *International Review of Administrative Sciences*, *80*(4), 746–765.

Huxham, C., & Vangen, S. (2000). Ambiguity, complexity and dynamics in the membership of collaboration. *Human Relations*, *53*(6), 771–806.

Innes, J. E., & Booher, D. E. (1999). Consensus building as role playing and bricolage: Toward a theory of collaborative planning. *Journal of the American Planning Association*, *65*(1), 9–26.

Isaacs, W. N. (2001). Toward an action theory of dialogue. *International Journal of Public Administration*, *24*(7–8), 709–748.

Jacques, O., & Noël, A. (2018). The case for welfare state universalism, or the lasting relevance of the paradox of redistribution. *Journal of European Social Policy*, *28*(1), 70–85.

Jensen, U. T., & Bro, L. L. (2018). How transformational leadership supports intrinsic motivation and public service motivation: The mediating role of basic need satisfaction. *American Review of Public Administration*, *48*(6), 535–549.

Jentoft, S. (2005). Fisheries co-management as empowerment. *Marine Policy*, *29*(1), 1–7.

Jentoft, S., McCay, B. J., & Wilson, D. C. (1998). Social theory and fisheries co-management. *Marine Policy*, *22*(4–5), 423–436.

Jessop, B. (2002a). Liberalism, neoliberalism, and urban governance: A state–theoretical perspective. *Antipode*, *34*(3), 452–472.

Jessop, B. (2002b). Governance and meta-governance in the face of complexity: On the roles of requisite variety, reflexive observation, and romantic irony in participatory governance. In H. Heinelt, P. Getimis, G. Kafkalis, R. Smith, & E. Swyngedouw (Eds.) *Participatory Governance in Multi-Level Context: Concepts and Experience*. Wiesbaden: VS Verlag für Sozialwissenschaften, pp. 33–58.

Ji, S. (2022). Role of managerial and political accountability in improving performance of local governments. *Public Performance & Management Review*, *45*(3), 499–531.

Jindra, C., & Vaz, A. (2019). Good governance and multidimensional poverty: A comparative analysis of 71 countries. *Governance*, *32*(4), 657–675.

Johns, L., Pelc, K. J., & Wellhausen, R. L. (2019). How a retreat from global economic governance may empower business interests. *Journal of Politics*, *81*(2), 731–738.

Johnson, C. (1982). *MITI and the Japanese Miracle: The Growth of Industrial Policy, 1925–1975*. Stanford: Stanford University Press.

Joshi, A., & Houtzager, P. P. (2012). Widgets or watchdogs? Conceptual explorations in social accountability. *Public Management Review*, *14*(2), 145–162.

Jütting, J. P., Kauffmann, C., McDonnell, I., Osterrieder, H., Pinaud, N., & Wegner, L. (2004). Decentralization and poverty in developing countries: Exploring the impact. Available at SSRN 583762.

Kahler, M. (2018). Global governance: Three futures. *International Studies Review*, *20*(2), 239–246.

Kania, J., & Kramer, M. (2011). Collective impact. *Stanford Social Innovation Review*, Winter.

Kania, J., & Kramer, M. (2013). Embracing emergence: How collective impact addresses complexity. *Stanford Social Innovation Review*. https://doi.org/10.48558/ZJY9-4D87.

Kanie, N., Griggs, D., Young, O., Waddell, S., Shrivastava, P., Haas, P. M., ... & Kőrösi, C. (2019). Rules to goals: Emergence of new governance strategies for sustainable development. *Sustainability Science, 14*(6), 1745–1749.

Kapucu, N. (2014). Complexity, governance and networks: Perspectives from public administration. *Complexity, Governance & Networks, 1*(1), 29–38.

Karpowitz, C. F., & Mendelberg, T. (2018). Do enclaves remediate social inequality? *Journal of Politics, 80*(4), 1134–1149.

Karpowitz, C. F., Mendelberg, T., & Shaker, L. (2012). Gender inequality in deliberative participation. *American Political Science Review, 106*(3), 533–547.

Karpowitz, C., Raphael, C., & Hammond IV, A. (2009). Deliberative democracy and inequality. *Politics & Society, 37*(4), 576–615.

Katzenstein, M. F., & Waller, M. R. (2015). Taxing the poor: Incarceration, poverty governance, and the seizure of family resources. *Perspectives on Politics, 13*(3), 638–656.

Kaufman, H. (1967). *The Forest Ranger: A Study in Administrative Behavior.* Baltimore: Resources for the Future.

Kaufmann, D., Kraay, A., & Mastruzzi, M. (June 24, 2008). Governance matters VII: Aggregate and individual governance indicators, 1996–2007. World Bank Policy Research Working Paper No. 4654, Available at SSRN: https://ssrn.com/abstract= 1148386 or http://dx.doi.org/10.2139/ssrn.1148386.

Keck, M. E., & Sikkink, K. (1998). *Activists beyond Borders: Advocacy Networks in International Politics.* Ithaca: Cornell University Press.

Kelly, B. B. (2019). *Power-sharing and Consociational Theory.* Berlin: Springer.

Kelman, H. C. (2005). Building trust among enemies: The central challenge for international conflict resolution. *International Journal of Intercultural Relations, 29*(6), 639–650.

Kemp, R., Loorbach, D., & Rotmans, J. (2007). Transition management as a model for managing processes of co-evolution towards sustainable development. *International Journal of Sustainable Development & World Ecology, 14*(1), 78–91.

Kemp, R., Parto, S., & Gibson, R. B. (2005). Governance for sustainable development: Moving from theory to practice. *International Journal of Sustainable Development, 8*(1–2), 12–30.

Keohane, R. O., & Victor, D. G. (2011). The regime complex for climate change. *Perspectives on Politics, 9*(1), 7–23.

Kern, F., Rogge, K. S., & Howlett, M. (2019). Policy mixes for sustainability transitions: New approaches and insights through bridging innovation and policy studies. *Research Policy, 48*(10), 103832.

Kerpershoek, E., Groenleer, M., & de Bruijn, H. (2016). Unintended responses to performance management in Dutch hospital care: Bringing together the managerial and professional perspectives. *Public Management Review, 18*(3), 417–436.

Kerwer, D. (2005). Rules that many use: Standards and global regulation. *Governance, 18*(4), 611–632.

Kettl, D. F. (2011). *Sharing Power: Public Governance and Private Markets.* Washington, DC: Brookings Institution Press.

Kickert, W. J., Klijn, E. H., & Koppenjan, J. F. M. (Eds.) (1997). *Managing Complex Networks: Strategies for the Public Sector.* Thousand Oaks: Sage.

Kienzle, B. (2019). Effective orchestration? The 1540 Committee and the WMD terrorism regime complex. *Global Policy, 10*(4), 486–496.

Kim, H., Jung, H., & Kim, S. Y. (2022). Does politicization influence senior public officials' work attitudes? Different forms and effects of politicization in the civil service. *Public Management Review*, *24*(7), 1100–1123.

Kim, R. E. (2020). Is global governance fragmented, polycentric, or complex? The state of the art of the network approach. *International Studies Review*, *22*(4), 903–931.

Kingsley, J. D. (1944) *Representative Bureaucracy: An Interpretation of the British Civil Service*. Yellow Springs, OH: Antioch Press.

Kirschke, S., & Newig, J. (2017). Addressing complexity in environmental management and governance. *Sustainability*, *9*(6), 983.

Kirschke, S., Borchardt, D., & Newig, J. (2017a). Mapping complexity in environmental governance: A comparative analysis of 37 priority issues in German water management. *Environmental Policy and Governance*, *27*(6), 534–559.

Kirschke, S., Newig, J., Völker, J., & Borchardt, D. (2017b). Does problem complexity matter for environmental policy delivery? How public authorities address problems of water governance. *Journal of Environmental Management*, *196*, 1–7.

Kleine, M. (2018). Informal governance and legitimacy in EU politics. *Journal of European Integration*, *40*(7), 873–888.

Kleinfeld, R., & Barham, E. (2018). Complicit states and the governing strategy of privilege violence: When weakness is not the problem. *Annual Review of Political Science*, *21*, 215–238.

Kleinhans, R. (2017). False promises of co-production in neighbourhood regeneration: The case of Dutch community enterprises. *Public Management Review*, *19*(10), 1500–1518.

Klijn, E. H., & Koppenjan, J. (2012). Governance network theory: Past, present and future. *Policy & Politics*, *40*(4), 587–606.

Klijn, E. H., & Koppenjan, J. (2014). Complexity in governance network theory. *Complexity, Governance & Networks*, *1*(1), 61–70.

Klijn, E. H., & Koppenjan, J. (2016). The impact of contract characteristics on the performance of public–private partnerships (PPPs). *Public Money & Management*, *36*(6), 455–462.

Klijn, E. H., & Skelcher, C. (2007). Democracy and governance networks: Compatible or not? *Public Administration*, *85*(3), 587–608.

Klijn, E. H., Steijn, B., & Edelenbos, J. (2010). The impact of network management on outcomes in governance networks. *Public Administration*, *88*(4), 1063–1082.

Knack, S., & Keefer, P. (1997). Does social capital have an economic payoff? A cross-country investigation. *Quarterly Journal of Economics*, *112*(4), 1251–1288.

Köhler, J., Geels, F. W., Kern, F., Markard, J., Onsongo, E., Wieczorek, A., ... & Wells, P. (2019). An agenda for sustainability transitions research: State of the art and future directions. *Environmental Innovation and Societal Transitions*, *31*, 1–32.

Koliba, C., Meek, J. W., & Zia, A. (2017). *Governance Networks in Public Administration and Public Policy*. London: Routledge.

Koliba, C. J., Mills, R. M., & Zia, A. (2011). Accountability in governance networks: An assessment of public, private, and nonprofit emergency management practices following Hurricane Katrina. *Public Administration Review*, *71*(2), 210–220.

Kooiman, J. (Ed.) (1993). *Modern Governance: New Government–Society Interactions*. Thousand Oaks: Sage.

Koop, C. (2011). Explaining the accountability of independent agencies: The importance of political salience. *Journal of Public Policy*, *31*(2), 209–234.

Koppell, J. G. (2005). Pathologies of accountability: ICANN and the challenge of "multiple accountabilities disorder". *Public Administration Review*, *65*(1), 94–108.

Koppenjan, J., & Klijn, E. H. (2004). *Managing Uncertainties in Networks: A Network Approach to Problem Solving and Decision Making*. London: Psychology Press.

Koppenjan, J., & Koliba, C. (2013). Transformations towards new public governance: Can the new paradigm handle complexity? *International Review of Public Administration, 18*(2), 1–8.

Korpi, W., & Palme, J. (1998). The paradox of redistribution and strategies of equality: Welfare state institutions, inequality, and poverty in the Western countries. *American Sociological Review, 63*(5), 661–687.

Kort, I. M., Verweij, S., & Klijn, E. H. (2016). In search for effective public–private partnerships: An assessment of the impact of organizational form and managerial strategies in urban regeneration partnerships using fsQCA. *Environment and Planning C: Government and Policy, 34*(5), 777–794.

Kosack, S., & Fung, A. (2014). Does transparency improve governance? *Annual Review of Political Science, 17*, 65–87.

Kraay, A., & McKenzie, D. (2014). Do poverty traps exist? Assessing the evidence. *Journal of Economic Perspectives, 28*(3), 127–148.

Krasner, S. D. (Ed.) (1983). *International Regimes*. Ithaca: Cornell University Press.

Kuhlmann, S., & Wayenberg, E. (2016). Institutional impact assessment in multi-level systems: Conceptualizing decentralization effects from a comparative perspective. *International Review of Administrative Sciences, 82*(2), 233–254.

Kumlin, S., & Rothstein, B. (2005). Making and breaking social capital: The impact of welfare-state institutions. *Comparative Political Studies, 38*(4), 339–365.

Kwon, H. J., & Kim, E. (2014). Poverty reduction and good governance: Examining the rationale of the Millennium Development Goals. *Development and Change, 45*(2), 353–375.

Lane, J. E. (2020). The principal–agent approach and public administration. In W. R. Thompson (Ed.) *Oxford Research Encyclopedia of Politics*. Oxford: Oxford University Press. https://doi.org/10.1093/acrefore/9780190228637.013.1462.

LaPorte, T. R. (2015). *Organized Social Complexity: Challenge to Politics and Policy*. Princeton: Princeton University Press.

Larson, A. M., & Soto, F. (2008). Decentralization of natural resource governance regimes. *Annual Review of Environment and Resources, 33*, 213–239.

Lavenex, S. (2020). The UN Global Compacts on migration and refugees: A case for experimentalist governance? *Global Governance: A Review of Multilateralism and International Organizations, 26*(4), 673–696.

Lee, K. N. (1999). Appraising adaptive management. *Conservation Ecology, 3*(2), 3.

Lee, S. (2022). When tensions become opportunities: Managing accountability demands in collaborative governance. *Journal of Public Administration Research and Theory, 32*(4), 641–655.

Lee, S., & Esteve, M. (2022). What drives the perceived legitimacy of collaborative governance? An experimental study. *Public Management Review*, 1–22.

Lee, S. Y., & Whitford, A. B. (2013). Assessing the effects of organizational resources on public agency performance: Evidence from the US federal government. *Journal of Public Administration Research and Theory, 23*(3), 687–712.

Lejano, R. P., & Ingram, H. (2009). Collaborative networks and new ways of knowing. *Environmental Science & Policy, 12*(6), 653–662.

Leonard, D. K. (2010). "Pockets" of effective agencies in weak governance states: Where are they likely and why does it matter? *Public Administration and Development: The International Journal of Management Research and Practice, 30*(2), 91–101.

Leonard, L., & Lidskog, R. (2021). Conditions and constrains for reflexive governance of industrial risks: The case of the South Durban industrial basin, South Africa. *Sustainability*, *13*(10), 5679.

Lessmann, C. (2012). Regional inequality and decentralization: An empirical analysis. *Environment and Planning A*, *44*(6), 1363–1388.

Lessmann, C., & Markwardt, G. (2010). One size fits all? Decentralization, corruption, and the monitoring of bureaucrats. *World Development*, *38*(4), 631–646.

Leventon, J., Duşe, I. A., & Horcea-Milcu, A. I. (2021). Leveraging biodiversity action from plural values: Transformations of governance systems. *Frontiers in Ecology and Evolution*, *9*, 609853.

Levi, M. (1998). A state of trust. In V. Braithwaite & M. Levi (Eds.) *Trust and Governance*. New York: Russell Sage Foundation, pp. 77–101.

Levin, K., Cashore, B., Bernstein, S., & Auld, G. (2012). Overcoming the tragedy of super wicked problems: Constraining our future selves to ameliorate global climate change. *Policy Sciences*, *45*(2), 123–152.

Levine, J. R. (2021). *Constructing Community*. Princeton: Princeton University Press.

Levy, M. A., Young, O. R., & Zürn, M. (1995). The study of international regimes. *European Journal of International Relations*, *1*(3), 267–330.

Lewicki, R. J., & Wiethoff, C. (2014). Trust, trust development, and trust repair. *Handbook of Conflict Resolution: Theory and Practice*, *1*(1), 86–107.

Lewin, K. (1943). Psychology and the process of group living. *Journal of Social Psychology*, *17*, 113–131.

Lewis, J. M., Ricard, L. M., & Klijn, E. H. (2018). How innovation drivers, networking and leadership shape public sector innovation capacity. *International Review of Administrative Sciences*, *84*(2), 288–307.

Lijphart, A. (1969). Consociational democracy. *World Politics*, *21*(2), 207–225.

Lijphart, A. (2012). *Patterns of Democracy*. New Haven: Yale University Press.

Lim, H. H. (2006). Representative bureaucracy: Rethinking substantive effects and active representation. *Public Administration Review*, *66*(2), 193–204.

Lin, T. H. (2015). Governing natural disasters: State capacity, democracy, and human vulnerability. *Social Forces*, *93*(3), 1267–1300.

Lind, E. A., & Tyler, T. R. (1988). *The Social Psychology of Procedural Justice*. Chem:Springer Science & Business Media.

Lindblom, C. E. (1959). The science of "muddling through". *Public Administration Review*, *19*(2), 79–88.

Lindblom, C. E., & Cohen, D. K. (1979). *Usable Knowledge: Social Science and Social Problem Solving*. New Haven: Yale University Press.

Linder, S. H., & Peters, B. G. (1984). From social theory to policy design. *Journal of Public Policy*, *4*(3), 237–259.

Linder, W. (2010). On the merits of decentralization in young democracies. *Publius: The Journal of Federalism*, *40*(1), 1–30.

Linder, W., & Bächtiger, A. (2005). What drives democratisation in Asia and Africa? *European Journal of Political Research*, *44*(6), 861–880.

Linnér, B. O., & Wibeck, V. (2021). Drivers of sustainability transformations: Leverage points, contexts and conjunctures. *Sustainability Science*, *16*(3), 889–900.

Lodge, M., & Wegrich, K. (Eds.) (2014). *The Problem-solving Capacity of the Modern State: Governance Challenges and Administrative Capacities*. Oxford: Oxford University Press.

Loeffler, E., & Bovaird, T. (2016). User and community co-production of public services: What does the evidence tell us? *International Journal of Public Administration, 39*(13), 1006–1019.

Lombard, M. (2013). Citizen participation in urban governance in the context of democratization: Evidence from low-income neighbourhoods in Mexico. *International Journal of Urban and Regional Research, 37*(1), 135–150.

Lönngren, J., & Van Poeck, K. (2021). Wicked problems: A mapping review of the literature. *International Journal of Sustainable Development & World Ecology, 28*(6), 481–502.

Loorbach, D. (2010). Transition management for sustainable development: A prescriptive, complexity-based governance framework. *Governance, 23*(1), 161–183.

Lowndes, V., & Wilson, D. (2001). Social capital and local governance: Exploring the institutional design variable. *Political Studies, 49*(4), 629–647.

Lustick, I. S. (1997). Lijphart, Lakatos, and consociationalism. *World Politics, 50*(1), 88–117.

Magalhães, P. C. (2014). Government effectiveness and support for democracy. *European Journal of Political Research, 53*(1), 77–97.

Maggetti, M., & Trein, P. (2019). Multilevel governance and problem-solving: Towards a dynamic theory of multilevel policy-making? *Public Administration, 97*(2), 355–369.

Maggetti, M., & Verhoest, K. (2014). Unexplored aspects of bureaucratic autonomy: A state of the field and ways forward. *International Review of Administrative Sciences, 80*(2), 239–256.

Mair, J., & Marti, I. (2009). Entrepreneurship in and around institutional voids: A case study from Bangladesh. *Journal of Business Venturing, 24*(5), 419–435.

Mair, J., & Seelos, C. (2017). Water is power. *Stanford Social Innovation Review, 2*(Spring 2017), 24–29.

Mair, J., Marti, I., & Ventresca, M. J. (2012). Building inclusive markets in rural Bangladesh: How intermediaries work institutional voids. *Academy of Management Journal, 55*(4), 819–850.

Majone, G. (2001). Nonmajoritarian institutions and the limits of democratic governance: A political transaction-cost approach. *Journal of Institutional and Theoretical Economics (JITE)/Zeitschrift für die gesamte Staatswissenschaft, 157*(1), 57–78.

Mandell, M. P., & Keast, R. (2009). A new look at leadership in collaborative networks: Process catalysts. In J. Raffel, P. Leisink, & A. Middlebrooks (Eds.) *Public Sector Leadership: International Challenges and Perspectives*. Cheltenham, UK and Northampton, MA, USA: Edward Elgar Publishing, pp. 163–178.

Mann, M. (1984). The autonomous power of the state: Its origins, mechanisms and results. *European Journal of Sociology/Archives Européennes de Sociologie, 25*(2), 185–213.

Maor, M. (2017). The implications of the emerging disproportionate policy perspective for the new policy design studies. *Policy Sciences, 50*(3), 383–398.

March, J. G., & Olsen, J. P. (1996). Institutional perspectives on political institutions. *Governance, 9*(3), 247–264.

Markard, J., Geels, F. W., & Raven, R. (2020). Challenges in the acceleration of sustainability transitions. *Environmental Research Letters, 15*(8), 081001.

Markard, J., Raven, R., & Truffer, B. (2012). Sustainability transitions: An emerging field of research and its prospects. *Research Policy, 41*(6), 955–967.

Marks, G. (1996). An actor-centred approach to multi-level governance. *Regional & Federal Studies, 6*(2), 20–38.

Marquette, H., & Peiffer, C. (2018). Grappling with the "real politics" of systemic corruption: Theoretical debates versus "real-world" functions. *Governance, 31*(3), 499–514.

Martindale, D. (2013). *The Nature and Types of Sociological Theory*. London: Routledge.

Martiskainen, M. (2017). The role of community leadership in the development of grassroots innovations. *Environmental Innovation and Societal Transitions, 22*, 78–89.

Marwell, N. P., & Morrissey, S. L. (2020). Organizations and the governance of urban poverty. *Annual Review of Sociology, 46*, 233–250.

Marwell, N. P., Marantz, E. A., & Baldassarri, D. (2020). The microrelations of urban governance: Dynamics of patronage and partnership. *American Journal of Sociology, 125*(6), 1559–1601.

Maryudi, A., Acheampong, E., Rutt, R. L., Myers, R., & McDermott, C. L. (2020). "A level playing field"?—What an environmental justice lens can tell us about who gets leveled in the Forest Law Enforcement, Governance and Trade Action Plan. *Society & Natural Resources, 33*(7), 859–875.

Massey, A., & Johnston-Miller, K. (2016). Governance: Public governance to social innovation? *Policy & Politics, 44*(4), 663–675.

Matthew, D. C. (2022). Against "institutional racism". *Philosophy & Social Criticism*, 01914537221114910.

Matthews, F. (2012). Governance and state capacity. In D. Levi-Faur (Ed.) *The Oxford Handbook of Governance*. Oxford: Oxford University Press, pp. 281–293.

Mattingly, D. C. (2019). *The Art of Political Control in China*. Cambridge: Cambridge University Press.

Mattli, W., & Woods, N. (Eds.) (2009). *The Politics of Global Regulation*. Princeton: Princeton University Press.

Mayntz, R. (1993). Governing failures and the problem of governability: Some comments on a theoretical paradigm. In J. Kooiman (Ed.) *Modern Governance: New Government–Society Interactions*. Thousand Oaks: Sage, pp. 9–20.

Mazepus, H., & van Leeuwen, F. (2020). Fairness matters when responding to disasters: An experimental study of government legitimacy. *Governance, 33*(3), 621–637.

McAdam, D., Tarrow, S., & Tilly, C. (2001). *Dynamics of Contention*. Cambridge: Cambridge University Press.

McCabe, B. J. (2022). Ready to rent: Administrative decisions and poverty governance in the Housing Choice Voucher program. *American Sociological Review*, 00031224221131798.

McCandless, S. A., & Guy, M. E. (2013). One more time: What did Woodrow Wilson really mean about politics and administration? *Administrative Theory & Praxis, 35*(3), 356–377.

McCubbins, M. D., & Schwartz, T. (1984). Congressional oversight overlooked: Police patrols versus fire alarms. *American Journal of Political Science, 28*(1), 165–179.

McCubbins, M. D., Noll, R. G., & Weingast, B. R. (1987). Administrative procedures as instruments of political control. *Journal of Law, Economics, and Organization, 3*(2), 243–277.

McDermott, M., Mahanty, S., & Schreckenberg, K. (2013). Examining equity: A multidimensional framework for assessing equity in payments for ecosystem services. *Environmental Science & Policy, 33*, 416–427.

References 219

McDonnell, E. M. (2017). Patchwork leviathan: How pockets of bureaucratic governance flourish within institutionally diverse developing states. *American Sociological Review, 82*(3), 476–510.

McDougall, C., & Banjade, M. R. (2015). Social capital, conflict, and adaptive collaborative governance: Exploring the dialectic. *Ecology and Society, 20*(1), 44.

McDougall, C., Jiggins, J., Pandit, B. H., Thapa Magar Rana, S. K., & Leeuwis, C. (2013). Does adaptive collaborative forest governance affect poverty? Participatory action research in Nepal's community forests. *Society & Natural Resources, 26*(11), 1235–1251.

McGarry, J. (2019). Classical consociational theory and recent consociational performance. *Swiss Political Science Review, 25*(4), 538–555.

McGinnis, M. D. (2011). An introduction to IAD and the language of the Ostrom workshop: A simple guide to a complex framework. *Policy Studies Journal, 39*(1), 169–183.

McGinnis, M. D., & Ostrom, E. (2012). Reflections on Vincent Ostrom, public administration, and polycentricity. *Public Administration Review, 72*(1), 15–25.

McLain, R. J., & Lee, R. G. (1996). Adaptive management: Promises and pitfalls. *Environmental Management, 20*(4), 437–448.

Mdee, A., & Harrison, E. (2019). Critical governance problems for farmer-led irrigation: Isomorphic mimicry and capability traps. *Water Alternatives, 12*(1), 30–45.

Meadows, D. (1999). *Leverage Points: Places to Intervene in a System.* Hartland, VT: The Sustainability Institute.

Meagher, K. (2012). The strength of weak states? Non-state security forces and hybrid governance in Africa. *Development and Change, 43*(5), 1073–1101.

Meier, K. J. (1975). Representative bureaucracy: An empirical analysis. *American Political Science Review, 69*(2), 526–542.

Meier, K. J. (1993). Latinos and representative bureaucracy testing the Thompson and Henderson hypotheses. *Journal of Public Administration Research and Theory, 3*(4), 393–414.

Meier, K. J., & O'Toole Jr, L. J. (2002). Public management and organizational performance: The effect of managerial quality. *Journal of Policy Analysis and Management, 21*(4), 629–643.

Meier, K. J., & O'Toole Jr, L. J. (2006). Political control versus bureaucratic values: Reframing the debate. *Public Administration Review, 66*(2), 177–192.

Meier, K. J., & Xu, X. (2022). Critical thoughts about critical mass in representative bureaucracy: A theoretical exploration and empirical illustration. *Governance.* https://doi.org/10.1111/gove.12711.

Meier, K. J., Compton, M., Polga-Hecimovich, J., Song, M., & Wimpy, C. (2019). Bureaucracy and the failure of politics: Challenges to democratic governance. *Administration & Society, 51*(10), 1576–1605.

Meier, K. J., O'Toole Jr, L. J., Boyne, G. A., & Walker, R. M. (2007). Strategic management and the performance of public organizations: Testing venerable ideas against recent theories. *Journal of Public Administration Research and Theory, 17*(3), 357–377.

Meier, K. J., O'Toole Jr, L. J. (2006). *Bureaucracy in a Democratic State: A Governance Perspective.* Baltimore: John Hopkins University Press.

Meyer-Sahling, J. H., & Mikkelsen, K. S. (2016). Civil service laws, merit, politicization, and corruption: The perspective of public officials from five East European countries. *Public Administration, 94*(4), 1105–1123.

Meyer-Sahling, J. H., Mikkelsen, K. S., & Schuster, C. (2018). Civil service management and corruption: What we know and what we don't. *Public Administration*, *96*(2), 276–285.

Michels, A. (2011). Innovations in democratic governance: How does citizen participation contribute to a better democracy? *International Review of Administrative Sciences*, *77*(2), 275–293.

Michels, A., & De Graaf, L. (2010). Examining citizen participation: Local participatory policy making and democracy. *Local Government Studies*, *36*(4), 477–491.

Michels, A., & De Graaf, L. (2017). Examining citizen participation: Local participatory policymaking and democracy revisited. *Local Government Studies*, *43*(6), 875–881.

Millard, J., Weerakkody, V., Missi, F., Kapoor, K., & Fernando, G. (2016, March). Social innovation for poverty reduction and sustainable development: Some governance and policy perspectives. In *Proceedings of the 9th International Conference on Theory and Practice of Electronic Governance*, pp. 153–162.

Milward, H. B., & Provan, K. G. (2000). Governing the hollow state. *Journal of Public Administration Research and Theory*, *10*(2), 359–380.

Mitlin, D., Hickey, S., & Bebbington, A. (2007). Reclaiming development? NGOs and the challenge of alternatives. *World Development*, *35*(10), 1699–1720.

Mitroff, I. I., & Featheringham, T. R. (1974). On systemic problem solving and the error of the third kind. *Behavioral Science*, *19*(6), 383–393.

Moe, T. M. (2006). Political control and the power of the agent. *Journal of Law, Economics, and Organization*, *22*(1), 1–29.

Mohai, P., Pellow, D., & Roberts, J. T. (2009). Environmental justice. *Annual Review of Environment and Resources*, *34*, 405–430.

Montes, G. C., & Paschoal, P. C. (2016). Corruption: What are the effects on government effectiveness? Empirical evidence considering developed and developing countries. *Applied Economics Letters*, *23*(2), 146–150.

Moon, C. I., & Prasad, R. (1994). Beyond the developmental state: Networks, politics, and institutions. *Governance*, *7*(4), 360–386.

Moon, K. K. (2018). Examining the relationships between diversity and work behaviors in US federal agencies: Does inclusive management make a difference? *Review of Public Personnel Administration*, *38*(2), 218–247.

Moore, M. H. (1995). *Creating Public Value: Strategic Management in Government*. Cambridge, MA: Harvard University Press.

Mora, C., Myers, R. A., Coll, M., Libralato, S., Pitcher, T. J., Sumaila, R. U., ... & Worm, B. (2009). Management effectiveness of the world's marine fisheries. *PLoS Biology*, *7*(6), e1000131.

Mosher, F. C. (1968). *Democracy and the Public Service*, 2nd ed. New York: Oxford University Press.

Mosley, J. E., & Park, S. (2022). Service providers' influence in collaborative governance networks: Effectiveness in reducing chronic homelessness. *Journal of Public Administration Research and Theory*, *32*(1), 130–149.

Mosley, P. (2012). *The Politics of Poverty Reduction*. Oxford: Oxford University Press.

Moynihan, D. P. (2006). What do we talk about when we talk about performance? Dialogue theory and performance budgeting. *Journal of Public Administration Research and Theory*, *16*(2), 151–168.

Moynihan, D. P., & Kroll, A. (2016). Performance management routines that work? An early assessment of the GPRA Modernization Act. *Public Administration Review*, *76*(2), 314–323.

Moynihan, D. P., & Pandey, S. K. (2005). Testing how management matters in an era of government by performance management. *Journal of Public Administration Research and Theory*, *15*(3), 421–439.

Moynihan, D. P., & Pandey, S. K. (2007). The role of organizations in fostering public service motivation. *Public Administration Review*, *67*(1), 40–53.

Moynihan, D. P., & Pandey, S. K. (2010). The big question for performance management: Why do managers use performance information? *Journal of Public Administration Research and Theory*, *20*(4), 849–866.

Moynihan, D. P., Pandey, S. K., and Wright, B. E. (2014). Transformational leadership in the public sector: Empirical evidence of its effects. In Y. K. Dwivedi, M. A. Shareef, S. K. Pandey, & V. Kumar (Eds.) *Public Administration Reformation: Market Demand from Public Organizations*. London: Routledge/Taylor and Francis, pp. 87–104.

Mulgan, G. (2006). The process of social innovation. *Innovations*, *1*(2), 145–162.

Mulgan, R. (2000). "Accountability": An ever-expanding concept? *Public Administration*, *78*(3), 555–573.

Musso, J., Weare, C., Bryer, T., & Cooper, T. (2011). Toward "strong democracy" in global cities? Social capital building, theory-driven reform, and the Los Angeles neighborhood council experience. *Public Administration Review*, *71*(1), 102–111.

Nabatchi, T., Sancino, A., & Sicilia, M. (2017). Varieties of participation in public services: The who, when, and what of coproduction. *Public Administration Review*, *77*(5), 766–776.

Nadasdy, P. (2003). Reevaluating the co-management success story. *Arctic*, *56*(4), 367–380.

Nagendra, H., & Ostrom, E. (2012). Polycentric governance of multifunctional forested landscapes. *International Journal of the Commons*, *6*(2), 104–133.

Nance, M. T. (2018). Re-thinking FATF: An experimentalist interpretation of the Financial Action Task Force. *Crime, Law and Social Change*, *69*(2), 131–152.

Natcher, D. C., Davis, S., & Hickey, C. G. (2005). Co-management: Managing relationships, not resources. *Human Organization*, *64*(3), 240–250.

Nederhand, J., Bekkers, V., & Voorberg, W. (2016). Self-organization and the role of government: How and why does self-organization evolve in the shadow of hierarchy? *Public Management Review*, *18*(7), 1063–1084.

Nelson, H. W., & Nikolakis, W. (2012). How does corporatization improve the performance of government agencies? Lessons from the restructuring of state-owned forest agencies in Australia. *International Public Management Journal*, *15*(3), 364–391.

Newig, J., Challies, E., Jager, N. W., Kochskaemper, E., & Adzersen, A. (2018). The environmental performance of participatory and collaborative governance: A framework of causal mechanisms. *Policy Studies Journal*, *46*(2), 269–297.

Newman, J., & Head, B. W. (2017). Wicked tendencies in policy problems: Rethinking the distinction between social and technical problems. *Policy and Society*, *36*(3), 414–429.

Nguyen, C. V., Giang, L. T., Tran, A. N., & Do, H. T. (2021). Do good governance and public administration improve economic growth and poverty reduction? The case of Vietnam. *International Public Management Journal*, *24*(1), 131–161.

Nicholson-Crotty, S., Nicholson-Crotty, J., & Fernandez, S. (2017). Will more black cops matter? Officer race and police-involved homicides of black citizens. *Public Administration Review*, *77*(2), 206–216.

Niemeyer, S. (2011). The emancipatory effect of deliberation: Empirical lessons from mini-publics. *Politics & Society*, *39*(1), 103–140.

Noble, B. F. (2000). Institutional criteria for co-management. *Marine Policy, 24*(1), 69–77.

Noordegraaf, M. (2016). Reconfiguring professional work: Changing forms of professionalism in public services. *Administration & Society, 48*(7), 783–810.

Noordegraaf, M., Douglas, S., Geuijen, K., & Van Der Steen, M. (2019). Weaknesses of wickedness: A critical perspective on wickedness theory. *Policy and Society, 38*(2), 278–297.

Norris, P. (2012). *Making Democratic Governance Work: How Regimes Shape Prosperity, Welfare, and Peace.* Cambridge: Cambridge University Press.

Norris, P. (2018). *Driving Democracy: Do Power-Sharing Institutions Work?* Cambridge: Cambridge University Press.

North, D. C. (1990). *Institutions, Institutional Change and Economic Performance.* Cambridge: Cambridge University Press.

Nunan, F., Menton, M., McDermott, C. L., Huxham, M., & Schreckenberg, K. (2021). How does governance mediate links between ecosystem services and poverty alleviation? Results from a systematic mapping and thematic synthesis of literature. *World Development, 146*, 105595.

Oates, W. E. (1972). *Fiscal Federalism.* New York: Harcourt, Brace, Jovanovich.

Öberg, S. A., & Bringselius, L. (2015). Professionalism and organizational performance in the wake of new managerialism. *European Political Science Review, 7*(4), 499–523.

O'Brien, C. M., Ferguson, J., & McVey, M. (2022). National action plans on business and human rights: An experimentalist governance analysis. *Human Rights Review, 23*(1), 71–99.

O'Flynn, I., & Russell, D. (2005). *Power Sharing: New Challenges for Divided Societies.* London: Pluto Press.

Oh, Y., & Bush, C. B. (2016). Exploring the role of dynamic social capital in collaborative governance. *Administration & Society, 48*(2), 216–236.

Olsen, J., & Feeney, M. K. (2022). The influence of legal mandates on public participation. *American Review of Public Administration, 52*(7), 486–497. 02750740221123105.

Olsson, P., Gunderson, L. H., Carpenter, S. R., Ryan, P., Lebel, L., Folke, C., & Holling, C. S. (2006). Shooting the rapids: Navigating transitions to adaptive governance of social-ecological systems. *Ecology and Society, 11*(1), 18.

Oosterlynck, S., Novy, A., Kazepov, Y., Cools, P., Saruis, T., Leubolt, B., & Wukovitsch, F. (2018). Improving poverty reduction: Lessons from the social innovation perspective. In B. Cantillon (Ed.) *Decent Incomes for All: Improving Policies in Europe.* Oxford: Oxford University Press, pp. 179–200.

Orsini, A., & Godet, C. (2018). Food security and biofuels regulations: The emulsifying effect of international regime complexes. *Journal of Contemporary European Research, 14*(1), 4–22.

Osborne, D., & Gaebler, T. (1993). *Reinventing Government.* London: Penguin.

Osborne, S. P. (2006). The new public governance? *Public Management Review, 8*(3), 377–387.

Osborne, S. P. (2018). From public service-dominant logic to public service logic: Are public service organizations capable of co-production and value co-creation? *Public Management Review, 20*(2), 225–231.

Osborne, S. P., Radnor, Z., & Strokosch, K. (2016). Co-production and the co-creation of value in public services: A suitable case for treatment? *Public Management Review, 18*(5), 639–653.

Ospina, S. M. (2017). Collective leadership and context in public administration: Bridging public leadership research and leadership studies. *Public Administration Review, 77*(2), 275–287.

Ospina, S. M., & Saz-Carranza, A. (2010). Paradox and collaboration in network management. *Administration & Society, 42*(4), 404–440.

Ostrom, E. (1990). *Governing the Commons: The Evolution of Institutions for Collective Action.* Cambridge: Cambridge University Press.

Ostrom, E. (2007). A diagnostic approach for going beyond panaceas. *Proceedings of the National Academy of Sciences, 104*(39), 15181–15187.

Ostrom, E. (2010). Beyond markets and states: Polycentric governance of complex economic systems. *American Economic Review, 100*(3), 641–672.

Ostrom, E. (2011). Background on the institutional analysis and development framework. *Policy Studies Journal, 39*(1), 7–27.

Overdevest, C., & Zeitlin, J. (2014). Assembling an experimentalist regime: Transnational governance interactions in the forest sector. *Regulation & Governance, 8*(1), 22–48.

Overman, S. (2016). Great expectations of public service delegation: A systematic review. *Public Management Review, 18*(8), 1238–1262.

Overman, S., & Van Thiel, S. (2016). Agencification and public sector performance: A systematic comparison in 20 countries. *Public Management Review, 18*(4), 611–635.

Page, E. C. (2012). *Policy without Politicians: Bureaucratic Influence in Comparative Perspective.* Oxford: Oxford University Press.

Page, S. (2016). A strategic framework for building civic capacity. *Urban Affairs Review, 52*(4), 439–470.

Page, S. B., Stone, M. M., Bryson, J. M., & Crosby, B. C. (2015). Public value creation by cross-sector collaborations: A framework and challenges of assessment. *Public Administration, 93*(3), 715–732.

Pahl-Wostl, C., Lebel, L., Knieper, C., & Nikitina, E. (2012). From applying panaceas to mastering complexity: Toward adaptive water governance in river basins. *Environmental Science & Policy, 23*, 24–34.

Painter, M., & Pierre, J. (Eds.) (2004). *Challenges to State Policy Capacity: Global Trends and Comparative Perspectives.* Berlin: Springer.

Panday, P. (2018). Making innovations work: Local government–NGO partnership and collaborative governance in rural Bangladesh. *Development in Practice, 28*(1), 125–137.

Pandey, S. K., Davis, R. S., Pandey, S., & Peng, S. (2016). Transformational leadership and the use of normative public values: Can employees be inspired to serve larger public purposes? *Public Administration, 94*(1), 204–222.

Papadopoulos, Y. (2010) Accountability and multi-level governance: More accountability, less democracy? *West European Politics, 33*(5), 1030–1049.

Park, S. M., & Rainey, H. G. (2008). Leadership and public service motivation in US federal agencies. *International Public Management Journal, 11*(1), 109–142.

Parkhurst, J. O. (2016). Appeals to evidence for the resolution of wicked problems: The origins and mechanisms of evidentiary bias. *Policy Sciences, 49*(4), 373–393.

Parks, R. B., Baker, P. C., Kiser, L., Oakerson, R., Ostrom, E., Ostrom, V., ... & Wilson, R. (1981). Consumers as coproducers of public services: Some economic and institutional considerations. *Policy Studies Journal, 9*(7), 1001–1011.

Parrado, S., Van Ryzin, G. G., Bovaird, T., & Löffler, E. (2013). Correlates of co-production: Evidence from a five-nation survey of citizens. *International Public Management Journal, 16*(1), 85–112.

Parsons, M., Taylor, L., & Crease, R. (2021). Indigenous environmental justice within marine ecosystems: A systematic review of the literature on indigenous peoples' involvement in marine governance and management. *Sustainability, 13*(8), 4217.

Pasha, O., Poister, T. H., Wright, B. E., & Thomas, J. C. (2017). Transformational leadership and mission valence of employees: The varying effects by organizational level. *Public Performance & Management Review, 40*(4), 722–740.

Pattberg, P. (2010). Public–private partnerships in global climate governance. *Wiley Interdisciplinary Reviews: Climate Change, 1*(2), 279–287.

Peiffer, C., & Alvarez, L. (2016). Who will be the "principled-principals"? Perceptions of corruption and willingness to engage in anticorruption activism. *Governance, 29*(3), 351–369.

Perreault, T. (2014). What kind of governance for what kind of equity? Towards a theorization of justice in water governance. *Water International, 39*(2), 233–245.

Perry, J. L. (2012). How can we improve our science to generate more usable knowledge for public professionals? *Public Administration Review, 72*(4), 479–482.

Perry, J. L., & Vandenabeele, W. (2015). Public service motivation research: Achievements, challenges, and future directions. *Public Administration Review, 75*(5), 692–699.

Perry, J. L., & Wise, L. R. (1990). The motivational bases of public service. *Public Administration Review, 50*, 367–373.

Persson, A., Rothstein, B., & Teorell, J. (2013). Why anticorruption reforms fail: Systemic corruption as a collective action problem. *Governance, 26*(3), 449–471.

Persson, A., Rothstein, B., & Teorell, J. (2019). Getting the basic nature of systemic corruption right: A reply to Marquette and Peiffer. *Governance, 32*(4), 799–810.

Peters, B. G. (1994). Managing the hollow state. *International Journal of Public Administration, 17*(3–4), 739–756.

Peters, B. G. (2005). The problem of policy problems. *Journal of Comparative Policy Analysis, 7*(4), 349–370.

Peters, B. G. (2010). Bureaucracy and democracy. *Public Organization Review, 10*(3), 209–222.

Peters, B. G., & Pierre, J. (Eds.) (2004). *Politicization of the Civil Service in Comparative Perspective: The Quest for Control*. London: Routledge.

Peters, B. G., & Pierre, J. (2016). *Comparative Governance: Rediscovering the Functional Dimension of Governing*. Cambridge: Cambridge University Press.

Peters, B. G., & Pierre, J. (2019). Populism and public administration: Confronting the administrative state. *Administration & Society, 51*(10), 1521–1545.

Peters, B. G., & Tarpey, M. (2019). Are wicked problems really so wicked? Perceptions of policy problems. *Policy and Society, 38*(2), 218–236.

Petersen, O. H., Hjelmar, U., & Vrangbæk, K. (2018). Is contracting out of public services still the great panacea? A systematic review of studies on economic and quality effects from 2000 to 2014. *Social Policy & Administration, 52*(1), 130–157.

Phillips, W., Lee, H., Ghobadian, A., O'Regan, N., & James, P. (2015). Social innovation and social entrepreneurship: A systematic review. *Group & Organization Management, 40*(3), 428–461.

Piattoni, S. (2010). *The Theory of Multi-level Governance: Conceptual, Empirical, and Normative Challenges*. Oxford: Oxford University Press.

Pierce, J. C., Lovrich Jr, N. P., & Moon Jr, C. D. (2002). Social capital and government performance: An analysis of 20 American cities. *Public Performance & Management Review*, *25*(4), 381–397.

Pierre, J. (Ed.) (2000). *Debating Governance: Authority, Steering, and Democracy.* Oxford: Oxford University Press.

Pierre, J., & Peters, B. G. (2020). *Governance, Politics and the State.* London: Bloomsbury Publishing.

Pierskalla, J. H., & Sacks, A. (2017). Unpacking the effect of decentralized governance on routine violence: Lessons from Indonesia. *World Development*, *90*, 213–228.

Pierson, P. (1996). The new politics of the welfare state. *World Politics*, *48*(2), 143–179.

Pitts, D. W. (2011). A little less conversation, a little more action: Using empirical research to promote social equity. *Journal of Public Administration Research and Theory*, *21*(suppl 1), i77–i82.

Platt, J. (1973). Social traps. *American Psychologist*, *28*(8), 641–651.

Plummer, R., & Fitzgibbon, J. (2004). Co-management of natural resources: A proposed framework. *Environmental Management*, *33*(6), 876–885.

Poister, T. H. (2010). The future of strategic planning in the public sector: Linking strategic management and performance. *Public Administration Review*, *70*, s246–s254.

Pollitt, C., & Bouckaert, G. (2017). *Public Management Reform: A Comparative Analysis: Into the Age of Austerity.* Oxford: Oxford University Press.

Pollitt, C., & Dan, S. (2011). The impacts of the New Public Management in Europe: A meta-analysis. COCOPS—COordinating for COhesion in the Public Sector of the Future, Working Paper No. 3.

Pollitt, C., & Hupe, P. (2011). Talking about government: The role of magic concepts. *Public Management Review*, *13*(5), 641–658.

Pomeroy, R. S., & Berkes, F. (1997). Two to tango: The role of government in fisheries co-management. *Marine Policy*, *21*(5), 465–480.

Pomeroy, R. S., Katon, B. M., & Harkes, I. (2001). Conditions affecting the success of fisheries co-management: Lessons from Asia. *Marine Policy*, *25*(3), 197–208.

Popper, K. R. (1963). Science as falsification. *Conjectures and Refutations*, *1*(1963), 33–39.

Porter, G. (2003). NGOs and poverty reduction in a globalizing world: Perspectives from Ghana. *Progress in Development Studies*, *3*(2), 131–145.

Powell, M., Yörük, E., & Bargu, A. (2020). Thirty years of the three worlds of welfare capitalism: A review of reviews. *Social Policy & Administration*, *54*(1), 60–87.

Pradilla, C. A., da Silva, J. B., & Reinecke, J. (2022). Wicked problems and new ways of organizing: How Fe y Alegria confronted changing manifestations of poverty. In A. A. Gümüsay, E. Marti, H. Trittin-Ulbrich, & C. Wickert (Eds.) *Organizing for Societal Grand Challenges*. Bingley: Emerald Publishing Limited, pp. 94–114.

Pressman, J. L., & Wildavsky, A. (1984). *Implementation.* Berkeley: University of California Press.

Provan, K. G., & Kenis, P. (2008). Modes of network governance: Structure, management, and effectiveness. *Journal of Public Administration Research and Theory*, *18*(2), 229–252.

Provan, K. G., & Milward, H. B. (1995). A preliminary theory of interorganizational network effectiveness: A comparative study of four community mental health systems. *Administrative Science Quarterly*, *40*(1), 1–33.

Putnam, R. D. (2000). *Bowling Alone: The Collapse and Revival of American Community.* New York: Simon and Schuster.

Putnam, R. D. with Leonardi, R., & Nanetti, R. Y. (2001). *Making Democracy Work: Civic Traditions in Modern Italy*. Princeton: Princeton University Press.

Quick, K. S. (2017). Locating and building collective leadership and impact. *Leadership, 13*(4), 445–471.

Raab, J., Mannak, R. S., & Cambré, B. (2015). Combining structure, governance, and context: A configurational approach to network effectiveness. *Journal of Public Administration Research and Theory, 25*(2), 479–511.

Radin, B. A. (2006). *Challenging the Performance Movement: Accountability, Complexity, and Democratic Values*. Washington, DC: Georgetown University Press.

Radosavljevic, S., Haider, L. J., Lade, S. J., & Schlüter, M. (2021). Implications of poverty traps across levels. *World Development, 144*, 105437.

Ragin, C., & Zaret, D. (1983). Theory and method in comparative research: Two strategies. *Social Forces, 61*(3), 731–754.

Rainey, H. G., & Steinbauer, P. (1999). Galloping elephants: Developing elements of a theory of effective government organizations. *Journal of Public Administration Research and Theory, 9*(1), 1–32.

Rangoni, B., & Zeitlin, J. (2021). Is experimentalist governance self-limiting or self-reinforcing? Strategic uncertainty and recursive rulemaking in European Union electricity regulation. *Regulation & Governance, 15*(3), 822–839.

Raustiala, K., & Victor, D. G. (2004). The regime complex for plant genetic resources. *International Organization, 58*(2), 277–309.

Raven, R. (2007). Niche accumulation and hybridisation strategies in transition processes towards a sustainable energy system: An assessment of differences and pitfalls. *Energy Policy, 35*(4), 2390–2400.

Reinicke, W. H. (1999). The other world wide web: Global public policy networks. *Foreign Policy*, (117) (Winter), 44–57.

Repenning, N. P., & Sterman, J. D. (2002). Capability traps and self-confirming attribution errors in the dynamics of process improvement. *Administrative Science Quarterly, 47*(2), 265–295.

Rethemeyer, R. K., & Hatmaker, D. M. (2008). Network management reconsidered: An inquiry into management of network structures in public sector service provision. *Journal of Public Administration Research and Theory, 18*(4), 617–646.

Rhodes, R. A. W. (1996). The new governance: Governing without government. *Political Studies, 44*(4), 652–667.

Rhodes, R. A. (1997). *Understanding Governance: Policy Networks, Governance, Reflexivity and Accountability*. Milton Keynes: Open University.

Rhodes, R. A. (2007). Understanding governance: Ten years on. *Organization Studies, 28*(8), 1243–1264.

Riccucci, N. M., & Van Ryzin, G. G. (2017). Representative bureaucracy: A lever to enhance social equity, coproduction, and democracy. *Public Administration Review, 77*(1), 21–30.

Riccucci, N. M., Van Ryzin, G. G., & Li, H. (2016). Representative bureaucracy and the willingness to coproduce: An experimental study. *Public Administration Review, 76*(1), 121–130.

Rice, T. W. (2001). Social capital and government performance in Iowa communities. *Journal of Urban Affairs, 23*(3–4), 375–389.

Richardson, M. D. (2019). Politicization and expertise: Exit, effort, and investment. *Journal of Politics, 81*(3), 878–891.

Rietig, K. (2018). The links among contested knowledge, beliefs, and learning in European climate governance: From consensus to conflict in reforming biofuels policy. *Policy Studies Journal, 46*(1), 137–159.

Rihoux, B., & Ragin, C. C. (2008). *Configurational Comparative Methods: Qualitative Comparative Analysis (QCA) and Related Techniques.* Thousand Oaks, CA: Sage.

Rijke, J., Brown, R., Zevenbergen, C., Ashley, R., Farrelly, M., Morison, P., & van Herk, S. (2012). Fit-for-purpose governance: A framework to make adaptive governance operational. *Environmental Science & Policy, 22*, 73–84.

Rijke, J., Farrelly, M., Brown, R., & Zevenbergen, C. (2013). Configuring transformative governance to enhance resilient urban water systems. *Environmental Science & Policy, 25*, 62–72.

Ringquist, E. J. (2005). Assessing evidence of environmental inequities: A meta-analysis. *Journal of Policy Analysis and Management, 24*(2), 223–247.

Rip, A., & Kemp, R. (1998). Technological change. *Human Choice and Climate Change, 2*(2), 327–399.

Rittel, H. W., & Webber, M. M. (1973). Dilemmas in a general theory of planning. *Policy Sciences, 4*(2), 155–169.

Ritz, A., Brewer, G. A., & Neumann, O. (2016). Public service motivation: A systematic literature review and outlook. *Public Administration Review, 76*(3), 414–426.

Roberts, A. (2011). *The Logic of Discipline: Global Capitalism and the Architecture of Government.* Oxford: Oxford University Press.

Roberts, A. (2020). *Strategies for Governing: Reinventing Public Administration for a Dangerous Century.* Ithaca: Cornell University Press.

Roberts, N. (2000). Wicked problems and network approaches to resolution. *International Public Management Review, 1*(1), 1–19.

Roberts, P. S. (2006). FEMA and the prospects for reputation-based autonomy. *Studies in American Political Development, 20*(1), 57–87.

Roberts, P. S. (2009). How security agencies control change: Executive power and the quest for autonomy in the FBI and CIA. *Public Organization Review, 9*, 169–198.

Roe, E. (2013). *Making the Most of Mess: Reliability and Policy in Today's Management Challenges.* Durham: Duke University Press.

Roe, E. (2016). Policy messes and their management. *Policy Sciences, 49*(4), 351–372.

Røiseland, A. (2022). Co-creating democratic legitimacy: Potentials and pitfalls. *Administration & Society, 54*(8), 1493–1515.

Roll, M. (Ed.). (2014). *The Politics of Public Sector Performance: Pockets of Effectiveness in Developing Countries.* London: Routledge.

Romzek, B. S., & Dubnick, M. J. (1987). Accountability in the public sector: Lessons from the Challenger tragedy. *Public Administration Review, 47*(3), 227–238.

Romzek, B. S., & Ingraham, P. W. (2000). Cross pressures of accountability: Initiative, command, and failure in the Ron Brown plane crash. *Public Administration Review, 60*(3), 240–253.

Romzek, B. S., & Johnston, J. M. (2005). State social services contracting: Exploring the determinants of effective contract accountability. *Public Administration Review, 65*(4), 436–449.

Romzek, B. S., LeRoux, K., & Blackmar, J. M. (2012). A preliminary theory of informal accountability among network organizational actors. *Public Administration Review, 72*(3), 442–453.

Rose-Ackerman, S. (2017). What does "governance" mean? *Governance, 30*(1), 23–27.

Rose, N., O'Malley, P., & Valverde, M. (2006). Governmentality. *Annual Review of Law and Social Science, 2*, 83–104.

Rotberg, R. I. (2014). Good governance means performance and results. *Governance*, *27*(3), 511–518.

Rothstein, B. (2005). *Social Traps and the Problem of Trust*. Cambridge: Cambridge University Press.

Rothstein, B. (2012). Good governance. In D. Levi-Faur (Ed.) *The Oxford Handbook of Governance*. Oxford: Oxford University Press, pp. 143–154.

Rothstein, B. O., & Teorell, J. A. (2008). What is quality of government? A theory of impartial government institutions. *Governance*, *21*(2), 165–190.

Ruano-Chamorro, C., Gurney, G. G., & Cinner, J. E. (2022). Advancing procedural justice in conservation. *Conservation Letters*, *15*(3), e12861.

Rudra, N. (2007). Welfare states in developing countries: Unique or universal? *Journal of Politics*, *69*(2), 378–396.

Rule, P., & John, V. M. (2015). A necessary dialogue: Theory in case study research. *International Journal of Qualitative Methods*, *14*(4), 1609406915611575.

Sabel, C. F., & Zeitlin, J. (2008). Learning from difference: The new architecture of experimentalist governance in the EU. *European Law Journal*, *14*(3), 271–327.

Sabharwal, M., Levine, H., & D'Agostino, M. (2018). A conceptual content analysis of 75 years of diversity research in public administration. *Review of Public Personnel Administration*, *38*(2), 248–267.

Sachs, J., McArthur, J. W., Schmidt-Traub, G., Kruk, M., Bahadur, C., Faye, M., & McCord, G. (2004). Ending Africa's poverty trap. *Brookings Papers on Economic Activity*, *2004*(1), 117–240.

Sager, F., & Rosser, C. (2009). Weber, Wilson, and Hegel: Theories of modern bureaucracy. *Public Administration Review*, *69*(6), 1136–1147.

Saleem, Z., & Donaldson, J. A. (2016). Pathways to poverty reduction. *Development Policy Review*, *34*(5), 671–690.

Sanginga, P. C., Kamugisha, R. N., & Martin, A. M. (2007). The dynamics of social capital and conflict management in multiple resource regimes: A case of the southwestern highlands of Uganda. *Ecology and Society*, *12*(1), 6.

Sanogo, T. (2019). Does fiscal decentralization enhance citizens' access to public services and reduce poverty? Evidence from Côte d'Ivoire municipalities in a conflict setting. *World Development*, *113*, 204–221.

Sawulski, J., & Kutwa, K. (2022). Does spending on social-welfare policies reduce poverty? An assessment of the European Union countries using impulse-response and efficiency methods. *Optimum. Economic Studies*, *1*(107), 64–83.

Scharpf, F. W. (1994). Games real actors could play: Positive and negative coordination in embedded negotiations. *Journal of Theoretical Politics*, *6*(1), 27–53.

Scharpf, F. W. (1999). *Governing in Europe: Effective and Democratic?* Oxford: Oxford University Press.

Schillemans, T. (2016). Calibrating public sector accountability: Translating experimental findings to public sector accountability. *Public Management Review*, *18*(9), 1400–1420.

Schillemans, T., & Busuioc, M. (2015). Predicting public sector accountability: From agency drift to forum drift. *Journal of Public Administration Research and Theory*, *25*(1), 191–215.

Schlosberg, D. (2013). Theorising environmental justice: The expanding sphere of a discourse. *Environmental Politics*, *22*(1), 37–55.

Schlosberg, D., & Collins, L. B. (2014). From environmental to climate justice: Climate change and the discourse of environmental justice. *Wiley Interdisciplinary Reviews: Climate Change*, *5*(3), 359–374.

Schmelzle, C., & Stollenwerk, E. (2018). Virtuous or vicious circle? Governance effectiveness and legitimacy in areas of limited statehood. *Journal of Intervention and Statebuilding*, *12*(4), 449–467.

Schmidt, V. A. (2013). Democracy and legitimacy in the European Union revisited: Input, output and "throughput". *Political Studies*, *61*(1), 2–22.

Schmidt, V., & Wood, M. (2019). Conceptualizing throughput legitimacy: Procedural mechanisms of accountability, transparency, inclusiveness and openness in EU governance. *Public Administration*, *97*(4), 727–740.

Schneider, H. (1999). Participatory governance for poverty reduction. *Journal of International Development, Special Issue: 1998 Annual Conference of the Development Studies Association*, *11*(4), 521–534.

Schott, C., Van Kleef, D., & Noordegraaf, M. (2016). Confused professionals? Capacities to cope with pressures on professional work. *Public Management Review*, *18*(4), 583–610.

Scott, J. C. (2020). *Seeing Like a State: How Certain Schemes to Improve the Human Condition have Failed*. New Haven: Yale University Press.

Scott, T. (2015). Does collaboration make any difference? Linking collaborative governance to environmental outcomes. *Journal of Policy Analysis and Management*, *34*(3), 537–566.

Scott, T. A., & Thomas, C. W. (2017). Unpacking the collaborative toolbox: Why and when do public managers choose collaborative governance strategies? *Policy Studies Journal*, *45*(1), 191–214.

Seim, J. (2017). The ambulance: Toward a labor theory of poverty governance. *American Sociological Review*, *82*(3), 451–475.

Selin, J. L. (2015). What makes an agency independent? *American Journal of Political Science*, *59*(4), 971–987.

Selznick, P. (1958). *Leadership in Administration: A Sociological Interpretation*. Berkeley: University of California Press.

Selznick, P. (1996). Institutionalism "old" and "new". *Administrative Science Quarterly*, *41*, 270–277.

Sen, S., & Nielsen, J. R. (1996). Fisheries co-management: A comparative analysis. *Marine Policy*, *20*(5), 405–418.

Sepulveda, C. F., & Martinez-Vazquez, J. (2011). The consequences of fiscal decentralization on poverty and income equality. *Environment and Planning C: Government and Policy*, *29*(2), 321–343.

Seyfang, G., & Haxeltine, A. (2012). Growing grassroots innovations: Exploring the role of community-based initiatives in governing sustainable energy transitions. *Environment and Planning C: Government and Policy*, *30*(3), 381–400.

Seyfang, G., & Smith, A. (2007). Grassroots innovations for sustainable development: Towards a new research and policy agenda. *Environmental Politics*, *16*(4), 584–603.

Shelby, T. (2012). Race. In D. Estlund (Ed.) *The Oxford Handbook of Political Philosophy*. Oxford: Oxford University Press, pp. 336–353.

Sher-Hadar, N., Lahat, L., & Galnoor, I. (2021). Conclusion: Collaborative governance as an arrangement for shaping and implementing policy. In N. Sher-Hadar, L. Lahat, & I. Galnoor (Eds.) *Collaborative Governance*. Cham: Palgrave Macmillan, pp. 277–293.

Shiffman, J. (2017). Four challenges that global health networks face. *International Journal of Health Policy and Management*, *6*(4), 183–189.

Shön, D., & Rein, M. (1994). *Frame Reflection: Toward the Resolution of Intractable Policy Controversies*. New York: Basic Books.

Shon, J., & Cho, Y. K. (2020). Fiscal decentralization and government corruption: Evidence from US states. *Public Integrity*, *22*(2), 187–204.

Sicilia, M., Sancino, A., Nabatchi, T., & Guarini, E. (2019). Facilitating co-production in public services: Management implications from a systematic literature review. *Public Money & Management*, *39*(4), 233–240.

Simon, H. A. (1946). The proverbs of administration. *Public Administration Review*, *6*(1), 53–67.

Simon, H. A. (1973). The structure of ill structured problems. *Artificial Intelligence*, *4*(3–4), 181–201.

Singh, P. K., & Chudasama, H. (2020). Evaluating poverty alleviation strategies in a developing country. *PloS One*, *15*(1), e0227176.

Sirianni, C. (2010). *Investing in Democracy: Engaging Citizens in Collaborative Governance*. Washington, DC: Brookings Institution Press.

Sjoberg, F. M., Mellon, J., & Peixoto, T. (2017). The effect of bureaucratic responsiveness on citizen participation. *Public Administration Review*, *77*(3), 340–351.

Skocpol, T., & Finegold, K. (1982). State capacity and economic intervention in the early New Deal. *Political Science Quarterly*, *97*(2), 255–278.

Slaughter, A. M. (2004). *A New World Order*. Princeton: Princeton University Press.

Slaughter, A. M., & Zaring, D. (2006). Networking goes international: An update. *Annual Review of Law and Social Science*, *2*, 211–229.

Smith, A., & Seyfang, G. (2013). Constructing grassroots innovations for sustainability. *Global Environmental Change*, *23*(5), 827–829.

Smith, A., Fressoli, M., & Thomas, H. (2014). Grassroots innovation movements: Challenges and contributions. *Journal of Cleaner Production*, *63*, 114–124.

Smith, A., Stirling, A., & Berkhout, F. (2005). The governance of sustainable socio-technical transitions. *Research Policy*, *34*, 1491–1510.

Smith, J. G. (2020). Theoretical advances in our understanding of network effectiveness. *Perspectives on Public Management and Governance*, *3*(2), 167–182.

Soifer, H. (2008). State infrastructural power: Approaches to conceptualization and measurement. *Studies in Comparative International Development*, *43*, 231–251.

Sørensen, E. (2017). Political innovations: Innovations in political institutions, processes and outputs. *Public Management Review*, *19*(1), 1–19.

Sørensen, E. (2020). *Interactive Political Leadership: The Role of Politicians in the Age of Governance*. Oxford: Oxford University Press.

Sørensen, E., & Torfing, J. (2005). The democratic anchorage of governance networks. *Scandinavian Political Studies*, *28*(3), 195–218.

Sørensen, E., & Torfing, J. (2009). Making governance networks effective and democratic through metagovernance. *Public Administration*, *87*(2), 234–258.

Sørensen, E., & Torfing, J. (Eds.) (2016). *Theories of Democratic Network Governance*. Berlin: Springer.

Sørensen, E., & Torfing, J. (2017). Metagoverning collaborative innovation in governance networks. *American Review of Public Administration*, *47*(7), 826–839.

Sørensen, E., & Torfing, J. (2021). Accountable government through collaborative governance? *Administrative Sciences*, *11*(4), 127.

Sørensen, E., Bryson, J., & Crosby, B. (2021). How public leaders can promote public value through co-creation. *Policy & Politics*, *49*(2), 267–286.

Sorrentino, M., Sicilia, M., & Howlett, M. (2018). Understanding co-production as a new public governance tool. *Policy and Society*, *37*(3), 277–293.

References

Soss, J., Fording, R. C., & Schram, S. F. (2011). *Disciplining the Poor: Neoliberal Paternalism and the Persistent Power of Race*. Chicago: University of Chicago Press.

Sowa, J. E., & Selden, S. C. (2003). Administrative discretion and active representation: An expansion of the theory of representative bureaucracy. *Public Administration Review*, *63*(6), 700–710.

Steffek, J. (2019). The limits of proceduralism: Critical remarks on the rise of "throughput legitimacy". *Public Administration*, *97*(4), 784–796.

Stern, P. (2011). Design principles for global commons: Natural resources and emerging technologies. *International Journal of the Commons*, *5*(2), 2133–232.

Stewart, D. W. (1985). Professionalism vs. democracy: Friedrich vs. Finer revisited. *Public Administration Quarterly*, *9*(1), 13–25.

Stinchcombe, A. L. (1997). On the virtues of the old institutionalism. *Annual Review of Sociology*, *23*(1), 1–18.

Stirling, A. (2006). Precaution, foresight and sustainability: Reflection and reflexivity in the governance of science and technology. In J.-P. Voß & R. Kemp (Eds.) *Reflexive Governance for Sustainable Development*. Cheltenham, UK and Northampton, MA, USA: Edward Elgar Publishing, pp. 225–272.

Stoker, G. (1998). Governance as theory: Five propositions. *International Social Science Journal*, *50*(155), 17–28.

Stoker, G. (2019). Can the governance paradigm survive the rise of populism? *Policy & Politics*, *47*(1), 3–18.

Stone, C. N., Henig, J. R., Jones, B. D., & Pierannunzi, C. (2001). *Building Civic Capacity: The Politics of Reforming Urban Schools*. Lawrence: University Press of Kansas.

Stone, D. (2004). Transfer agents and global networks in the "transnationalization" of policy. *Journal of European Public Policy*, *11*(3), 545–566.

Storeng, K. T., & de Bengy Puyvallée, A. (2018). Civil society participation in global public private partnerships for health. *Health Policy and Planning*, *33*(8), 928–936.

Strebel, M. A., Kübler, D., & Marcinkowski, F. (2019). The importance of input and output legitimacy in democratic governance: Evidence from a population-based survey experiment in four West European countries. *European Journal of Political Research*, *58*(2), 488–513.

Stuart, F. (2014). From "rabble management" to "recovery management": Policing homelessness in marginal urban space. *Urban Studies*, *51*(9), 1909–1925.

Suiseeya, K. R. M., & Caplow, S. (2013). In pursuit of procedural justice: Lessons from an analysis of 56 forest carbon project designs. *Global Environmental Change*, *23*(5), 968–979.

Sun, R., & Henderson, A. C. (2017). Transformational leadership and organizational processes: Influencing public performance. *Public Administration Review*, *77*(4), 554–565.

Sun, R., & Wang, W. (2017). Transformational leadership, employee turnover intention, and actual voluntary turnover in public organizations. *Public Management Review*, *19*(8), 1124–1141.

Sunshine, J., & Tyler, T. R. (2003). The role of procedural justice and legitimacy in shaping public support for policing. *Law & Society Review*, *37*(3), 513–548.

Susskind, L., & Cruikshank, J. (1987). *Breaking the Impasse*. New York: Basic Books.

Sutton, R. I., & Staw, B. M. (1995). What theory is not. *Administrative Science Quarterly*, *40*(3), 371–384.

Tavits, M. (2006). Making democracy work more? Exploring the linkage between social capital and government performance. *Political Research Quarterly, 59*(2), 211–225.

Tendler, J. (1997). *Good Government in the Tropics*. Baltimore and London: Johns Hopkins University Press.

Termeer, C. J., & Dewulf, A. (2019). A small wins framework to overcome the evaluation paradox of governing wicked problems. *Policy and Society, 38*(2), 298–314.

Termeer, C. J. A. M., & Metze, T. A. P. (2019). More than peanuts: Transformation towards a circular economy through a small-wins governance framework. *Journal of Cleaner Production, 240*, 118272.

Termeer, C. J., Dewulf, A., Breeman, G., & Stiller, S. J. (2015). Governance capabilities for dealing wisely with wicked problems. *Administration & Society, 47*(6), 680–710.

Teubner, G. (1982). Substantive and reflexive elements in modern law. *Law & Society Review, 17*, 239–285.

Theobald, N. A., & Haider-Markel, D. P. (2009). Race, bureaucracy, and symbolic representation: Interactions between citizens and police. *Journal of Public Administration Research and Theory, 19*(2), 409–426.

Thiel, A. (2017). The scope of polycentric governance analysis and resulting challenges. *Journal of Self-Governance and Management Economics, 5*(3), 52–82.

Thomann, E., Hupe, P., & Sager, F. (2018). Serving many masters: Public accountability in private policy implementation. *Governance, 31*(2), 299–319.

Tiebout, C. M. (1956). A pure theory of local expenditures. *Journal of Political Economy, 64*(5), 416–424.

Toke, D. (2010). Politics by heuristics: Policy networks with a focus on actor resources, as illustrated by the case of renewable energy policy under New Labour. *Public Administration, 88*(3), 764–781.

Torfing, J. (2016). *Collaborative Innovation in the Public Sector*. Washington, DC: Georgetown University Press.

Torfing, J. (2019). Collaborative innovation in the public sector: The argument. *Public Management Review, 21*(1), 1–11.

Torfing, J. (2023). *Rethinking Public Governance*. Cheltenham, UK and Northampton, MA, USA: Edward Elgar Publishing.

Torfing, J., & Ansell, C. (2017). Strengthening political leadership and policy innovation through the expansion of collaborative forms of governance. *Public Management Review, 19*(1), 37–54.

Torfing, J., Peters, B. G., Pierre, J., & Sørensen, E. (2012). *Interactive Governance: Advancing the Paradigm*. Oxford: Oxford University Press.

Torfing, J., Sørensen, E., & Røiseland, A. (2019). Transforming the public sector into an arena for co-creation: Barriers, drivers, benefits, and ways forward. *Administration & Society, 51*(5), 795–825.

Tortola, P. D. (2017). Clarifying multilevel governance. *European Journal of Political Research, 56*(2), 234–250.

Tosun, J., Koos, S., & Shore, J. (2016). Co-governing common goods: Interaction patterns of private and public actors. *Policy and Society, 35*(1), 1–12.

Townsend, J. G., Porter, G., & Mawdsley, E. (2002). The role of the transnational community of non-government organizations: Governance or poverty reduction? *Journal of International Development, 14*(6), 829–839.

Treisman, D. (2007). *The Architecture of Government: Rethinking Political Decentralization*. Cambridge: Cambridge University Press.

Triantafillou, P. (2020). Trapped in the complexity bowl? Public governance and the liberal art of governing. *International Journal of Public Administration, 43*(14), 1228–1236.

Turnbull, N. (2006). How should we theorise public policy? Problem solving and problematicity. *Policy and Society, 25*(2), 3–22.

Turnbull, N. (2013). The questioning theory of policy practice: Outline of an integrated analytical framework. *Critical Policy Studies, 7*(2), 115–131.

Turnbull, N., & Hoppe, R. (2019). Problematizing "wickedness": A critique of the wicked problems concept, from philosophy to practice. *Policy and Society, 38*(2), 315–337.

Tyler, T. R. (1998). Trust and democratic governance. In V. Braithwaite & M. Levi (Eds.) *Trust and Governance.* New York: Russell Sage Foundation, pp. 269–294.

Ulibarri, N. (2015). Tracing process to performance of collaborative governance: A comparative case study of federal hydropower licensing. *Policy Studies Journal, 43*(2), 283–308.

Van Bueren, E. M., Klijn, E. H., & Koppenjan, J. F. (2003). Dealing with wicked problems in networks: Analyzing an environmental debate from a network perspective. *Journal of Public Administration Research and Theory, 13*(2), 193–212.

van der Does, R. (2022). Citizen involvement in public policy: Does it matter how much is at stake? *Public Administration.* https://doi.org/10.1111/padm.12846.

Van der Voet, J. (2014). The effectiveness and specificity of change management in a public organization: Transformational leadership and a bureaucratic organizational structure. *European Management Journal, 32*(3), 373–382.

Van der Voet, J., Kuipers, B. S., & Groeneveld, S. (2016). Implementing change in public organizations: The relationship between leadership and affective commitment to change in a public sector context. *Public Management Review, 18*(6), 842–865.

Van Dooren, W., Bouckaert, G., & Halligan, J. (2015). *Performance Management in the Public Sector.* London: Routledge.

Van Eijk, C. J., & Steen, T. P. (2014). Why people co-produce: Analysing citizens' perceptions on co-planning engagement in health care services. *Public Management Review, 16*(3), 358–382.

Vangen, S. (2017). Developing practice-oriented theory on collaboration: A paradox lens. *Public Administration Review, 77*(2), 263–272.

Vangen, S., & Huxham, C. (2003). Nurturing collaborative relations: Building trust in interorganizational collaboration. *Journal of Applied Behavioral Science, 39*(1), 5–31.

Van Ham, H., & Koppenjan, J. (2001). Building public–private partnerships: Assessing and managing risks in port development. *Public Management Review, 3*(4), 593–616.

Van Kersbergen, K., Vis, B., & Hemerijck, A. (2014). The great recession and welfare state reform: Is retrenchment really the only game left in town? *Social Policy & Administration, 48*(7), 883–904.

Van Knippenberg, D., & Sitkin, S. B. (2013). A critical assessment of charismatic–transformational leadership research: Back to the drawing board? *Academy of Management Annals, 7*(1), 1–60.

Van Vliet, O., & Wang, C. (2015). Social investment and poverty reduction: A comparative analysis across fifteen European countries. *Journal of Social Policy, 44*(3), 611–638.

Van Wart, M. (2013). Lessons from leadership theory and the contemporary challenges of leaders. *Public Administration Review, 73*(4), 553–565.

van Wijk, J., van Wijk, J., Drost, S., & Stam, W. (2020). Challenges in building robust interventions in contexts of poverty: Insights from an NGO-driven multi-stakeholder network in Ethiopia. *Organization Studies*, *41*(10), 1391–1415.

Vatn, A., & Vedeld, P. (2012). Fit, interplay, and scale: A diagnosis. *Ecology and Society*, *17*(4), 12.

Verbruggen, P. (2013). Gorillas in the closet? Public and private actors in the enforcement of transnational private regulation. *Regulation & Governance*, *7*(4), 512–532.

Verhoest, K. (2005). Effects of autonomy, performance contracting, and competition on the performance of a public agency: A case study. *Policy Studies Journal*, *33*(2), 235–258.

Verkuil, P. R. (2017). *Valuing Bureaucracy: The Case for Professional Government*. Cambridge: Cambridge University Press.

Verschuere, B., Brandsen, T., & Pestoff, V. (2012). Co-production: The state of the art in research and the future agenda. *VOLUNTAS: International Journal of Voluntary and Nonprofit Organizations*, *23*(4), 1083–1101.

Verweij, M., Douglas, M., Ellis, R., Engel, C., Hendriks, F., Lohmann, S., ... & Thompson, M. (2006). Clumsy solutions for a complex world: The case of climate change. *Public Administration*, *84*(4), 817–843.

Vihma, P., & Toikka, A. (2021). The limits of collaborative governance: The role of inter-group learning and trust in the case of the Estonian "Forest War". *Environmental Policy and Governance*, *31*(5), 403–416.

Vining, A. R., Laurin, C., & Weimer, D. (2015). The longer-run performance effects of agencification: Theory and evidence from Québec agencies. *Journal of Public Policy*, *35*(2), 193–222.

Voorberg, W. H., Bekkers, V. J., & Tummers, L. G. (2015). A systematic review of co-creation and co-production: Embarking on the social innovation journey. *Public Management Review*, *17*(9), 1333–1357.

Voorn, B., Van Genugten, M., & Van Thiel, S. (2019). Multiple principals, multiple problems: Implications for effective governance and a research agenda for joint service delivery. *Public Administration*, *97*(3), 671–685.

Voß, J. P., & Bornemann, B. (2011). The politics of reflexive governance: Challenges for designing adaptive management and transition management. *Ecology and Society*, *16*(2), 9.

Voß, J. P. and Kemp, R. (2006). Sustainability and reflexive governance: An introduction. In J. P. Voß, D. Bauknecht, & R. Kemp (Eds.) *Reflexive Governance for Sustainable Development*. Cheltenham, UK and Northampton, MA, USA: Edward Elgar Publishing, pp. 3–28.

Waardenburg, M., Groenleer, M., de Jong, J., & Keijser, B. (2020). Paradoxes of collaborative governance: Investigating the real-life dynamics of multi-agency collaborations using a quasi-experimental action-research approach. *Public Management Review*, *22*(3), 386–407.

Wacquant, L. (2009). *Punishing the Poor*. Durham: Duke University Press.

Wagenaar, H. (2007). Governance, complexity, and democratic participation: How citizens and public officials harness the complexities of neighborhood decline. *American Review of Public Administration*, *37*(1), 17–50.

Walters, C. J. (1986). *Adaptive Management of Renewable Resources*. New York: Macmillan.

Walters, W. (2004). Some critical notes on "governance". *Studies in Political Economy*, *73*(1), 27–46.

Wälti, S., Küjbler, D., & Papadopoulos, Y. (2004). How democratic is "governance"? Lessons from Swiss drug policy. *Governance, 17*(1), 83–113.

Walton, O. E., Davies, T., Thrandardottir, E., & Keating, V. C. (2016). Understanding contemporary challenges to INGO legitimacy: Integrating top-down and bottom-up perspectives. *VOLUNTAS: International Journal of Voluntary and Nonprofit Organizations, 27*(6), 2764–2786.

Waluyo, B. (2021). The tides of agencification: Literature development and future directions. *International Journal of Public Sector Management, 35*(1), 34–60.

Walzer, N., Weaver, L., & McGuire, C. (2016). Collective impact approaches and community development issues. *Community Development, 47*(2), 156–166.

Wang, H., Ran, B., & Li, Y. (2022). Street-level collaborative governance for urban regeneration: How were conflicts resolved at grassroot level? *Journal of Urban Affairs*, 1–21. https://doi.org/10.1080/07352166.2022.2133725.

Wang, H., Xiong, W., Wu, G., & Zhu, D. (2018). Public–private partnership in Public Administration discipline: A literature review. *Public Management Review, 20*(2), 293–316.

Wang, W. (2016). Exploring the determinants of network effectiveness: The case of neighborhood governance networks in Beijing. *Journal of Public Administration Research and Theory, 26*(2), 375–388.

Warren, M. E. (2009). Governance-driven democratization. *Critical Policy Studies, 3*(1), 3–13.

Warsen, R., Nederhand, J., Klijn, E. H., Grotenbreg, S., & Koppenjan, J. (2018). What makes public–private partnerships work? Survey research into the outcomes and the quality of cooperation in PPPs. *Public Management Review, 20*(8), 1165–1185.

Waterman, R. W., & Meier, K. J. (1998). Principal–agent models: An expansion? *Journal of Public Administration Research and Theory, 8*(2), 173–202.

Weaver, L. (2016). Possible: Transformational change in collective impact. *Community Development, 47*(2), 274–283.

Weber, E. P., & Khademian, A. M. (2008). Wicked problems, knowledge challenges, and collaborative capacity builders in network settings. *Public Administration Review, 68*(2), 334–349.

Weber, M. (1978). *Economy and Society: An Outline of Interpretive Sociology.* Berkeley: University of California Press. Volume 2.

Weible, C. M. (2008). Expert-based information and policy subsystems: A review and synthesis. *Policy Studies Journal, 36*(4), 615–635.

Weible, C. M., and Sabatier, P. A. (2009). Coalitions, science, and belief change: Comparing adversarial and collaborative policy subsystems. *Policy Studies Journal, 37*(2), 195–212.

Weick, K. E. (1984). Small wins: Redefining the scale of social problems. *American Psychologist, 39*(1), 40–49.

Weick, K. E. (1989). Theory construction as disciplined imagination. *Academy of Management Review, 14*(4), 516–531.

Weick, K. E. (2007). The generative properties of richness. *Academy of Management Journal, 50*(1), 14–19.

Weiss, T. G., & Wilkinson, R. (2014). Rethinking global governance? Complexity, authority, power, change. *International Studies Quarterly, 58*(1), 207–215.

Werlin, H. H. (2003). Poor nations, rich nations: A theory of governance. *Public Administration Review, 63*(3), 329–342.

Westley, F., Antadze, N., Riddell, D. J., Robinson, K., & Geobey, S. (2014). Five configurations for scaling up social innovation: Case examples of nonprofit organizations from Canada. *Journal of Applied Behavioral Science*, *50*(3), 234–260.

Whitford, A. B. (2002). Decentralization and political control of the bureaucracy. *Journal of Theoretical Politics*, *14*(2), 167–193.

Wildavsky, A. B. (1979). *Speaking Truth to Power*. Piscataway, NJ: Transaction Publishers.

Willems, T., Verhoest, K., Voets, J., Coppens, T., Van Dooren, W., & Van den Hurk, M. (2017). Ten lessons from ten years PPP experience in Belgium. *Australian Journal of Public Administration*, *76*(3), 316–329.

Willetts, P. (2010). *Non-governmental Organizations in World Politics: The Construction of Global Governance*. London: Routledge.

Williams, B. N., Kang, S. C., & Johnson, J. (2016). (Co)-contamination as the dark side of co-production: Public value failures in co-production processes. *Public Management Review*, *18*(5), 692–717.

Williams, D. S., Celliers, L., Unverzagt, K., Videira, N., Máñez Costa, M., & Giordano, R. (2020). A method for enhancing capacity of local governance for climate change adaptation. *Earth's Future*, *8*(7), e2020EF001506.

Wilson, J. Q. (1989). *Bureaucracy: What Government Agencies Do and Why They Do it*. London: Hachette UK.

Wilson, W. (1887). The study of administration. *Political Science Quarterly*, *2*(2), 197–222.

Wolf, P. J. (1993). A case survey of bureaucratic effectiveness in US cabinet agencies: Preliminary results. *Journal of Public Administration Research and Theory*, *3*(2), 161–181.

Wolff, T. (2016). Ten places where collective impact gets it wrong. *Global Journal of Community Psychology Practice*, *7*(1), 1–13.

Wolff, T., Minkler, M., Wolfe, S. M., Berkowitz, B., Bowen, L., Butterfoss, F. D., & Lee, K. S. (2017). Collaborating for equity and justice: Moving beyond collective impact. *Nonprofit Quarterly*, *9*, 42–53.

Wondolleck, J. M., & Yaffee, S. L. (2000). *Making Collaboration Work: Lessons from Innovation in Natural Resource Management*. Washington, DC: Island Press.

Wood, B. D., & Waterman, R. W. (1991). The dynamics of political control of the bureaucracy. *American Political Science Review*, *85*(3), 801–828.

Wooldridge, B., & Gooden, S. (2009). The epic of social equity: Evolution, essence, and emergence. *Administrative Theory & Praxis*, *31*(2), 222–234.

Wright, B. E., Moynihan, D. P., & Pandey, S. K. (2012). Pulling the levers: Transformational leadership, public service motivation, and mission valence. *Public Administration Review*, *72*(2), 206–215.

Wu, X., Ramesh, M., & Howlett, M. (2015). Policy capacity: A conceptual framework for understanding policy competences and capabilities. *Policy and Society*, *34*(3–4), 165–171.

Wu, X., Ramesh, M., & Howlett, M. (2018). Policy capacity: Conceptual framework and essential components. In X. Wu, M. Howlett, & M. Ramesh (Eds.) *Policy Capacity and Governance: Studies in the Political Economy of Public Policy*. Cham: Palgrave Macmillan, https://doi.org/10.1007/978-3-319-54675-9_1

Yen, W. T., Liu, L. Y., & Won, E. (2022). The imperative of state capacity in public health crisis: Asia's early COVID-19 policy responses. *Governance*, *35*(3), 777–798.

Yesilkagit, K., & Van Thiel, S. (2008). Political influence and bureaucratic autonomy. *Public Organization Review*, *8*(2), 137–153.

References

Young, O. R. (1999a). *The Effectiveness of International Environmental Regimes: Causal Connections and Behavioral Mechanisms*. Cambridge, MA: MIT Press.

Young, O. R. (1999b). *Governance in World Affairs*. Ithaca: Cornell University Press.

Young, O. R. (2002). *The Institutional Dimensions of Environmental Change: Fit, Interplay, and Scale*. Cambridge, MA: MIT Press.

Young, O. R. (2019). Constructing diagnostic trees: A stepwise approach to institutional design. *Earth System Governance, 1*, 100002.

Young, O. R. (2021). *Grand Challenges of Planetary Governance: Global Order in Turbulent Times*. Cheltenham, UK and Northampton, MA, USA: Edward Elgar Publishing.

Young, Y. (2014). Social context and social capital: Governance, inequality, and the individual experience. *International Journal of Sociology, 44*(2), 37–62.

Zürn, M. (2018a). *A Theory of Global Governance: Authority, Legitimacy, and Contestation*. Oxford: Oxford University Press.

Zürn, M. (2018b). Contested global governance. *Global Policy, 9*(1), 138–145.

Index

Abbott, K. W. 108, 116–18
Abend, G. 5
Aberbach, J. 33
Abson, D. J. 168
accountability 2, 30, 36, 41–6, 52, 60–61, 63, 65–6, 69, 73, 77–8, 91, 94–5, 97, 101, 114–15, 118, 122, 125–6, 128, 175–6, 181–2, 184
  for results 54–5, 176
  social 44–6, 78, 181, 188
active representation 145–7
adaptive governance 24, 160–62, 169, 172, 183
Adler, P. S. 90
administrative agencies
  administrative conditions 47–62
  political conditions 30–46
administrative politicalization 37
Advocacy Coalition Framework 100
advocacy networks 116, 177
agencification 49–50, 175
Agranoff, R. 73
Agrawal, A. 154
Ahmed, S. M. 136
Aleksovska, M. 42–3
Alford, J. 15, 80
Allen, C. R. 160
Alonso, J. M. 52
Altunba, Y. 67
Andersson, K. P. 158
Andonova, L. B. 114–15
Andrews, M. 18, 24, 129
Ansell, C. 75–6, 81–2, 142
anti-politics 89, 104
Araral, E. 156
Aristotle 9
Armitage, D. 162
Arnstein, S. R. 78
Arora, P. 130
Asadullah, M. N. 124, 128
Åström, J. 94
auditing 34, 118

autonomy 37–9, 46, 49–50, 55, 60, 62, 97, 109, 118, 129–30, 157, 175, 181, 184

Bache, I. 113
Bächtiger, A. 103
Bäckstrand, K. 97
Bali, A. S. 25
Balogh, S. 75–6
bandwagon effects (small wins) 22
Banjade, M. R. 92
Bardhan, P. 67
Barham, E. 101
Barnett, M. 109
Barrett, C. B. 18
Barrett, G. 79–80, 95
Bartley, T. 66, 120
Bass, B. M. 58, 62
Bauer, M. W. 37
Beck, U. 169, 173
Becker, S. 37
Behn, R. D. 41–2, 53
Berardo, R. 163
Berkes, F. 158–9
Bernstein, S. 117
Berrone, P. 139
Berwick, E. 64
Besley, T. J. 130
Bevir, M. 4, 186
Bianchi, C. 21
bicameralism 39
Biermann, F. 106, 123
Boin, A. 57
Boix, C. 91
Böker, M. 97–8
Bornemann, B. 170–71
Bornstein, A. 143–4
Börzel, T. A. 65
Bostic, A. 133
Bours, S. A. 22
Bovaird, T. 80

238

Index

Bovens, M. 42
Bown, N. 159
boycott campaigns 119
Boyne, G. A. 53
BRAC 140
Bradbury, M. 146–7
Brady, D. 133
Braithwaite, V. 94, 185
Brandsen, T. 80, 92–3
Brass, J. N. 139
Brehm, J. O. 60
Breitmeier, H. 163
Brewer, G. A. 56–7
bribery 67–8, *see also* corruption
Briggs, X. D. S. 94–5
Bringselius, L. 61
Brinkerhoff, D. W. 44
Bro, L. L. 57–8
Bryson, J. M. 51, 77
Buller, J. 38
bureaucracy 8, 31–2, 34–41, 45–6, 60,
     94, 109, 121, 123, 126, 129–30,
     145–6, 150, 152, 175, 178, 183–4,
     187
bureaucratic accountability 43
Buse, K. 115
Busuioc, M. 42

Caillier, J. G. 58
Canare, T. 132
capability trap 18
Capano, G. 25–6, 64
Caplow, S. 148
Carlisle, K. 157
Carlsson, L. 158–9, 163
Carpenter, D. 38
Cashore, B. 119, 121
Cento Bull, A. 91
centralization 65–8, 71, 84, 158
Cepiku, D. 72
Chan, K. M. 169
Chang, E. C. 34
Chhotray, V. 43
child labor 12
Cho, Y. K. 67
Choi, S. 142
Chong, A. 130
Christensen, T. 57, 59
Christia, F. 64
Cingolani, L. 49

civic capacity 94–5, 104
Clarke, N. 89
clientelism 30, 32, 34, 36–7, 45, 127,
     130–31, 175
climate change 12, 111
climate justice 148
Coasean bargaining 150
Coccia, M. 128
co-creation 81–2, 85, 98, 105, 181
cognitive bias 143–4, 151
Cohen, D. K. 5
collaborative governance 10, 23–4, 75–8,
     82, 85–6, 88, 92, 99–100, 105,
     135–6, 142, 176–7, 181, 183
collective impact 95, 126, 136–7, 151,
     180
Collier, D. 185
co-management 158–9, 162–3, 172, 179,
     181
common pool resources 154, 171, 179,
     186
commons 153–73
community-based strategies 135–41
complex adaptive systems 24
complexity 15–16, 19–20, 23–4, 27–8,
     69–70, 72–6, 79, 112, 165, 185,
     189
conflict management 98–103, 109, 177
Conklin, J. 21
consociationalism 102–3, 105
contracting 48–9, 51–2, 55, 61, 74, 176
co-production 80–82, 85, 98, 147, 181
corporatization *see* agencification
corruption 2, 17, 30, 32–4, 37, 44–6,
     66–8, 87, 92, 101, 127, 150, 160,
     175, 181, 183
Cortright, D. 100–101
cost–benefit analysis 16
coupling (small wins) 22
COVID-19 64
Cox, M. 154, 156, 186
Craig, D. A. 127
Crawford, G. 132
Crick, B. 89
Cristofoli, D. 71
critical theory 188–9
Crook, R. 131
Crosby, B. C. 77
Cross, M. D. 113
Crowley, K. 13

Cucciniello, M. 44
Curato, N. 97–8

Dahlström, C. 31–3
Dan, S. 48
De Búrca, G. 121–2
De Graaf, L. 95–6
decentralization 40, 47, 49, 65–8, 71, 84,
    92, 103, 108, 115, 125–6, 131–2,
    134, 141, 150, 158–9, 171, 176,
    178, 180–81
delegation 49–50
deliberation 2, 51, 77, 79, 83, 86, 90,
    96–8, 104–5, 119, 142, 160,
    169–70
deliberative democracy 75, 90, 104
Dellmuth, L. M. 112
democracy cube 78
democratic deficit 87, 89, 111
democratic legitimacy 10, 83, 86–105
Department of Agriculture 146
depoliticization 38, 89, 96, 104, 182, 189
descriptive theory 27, 185–6
design by patching 25
Destler, K. N. 54
development studies 79, 139
developmental states 129–31
Dewey, J. 7
Dewulf, A. 22
diagnosis 7–10, 144, 156, 174–6, 180,
    185–6
diagnostic approach 1, 8–9, 14–15,
    19–20, 29, 46, 156, 169, 174–6,
    179–80, 185, 187, 190
dialogical view 1, 8–9, 14, 174–6,
    179–80, 185, 187
dialogue 7–10, 17, 21, 54, 75, 88, 174–6,
    180, 185–6, 191
Dietz, T. 161
Digdowiseiso, K. 132
Dincecco, M. 64
Dingwerth, K. 108, 119
Dixon, R. 48
Djelic, M. L. 118
Doberstein, C. 77, 83, 88–9
domestic violence 12
Doorenspleet, R. 66
Douglas, M. 23
Dryzek, J. S. 96
Dubnick, M. J. 43, 54–5

Duit, A. 24
Dunlop, C. A. 16
Dunn, W. N. 9, 16
Dzur, A. W. 96

Eberlein, B. 119, 121
economic growth 12, 64, 126–7, 129–30,
    150, 178, 181
Edelenbos, J. 24, 79
Elbanna, S. 51
Emerson, K. 75–6
employee turnover 58, 141–2
energizing (small wins) 22
environmental issues 22, 77, 97, 111,
    121, 148–50, 153–7, 161, 163,
    169, 172–3, 178–9
environmental justice 126, 148–50, 152,
    178–9
e-petitioning 94
epistemic communities 112–13
Equal Opportunity Employment
    Commission 146
equity 11, 126, 141, 144–6, 148–9,
    151–2, 178, 184
Ersoy, A. 170
Esping-Andersen, G. 132
ethnicity 91–2, 103, 105, 127, 141, 147,
    151, 177, 181, 189
European Union 87–8, 100, 113, 122,
    132–3
Evans, P. 44, 130, 181, 183
evidence-based policy making 6–7, 21,
    174
experimentalist governance 121–3, 125,
    178
explanatory theory 189–91
externally directed regimes 76
extrinsic motivation 58, 61

Faguet, J. P. 66
failed states 101, 127
fairness 147–8
Fan, C. S. 67
Farrell, D. 97
Favero, N. 50
Favoreu, C. 51
Fazekas, M. 49
Featheringham, T. R. 15
federalism 67, 103, 105, 177, 189

Index

Federation of Organic Agricultural
  Movements 119
Feeney, M. K. 78
Feindt, P. H. 169
Feldman, M. S. 142
Feola, G. 167
Ferguson, J. 89
Financial Action Task Force 122
Finegold, K. 64
Finnemore, M. 109
Fischer, J. 168
Fisher, J. 99
fisheries 3, 91, 121, 153, 155–6, 158–60
Fledderus, J. 81
Flinders, M. 38, 89
Folke, C. 161
forestry 49, 92, 99, 121–2, 141
formal politicalization 36
forum shopping 110
Fox, J. A. 44–5
fragmentation 48, 50, 60, 76, 95, 103,
  106–8, 110, 112, 124, 136, 138,
  157, 167, 177
frame reflection 16, 27, 171
framing 11, 16, 23, 26, 40, 73, 83, 166
Frederickson, H. G. 3, 145
Friedrich–Finer debate 39
Fukuyama, F. 2, 37, 92
functional politicalization 36–7
44, 78, 97

Gaebler, T. 47
Gailmard, S. 32
Galaz, V. 24
Gash, A. 75
Gates, S. 60
Gaventa, J. 79–80, 95
Geddes, B. 34
George, A. L. 7
George, B. 51
George, C. 148
Gerring, J. 68, 183
Geyer, R. 19
Giessen, L. 121
Giest, S. 162
Gjaltema, J. 82
global cooperation 106–25, 177
global governance 2, 6, 11, 106–8,
  124–5, 177–8, 180
    basic structure of 108–12

institutional mechanisms of 116–24
  networks 112–16
global regulation 118–19
globalization 101, 113–14, 119, 124
goal-based governance 108, 123–5
Godet, C. 111
Goldsmith, A. A. 129
good governance 2, 6, 30, 32, 66, 68, 84,
  100–102, 104, 126–9, 150, 178,
  180
Goodsell, C. T. 56, 94
governance
    of the commons 153–63
    as deepening of democracy 90–98
    definition of 4
    as management of conflict 98–103
    as politics 86–90
    theories 1–11, 174–91, see also
        individual theories
governance gap 11, 107, 119, 177
governance theories 1–11, 174–91, see
    also individual theories
governance triangle 118
Grafton, R. Q. 91
Gram Vikas 140
grassroots innovation 167–8, 173, 179
Greve, C. 74
Griffith, D. M. 144
Grin, J. 170
Grindle, M. S. 56, 63, 128
Gruby, R. L. 157
Gruendel, A. 13
Gugushvili, D. 133
Gulbrandsen, L. H. 121
Gunderson, L. 161
Gupta, D. 141
Gustafson, P. 78, 96
Gustavson, M. 34
Guy, M. E. 31

Haas, P. M. 112
Haggard, S. 129
Haider-Markel, D. P. 147
Hale, T. 107
Hall, S. 170
Halleröd, B. 127–8
Han, Y. 55
Hanleybrown, F. 137
Hardin, G. 17, 153–6, 171
Hardin, R. 93

Harlow, C. 69
Harmer, A. M. 115
Harrison, E. 18
Hassan, M. S. 128
Haxeltine, A. 168
Head, B. W. 13–15, 20–21
Hegre, H. 102
Henderson, A. C. 58
Hendriks, C. M. 96, 170
Henry, P. J. 143
Herd, P. 134–5
Herian, M. N. 148
Hertting, N. 78, 96
Hickel, J. 123
Hickey, S. 45
Hilderbrand, M. E. 56, 63
Hindera, J. J. 146–7
Hirsch, D. 133
Hisschemöller, M. 16
Hodge, G. A. 74
hollow state 51–2, 65
Holmberg, S. 32
homelessness 12, 18, 23, 72, 77, 88–9, 134
Hong, S. 55
Honingh, M. 80–81
Hood, C. 33, 48
Hoppe, R. 15–16, 21
Houtzager, P. 44, 184
Howlett, M. 65, 162
Huang, W. L. 78
Huber, J. D. 39
Hui, I. 88
Hulme, D. 187
human rights 111, 122
Hupe, P. 3
Hustedt, T. 37
hybrid governance 101, 121

ill-structured problems 16, 27, 174–5
incentive design 40, 61, 175
income inequality 12
independently convened regimes 76
inequality 126–52, 178
Ingram, H. 162–3
Institutional Analysis and Development 154
institutional bias 126, 143–4, 151, 178
institutional complexity 23–4
institutional racism 143–4

institutionalism 10, 25, 47, 55, 61–2, 70, 129
instrumental theory 188–91
international coordination 106–25, 177
international organizations 6, 107–12, 114, 117–18, 120, 124–6, 177, 184, see also multinational corporations
  INGOs 111–12, 116, 124–5
intractable problems 16–17, 27, 76, 107
Isaacs, W. N. 9
islands of excellence 35–6

Jensen, U. T. 57–8
Jentoft, S. 159
Jessop, B. 82
Ji, S. 55
Johns, L. 119
Jones, B. 91
Joshi, A. 44
Jütting, J. P. 131–2

Kahler, M. 107
Kania, J. 136
Kanie, N. 123
Karpowitz, C. F. 142–3
Katzenstein, M. F. 134
Keck, M. E. 116
Kellough, J. E. 146–7
Kelman, H. C. 99
Kemp, R. 167, 170
Kenis, P. 70–72
Keohane, R. O. 111
Kerpershoek, E. 61
Kerr, N. N. 34
Kerwer, D. 118
Khademian, A. M. 142
Kienzle, B. 117
Kim, E. 128
Kim, R. E. 36
King, S. 45
Kingsley, D. 145
Kirschke, S. 19
Kleine, M. 88
Kleinfeld, R. 101
Klijn, E. H. 23–4, 70, 74, 89
Köhler, J. 164
Koliba, C. 73
Koppell, J. G. 43

Index 243

Koppenjan, J. F. 23–4, 70, 74
Korpi, W. 133
Kort, I. M. 74
Kosack, S. 44
Kramer, M. 136
Kroll, A. 54
Kuhlmann, S. 66
Kuhn, T. 185
Kumlin, S. 92
Kwon, H. J. 128
Kwon, S. W. 90

ladder of participation 78
Lapuente, V. 31–2
Larson, A. M. 158
learning-by-doing (small wins) 22
Lee, R. G. 160
Lee, S. Y. 38, 60
legal accountability 43
legitimacy 10, 24, 30, 57, 70, 72, 77–8,
        86–8, 104–5, 107–8, 111, 117,
        119, 121, 147–8, 169, 177–8,
        181–2, 184
    democratic 10, 83, 86–105
Lejano, R. P. 162–3
Leonard, D. K. 35
Leonard, L. 170
Lessmann, C. 68, 132
Leventon, J. 168–9
leverage points 168–9, 173
Levin, K. 15, 22
Levine, J. R. 139
Levy, M. A. 110
Lewin, K. 1
Lewis, J. M. 26–7
Lidskog, R. 170
Light, S. S. 161
Lijphart, A. 102–3
Lim, H. H. 147
Lin, T. H. 64
Lind, E. A. 147
Lindblom, C. E. 5, 13
Linder, S. H. 25
Linder, W. 66, 103
Linnér, B. O. 169
Lodge, M. 33
Loeffler, E. 80
logic of attraction (small wins) 22
Lombard, M. 79
Lönngren, J. 14

Loorbach, D. 165
Lowndes, V. 92
Lubell, M. 163

Maggetti, M. 8–9, 69
Mahon, J. E. 185
Mair, J. 139–40
managerialism 50
Mann, M. 63–4
Markard, J. 165
Markovic, J. 71
Markwardt, G. 68
Marquette, H. 33–4
Marti, I. 139–40
Martinez-Vazquez, J. 132
Martiskainen, M. 168
Mattingly, D. 184–5
Mattli, W. 120
Mayntz, R. 83
McAdam, D. 187
McCabe, B. J. 134
McCandless, S. A. 31
McCubbins, M. D. 40
McDermott, M. 149
McDonnell, E. M. 35–6
McDougall, C. 92
McGuire, M. 73
McLain, R. J. 160
Mdee, A. 18
Meadows, D. 168
Meagher, K. 101–2
media 26, 38, 103
Meier, K. J. 36, 41, 146–7
Mendelberg, T. 142–3
meritocracy 33–4, 181
messy problems 15–17, 27, 174
meta-governance 82–3, 85, 176–7, 184
Metze, T. A. P. 22
Michels, A. 95–6
Millar, H. 89
Millard, J. 138
Millennium Development Goals 123–4
Milward, H. B. 70–71
mini-publics 97–8, 104
mission orientation 55–7
Mitroff, I. I. 15
Moe, T. M. 40
Moon, C. I. 129–31, 141–2
Moore, M. H. 51
Mora, C. 160

Mosher, F. 145
Mosley, J. E. 72
motivated reasoning 54
Moynihan, D. P. 38, 50, 53–4, 59, 134–5
muddling through 19, 25
multilateral environmental agreements 112–13
multi-level governance 8, 68–9, 73, 84, 162
multinational corporations 119–20
Musso, J. 95

Nabatchi, T. 75–6, 80
Nagendra, H. 158
natural resource management 75, 93, 129, 158, 160
Nederhand, J. 83
Nelson, H. W. 49
neoliberalism 48, 79, 134, 138, 151, 182
network administrative organization 71–2
network governance 23–4, 27, 70–75, 77, 83–4, 114, 125, 176, 183–4, 189
networks 23–4, 70, 162–3
    advocacy 116, 177
    effectiveness 70–73
    global governance 112–16
    management and accountability 73
    public–private partnerships 73–5, 107, 114–16, 118, 124–5, 177, 189
    regulatory 113, 177
New Public Governance 182
New Public Management 10, 38, 47–55, 57–8, 61–2, 84, 89, 104, 134, 138, 175–6, 180, 182
New York Police Department 143–4
Newig, J. 79
Nicholson-Crotty, S. 146
Nielsen, J. R. 159
Niemeyer, S. 96
Nikolakis, W. 49
non-governmental organizations 108, 111–12, 114, 116–18, 121, 124, 126, 138–41, 151, 159, 167, 178, 184
    international 111–12, 116, 124–5
Noordegraaf, M. 23, 60
Norris, P. 100, 103, 131
North, D. 127

Nunan, F. 135
Nunes, R. 167
Nygård, H. M. 102

Öberg, S. A. 61
Olsen, J. 78
Olsson, P. 162
Oosterlynck, S. 138
orchestration 108, 116–18, 125, 140, 177–8, 180, 184
Orsini, A. 111
Osborne, D. 47
Osborne, S. P. 70, 80–81
Ostrom, E. 153–8, 171–2, 179, 186
Ostrom, V. 157
O'Toole Jr, L. J. 41
Overdevest, C. 122
Overman, S. 49

Page, S. 40–41, 95
Pahl-Wostl, C. 187
Palme, J. 133
Panday, P. 140
pandemics 12
Pandey, S. K. 38, 50, 54, 57, 59
Papadopoulos, Y. 69
Park, S. 58, 72
Parrado, S. 81
participatory governance 19, 78–80, 85, 96–7, 104, 135–6, 142, 183
Pasha, O. 57
passive representation 145–6
paternalism 126, 134, 151, 180
Pattberg, P. 106, 115, 119
Patty, J. W. 32
peer review 122, 125
Peiffer, C. 33–4
Pellikaan, H. 66
performance management 21, 48, 50, 53–5, 58, 61–2, 176
Perreault, T. 144
Perry, J. L. 5–6, 59
personnel 59–60
Persson, A. 34
Peters, B. G. 3–4, 14–15, 20, 25, 36–7, 182
Petersen, O. H. 52
Piattoni, S. 68–9
Pierre, J. 3–4, 36–7, 182

Pierskalla, J. H. 103
Pitts, D. W. 144
Platt, J. 17
pledge-based governance 108
pockets of effectiveness 35–6
Poister, T. H. 51
police 143–4, 147–8
policy design 25–6, 28, 135
policy problems 25–6
political accountability 43
political support 37–9
political violence 100–102
politicization 36–7
Pollitt, C. 3, 48
polycentricity 26, 68, 111, 155–8, 171–2, 181
Pomeroy, R. S. 159
Popper, K. R. 6
population growth 111
populism 37, 45, 89, 107, 182
Porter, D. 127
Posner, D. N. 91
poverty 12, 17–18, 123–4, 126–52, 178
poverty trap 17–18, 127–8
power-sharing 86, 102–3, 105, 158, 177, 181
Pradilla, C. A. 140
Prasad, R. 129–31
precautionary principle 170
principal–agent theory 33–4, 39–42, 46, 48, 52, 55, 61, 117, 175
principles-based governance 107
privatization 49
problem-driven iterative adaptation 24
procedural justice 126, 142, 145, 147–9, 152
professional accountability 43
professionalism 31, 50, 60–61, 91, 113, 175–6, 183
property rights 110, 127, 153, 159, 171
proportional representation 102–3
Provan, K. G. 70–72
public agencies
    administrative conditions 47–62
    political conditions 30–46
public innovation 26–8
public participation 79, 86, 90, 94–5, 148, 181
public policy networks 114

public problems 12–29, *see also individual problems*
    diagnosing 12–20
    problem-solving 20–27
public service motivation 59–60
public–private partnerships 73–5, 107, 114–16, 118, 124–5, 177, 189
purchaser–provider split 51
Putnam, R. D. 90–91

Qualitative Comparative Analysis 71–2, 163

Raab, J. 71, 188
racism 143–6, 149–50
Radaelli, C. M. 16
radial theory 185
Radin, B. A. 53
Ragin, C. 187
Rainey, H. G. 56, 58, 142
Rangoni, B. 122
Rauch, J. E. 130
Raustiala, K. 110
Rawlings, R. 69
Rawls, J. 144
recruitment 31, 33, 36, 59, 81, 130
redistribution 93, 133
Reed, M. G. 148
reflexive governance 169–71, 173
reflexivity 21, 140, 169–70
regime complexes 109–11
regionalism 105, 107
regulation
    global 118–19
    private and hybrid forms of 119–21
    regulatory networks 113, 177
regulatory networks 113, 177
Rein, M. 16–17
Reinicke, W. 114
religion 92, 105, 114, 140
rent-seeking 129
Repenning, N. P. 18
representative bureaucracy 126, 145–7, 152, 178, 184
reputation 37–9
resilience 21
responsiveness 21
revitalization 21
Rhodes, R. A. 2, 65, 70, 186

Riccucci, N. M. 146–7
Riechers, M. 168
Rietig, K. 100
Rihani, S. 19
Rijke, J. 161
Ringquist, E. J. 149
Risse, T. 65
Rittel, H. W. 13–15, 20
Ritz, A. 59
Roberts, A. 48, 181
Roberts, N. 20
Roberts, P. S. 38
robustness (small wins) 22
Roe, E. 16
Røiseland, A. 98
Romzek, B. S. 43, 52
Rosser, C. 31
Rotberg, R. I. 32
Rothstein, B. 17, 92
rule of law 66, 86, 91, 127–8
rules-based governance 107, 123

Sabatier, P. A. 100
Sachs, J. 127–8
Sacks, A. 103
Sager, F. 31
Sahlin-Andersson, K. 118
Salomonsen, H. H. 37
Sandström, A. 163
Sanginga, P. C. 93
Savoia, A. 128
scaling 156–7
Scharpf, F. W. 83, 87
Schillemans, T. 42–3
Schlosberg, D. 149
Schmelzle, C. 87
Schmidt, V. 87–8
Schwartz, T. 40
Scott, T. A. 77
Seelos, C. 140
Selden, S. C. 56–7, 146
self-efficacy 81
self-governance 82–3, 85, 153–4, 171–2, 179, 181–2, 184
self-initiated regimes 76
Selznick, P. 56
Sen, S. 159
Sepulveda, C. F. 132
Seyfang, G. 167–8
shadow networks 162

shadow of hierarchy 83, 121
Shelby, T. 143
Shiffman, J. 114
Shipan, C. R. 39
Shön, D. 16–17
Shon, J. 67
Sicilia, M. 81
Sikkink, K. 116
Simon, H. A. 6
Sitkin, S. B. 58
Skelcher, C. 89
Skocpol, T. 64
Slaughter, A. M. 113
small wins 22–3, 28
Smith, A. 166–8
Smith, G. 88
Smith, J. G. 73
Snidal, D. 108, 116–18
social accountability 44–6, 78, 181, 188
social capital 92–5, 104, 136, 162, 181, 184
social equity 144–6, 152
social innovation 82, 126, 138–9, 151
social learning 16, 113
social network analysis 70, 172
social psychology 1, 6, 126, 147, 152, 184
social traps 17–18
social welfare 126, 131–5, 151
socialization 56, 108, 113
soft governance 88, 115
soft law 108, 118, 125
Soifer, H. 64
Sørensen, E. 26, 70, 76–8, 83, 88
Sorrentino, M. 80
Soss, J. 134
Soto, F. 158
Sowa, J. E. 146
Stacey Diagram 19
stakeholder relations 15
standards-based governance 108
state, governance and 63–9
state capacity 63–5, 84, 87, 101, 131, 150, 176, 181
state–society synergy 11, 44, 181–5
steering 3, 52, 121, 124
Steffek, J. 88
Steinbauer, P. 56
Sterman, J. D. 18
Stern, P. 155

Index 247

Stirling, A. 169
Stoker, G. 8, 43, 89
Stollenwerk, E. 87
Stone, C. N. 94
strategic complexity 23
strategic management 50–51
strategic planning 50–51
Stuart, F. 134
substantive complexity 23
Suiseeya, K. R. M. 148
Sun, R. 58
Sundström, A. 34
Sunshine, J. 148
sustainability transitions 164–73, 179, 188
Sustainable Development Goals 123
Sverrisson, A. S. 131
Swallow, B. M. 18
symbolic representation 147

Tallberg, J. 112
Tanaka, S. 115
Tarpey, M. 14–15
Tavits, M. 91
Termeer, C. J. 21–2
terrorism 127
Theobald, N. A. 147
theory, *see also individual theories*
    definition of 5–6
    as warranted assertibility 7–9
Thiel, A. 157
Thomas, C. W. 77
Thornton, J. 67
Tiebout model 67
Torfing, J. 26, 70, 76–8, 81–3
Tortola, P. D. 69
Tosun, J. 65
Tragedy of the Commons 153, 171
transactional leadership 57–8
transformational leadership 57–8, 176
transition management 164–72
Transition Movement 167
transition towns movement 168
transnational regulation 113, 118, 121–2, 124–5, 178
transparency 34, 42–4, 46, 49, 72, 95, 109, 119–20, 160
Trein, P. 8–9, 69
Treisman, D. 66
Triantafillou, P. 20, 182

trust 72–4, 81–2, 91, 93–4, 99–100, 104, 147, 159, 162, 176, 184
Turnbull, N. 15, 190
Tyler, T. R. 93, 147–8

United Nations 111, 114
universalism 7, 92–3, 126, 132–4, 151

value-based institutions 55–61
Van der Does, R. 78
Van der Voet, J. 58
Van Dooren, W. 53
Van Knippenberg, D. 58
van Meerkerk, I. 24
Van Poeck, K. 14
Van Ryzin, G. G. 146
Van Vliet, O. 133–4
van Wijk, J. 140
Vangen, S. 76
Vatn, A. 156–7
Vedeld, P. 156–7
Verhoest, K. 48
Verschuere, B. 81
Victor, D. G. 110–11
Vining, A. R. 49
violent conflict 100–102, 177
Voorberg, W. H. 81
Voß, J. P. 170–71

Wacquant, L. 134
Wagenaar, H. 19, 79
Waller, M. R. 134
Wälti, S. 90
Walton, O. E. 111–12
Wang, C. 134
Wang, H. 74, 99–100
Wang, W. 58, 71
warranted assertibility 7–9, 29
Wayenberg, E. 66
weak states 100–101, 105
Weaver, L. 137
Webber, M. M. 13, 15, 20
Weber, M. 31, 187
Weberian ideas 31–3, 36, 45, 51, 84, 101, 105, 109, 126, 129–31, 150, 175, 178, 181, 183
Weible, C. M. 100
Weick, K. E. 22, 185
Weiland, S. 169

Weiss, T. G. 106
welfare state 92, 126, 132–5, 138, 151, 178, 182
Werlin, H. H. 66
Westley, F. 138–9
Wetterberg, A. 44
Whitford, A. B. 38, 60
Wibeck, V. 169
wicked problems 10, 12–15, 17, 19–23, 27–8, 71, 174, 186
Wildavsky, A. B. 15–16, 22–3, 69
Wilkinson, R. 106
Willetts, P. 106, 111
Williams, B. N. 82
Williams, D. S. 169
Wilson, D. 92
Wilson, J. Q. 38, 60
Wilson, W. 31
Wilsonian ideas 31, 33, 45, 51
Wise, L. R. 59
Wolf, P. J. 38, 60
Wolff, T. 137

women 101, 111, 116, 140, 147
Woo, J. J. 25–6
Wood, M. 88–9
Woods, N. 120
World Bank 2, 124, 126–8, 150, 180
World Health Organization 124
Wright, E. O. 97
Wu, X. 65

Xiang, W. N. 21
Xu, X. 147

Yen, W. T. 64
Young, C. D. 146–7
Young, O. R. 2, 9, 17, 107, 109–10, 156, 163
Young, Y. 91–2

Zaret, D. 187
Zeitlin, J. 122
Zürn, M. 106–7